A Buddhist Exploration of Sex
from Celibacy to Polyamory and
Everything in Between

BRAD WARNER

New World Library
Novato, California

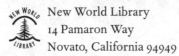 New World Library
14 Pamaron Way
Novato, California 94949

Text design by Tona Pearce Myers

Library of Congress Cataloging-in-Publication Data
Warner, Brad.
Sex, sin, and Zen : a Buddhist exploration of sex from celibacy to poly-amory and everything in between / Brad Warner.
    p.   cm.
Includes bibliographical references.
ISBN 978-1-57731-910-8 (pbk. : alk. paper)
    1. Sex—Religious aspects—Buddhism. I. Title.
BQ4570.S48W37 2010
294.3'422—dc22   2010020429

First printing, September 2010
ISBN 978-1-57731-910-8
Printed in Canada on 100% postconsumer-waste recycled paper

g New World Library is a proud member of the Green Press Initiative.

10 9 8 7 6 5 4 3 2 1

CONTENTS

BROKENHEARTED ZEN

Every night I tell myself
I am the cosmos
I am the wind
That don't bring you back again.

— Chris Bell, "I Am the Cosmos"

My chest hurts. That's the thought that keeps recurring as I sit cross-legged and stock-still in front of a room full of dedicated meditators. A wood-burning stove in the corner keeps the early-morning mountain chill at bay, the sun is shining, and it is calm and peaceful, with only the pine logs crackling sutras to disturb the quiet.

I want to die. Or cry. Or cry myself to death.

My chest *hurts*.

I'm the leader of this three-day retreat at the Southern Dharma Retreat Center near Asheville, North Carolina. I'm supposed to be the calmest and most in-control guy in the room. These people have paid good money, and some have traveled long distances, just to be in my presence, just to have me give them the secret to being as together as I am. They look up to me, respect me. And all I want to do is evaporate, disappear, dissolve into the ether, never to be seen again. What's even worse is it's all because of some girl.

What a fucking Zen master I am.

That day I finally understood exactly why they call it "heartbreak." My heart hurt just as if someone had punched a hole through my chest and ripped it out still beating, as in some Aztec sacrifice ritual. Sometimes it hurt really bad. Sometimes it was just a dull persistent pain. Sometimes it hurt for a while and kind of came to a crescendo and then stopped just as suddenly as it had begun. I tried as best I could to let go. Sometimes I found myself obsessing over some fantasy, maybe one in which we got back together or I told her exactly how I felt. Or maybe one in which she was happily meditating next to some bearded douche-nozzle at the retreat center where she was staying who liked to tell his friends he was "a very *spiritual* person," after which he fucked her from behind like a hyena in heat while she squealed Sanskrit chants of ecstasy he'd taught her during phony-baloney "tantric" rituals.

What's that you say? As a so-called Zen master I should be above such matters? I should be able to allow my thoughts to simply float past like clouds in a clear blue sky? I should be beyond the tawdry things of the world like romantic entanglements? Otherwise why would anyone care what I had to say about Zen?

That's what I would have thought, too. But I wasn't like that. In my twenty-five years of Zen practice and training no such perfection had come. And yet I handled this breakup differently from how I'd handled them before. I've never been a good breaker-upper. I remember when Becky Wagner dumped me and I couldn't get on the phone to her because I was sharing a punk rock house that had one telephone and Logan, one of my housemates, was on it. So I ran, literally almost blinded by tears, to the gas station on the corner and kept feeding quarters into the pay phone to leave increasingly distraught messages on her answering machine.

This time I'd been able to accept what needed to be accepted. I didn't beg, I didn't plead. Not much, at least. As one Zen monk said, "A man never got a woman back by begging on his knees."* I didn't yell or go red-faced with rage. When thoughts appeared in my mind

---

* Leonard Cohen, ordained by Joshu Sasaki Roshi, from the song "I'm Your Man."

of my love rolling around in the back of the ashram with one of those god-awful generic "mystical dude" types that always stink up those places with their patchouli-stench presence, I let them pass, knowing they were just thoughts in my head* and that any corresponding reality that might have existed was far different from what I was imagining.**

Oh, I could allow these thoughts and worse to pass. That's true. But I couldn't stop them from coming up. And that doesn't mean those thoughts didn't hurt when they did come up. Or that it didn't hurt when I dropped them. This, too, is part of the process. Dropping thoughts like that often hurts worse than holding on to them, since dropping thoughts you're convinced are correct is like denying the existence of your self.

So maybe you're wondering, if this Zen stuff can't even cure a broken heart, what the hell good is it? Sometimes I wonder that myself. But Zen practice has shown me the clear way never to have a broken heart ever again. Wanna know the secret? Never fall in love. Some Buddhist practitioners have put this into effect very successfully and live absolutely free from heartbreak. We'll talk about them in a little bit. But that's not the answer you wanted, is it? Maybe you wanted a magic mantra that would make it all go away. Sometimes the true answer isn't one we like. But it's always the best answer because it's true.

A lot of what gets written about Zen is based on abstractions and idealism. Too many people who write about it don't have a clue. They write all about the way things can be, or might be, or should be, not how they really are. Because very often they don't even know how they really are. The caricatures of Zen in pop culture are even worse, picking up on these abstractions and turning them into parody. I'm not interested in telling you what I might be like or what I could be

---

* Probably.
** I hope they got deep, painful splinters in their unmentionables.

like if only I did this or that. I'm interested in reporting on what life is actually like.

Still I sat there, leading the retreat. And I sat. And sat. And when the bell rang, I got up and joined everyone for the formal walking practice that punctuates each round of zazen. And then I sat some more.

And as I sat things changed, as they always do. Thoughts and sensations, feelings and perceptions, flowed through like a Technicolor river. Some were pleasant. Some were not. Most were neither. They just were. Sometimes nothing seemed to go on in the conscious portion of my brain for a long, long time. I didn't pass out or enter some mystical zone. It's just that the thoughts sort of gave up. And sometimes after a long while of feeling great my chest would start to hurt again. So it goes.

But I made it through. Just like everyone else at the retreat. We all survived. All of us, with our broken hearts, our family issues, our fears, our desires, our aspirations, our losses: we all sat through them together, and it was beautiful.

Let me tell you about that retreat in the back hills of North Carolina, though, because it was a really special one. There were more women than men, a first for any retreat I've run, if not for Zen retreats in general. Two devout Christians stayed through the whole thing and sat just as hard as anybody else. It was a group, for once, not made up entirely of white folks. Motley heavy-metal dudes mixed with middle-aged ladies. I loved hearing the language of the bodhisattvas spoken in that melodic lilting down-home drawl. It was an astounding scene — a truly Southern dharma retreat!

We did a ton of zazen, raked a bunch of leaves, cut some wood, talked, read bits of Joshu Sasaki's *Buddha Is the Center of Gravity*, ate spectacularly good food, walked, and talked some more. Many corn muffins and beans were consumed. Many farts were stifled in the silence of the zendo. Demons were wrestled with and conquered. Poetry was exchanged and dead dogs duly mourned. Live Buddha cats purred as they were petted. The sun shone. The rain rained. The wind howled and roared. Sexy white-butted deer trotted down mountainsides, followed by Carolina panthers. Doubts were raised about the wisdom of swallowing the Kool-Aid given by trusted teachers.

A lot more happened than just my silly little broken heart.

Sex is a big part of all of our lives. So are romance and heartache and all the rest of what goes along with it. Even when we give up sex and become celibate — something I have never tried* — sex seems to follow us.

Zen has been a big part of my life since not too long after the time I first discovered sex. I'm not quite certain which came first, my first period of zazen or the loss of my virginity. I had a girlfriend in high school, and we got naked together. But because I was too mortified to ask the old guy behind the counter at Brenneman's corner drugstore in Wadsworth, Ohio, to sell me some condoms, we never actually went all the way. That didn't happen until I got to college and you could buy rubbers at the university bookstore without having to ask someone for them. College was also the place where I discovered Zen practice through a wonderful potty-mouthed bodhisattva named Tim. So most of my personal encounters with sexuality have been informed in some way by Buddhist philosophy and practice.

I don't claim to be any kind of expert on human sexuality. A lot of the theories current these days about gender and sexuality leave me a little confused. I simply don't have enough interest in them to sustain the kind of study needed to understand them thoroughly. I'm a bit of a fuddy-duddy, I suppose. It's not that I hate the whole idea of there being, like, two dozen different genders and whatever else they're saying nowadays. I just really don't care.

I know that probably sounds blasphemous to some of you.

---

* Not by choice, anyway.

Please understand that I have no difficulty with any of the ways people choose to define themselves in terms of gender, sexual orientation, or whatever other factors we use to enhance our ego-based notions of self. I understand the social usefulness of these new ways of defining ourselves, and I'm not against them in any way. Others have written about that subject far more eloquently than I ever could. It's just that I personally don't have a whole lot of interest in ego-based notions of self. But who you choose to fuck and how you choose to do it, well, that's none of my business or anyone else's other than the people you fuck.

You should always be true to who you really are and never just accept what society tells you that you ought to be. But it takes a lot of work to discover exactly who you are.

This book represents my best effort at giving a very personal Buddhism-informed view on the subject of sexuality. Ultimately, though, it's my personal take. The opinions expressed in this book are not necessarily those of Buddha, the Soto School of Zen, or their supporters, adherents, and affiliates. And yet it's a view informed by more than twenty-five years of serious Zen practice, as well as about the same number of years of sexual experience.

This is not a textbook about the history of Buddhist approaches to sex. If you want that, check out *The Red Thread* by Bernard Faure or *Lust for Enlightenment* by John Stevens. I did! Most of what you'll read here about the approach Buddhism has taken throughout its history to matters of sexuality comes from these books.

This book consists of two different types of chapters. The main chapters look at aspects of sexuality and discuss them from a Buddhist angle. But after I'd written those it occurred to me that it might also be useful to discuss certain aspects of Buddhism from a sexual angle. The chapters where I do this are titled "Sexual Angles on Buddhism," with a subtitle regarding the specific topic under examination. Sometimes I've repeated information in these chapters that can also be found in the main book chapters. But when I've done so I've tried to look at that information from a different perspective. So I hope you'll bear with me.

I'm trying to provide something entirely different from any other book I've seen on the topic of Buddhism and sexuality. No other Zen monk that I know of has ever written a comprehensive book about sex. Even Dogen, the thirteenth-century monk who wrote about nearly every aspect of the lives of Buddhists, both monks and laypeople, barely even mentions sex.

You can think of this, perhaps, as a pioneering work — a seminal one, even.* And it has all the pitfalls such works always have. I hope that someday someone better qualified will write a more comprehensive book that addresses all the issues I leave out of this one, a book that's better informed about contemporary thinking regarding sex and gender, that gives something closer to the view that perhaps most Buddhists would take on the subject rather than one individual's opinions, or that gives the female perspective on these matters. A book on Buddhist sexuality by someone who isn't as poor an excuse for a Zen monk as I am might be good, too.

Unfortunately, I am unable to deliver on any of these counts. Still, I hope this book does you a little bit of good, or at least makes you laugh.

---

* Heh, heh! Seminal!

Chapter 1

THE PIECE OF ASS CHANT

We reflect on the effort that brought us this piece of ass and consider how
* it comes to us.*
We reflect on our virtue and practice and whether we are worthy of this
* piece of ass.*
We consider sexual greed to be the obstacle to freedom of mind.
We consider this piece of ass to be good medicine to sustain our lives.
For the sake of attaining the Truth we now receive this piece of ass.

The above is a paraphrase of what is known as the Five Reflections. It's the standard chant intoned by Zen monks before every meal during temple practice. Of course, in the orthodox version the words *piece of ass* would be replaced by the word *food*.

The reason we chant this (the original version) before eating is because eating is literally vital; it's indispensable for survival. If you stop eating for long, you die.

Sex, on the other hand, is not essential. You can live to be a hundred without ever getting a single piece of nookie and do just fine. But most of us don't think of sex that way. Most of us consider sex almost as crucial as food, water, or air. We'll spend incredible amounts of time, effort, and energy to get it. But when we do get some we often find ourselves in just as much of a quandary as we were in when we didn't have any.

Rewriting the Buddhist meal chant as a chant of thankfulness for sex and chanting it each time we get some action may not be the best way to deal with the problems that sex inevitably introduces into our lives, along with the pleasure it gives. But it may be useful whenever having sex to reflect briefly on how privileged we are just to be able to do it, and to accept it with gratitude and grace.

A lot went into that sex! Not only was there the obvious stuff, like going to the bar, getting up your nerve to talk to the person, getting the cold shoulder but trying again, getting rid of his or her friend, the dinner, the movie, the make-out session with the dog trying to hump your leg the whole time, and so on. But just the simple fact that you have a body and mind healthy enough to enjoy sex and the opportunity to do it at all is nothing to take for granted. Not everyone has that. And there will come a time when you won't have it either.

The reason Buddhists chant a verse of reflection and thankfulness before each meal is because most of us take eating very lightly. We sit in front of the TV shoving handfuls of Fritos in our mouths without even the slightest awareness of what a great and rare privilege it is just to be able to have food. We complain about our food when there are plenty of humans and other sentient beings who would do anything just to be able to eat. The meal verse is intended to remind us that eating is a significant matter. Even the strictest vegan in the world has to take life to sustain his or her own life. Carrots and potatoes are living things too.

Most of us don't take sex as lightly as we take eating. But we do often come to it with very little awareness of how very special it is. Sure, maybe we feel lucky to get a really hot piece of ass. We may be thankful to be with someone we love. But there are plenty of times when we quickly forget what a wonderful thing it is just to be able to have sex at all when we're caught up in the moment. That's not necessarily a bad thing. Still, a bit of reflection can never hurt.

And there are a lot of times when we approach sex in a dangerously unreflective way. We get so caught up in our carnal desires that nothing much else matters. We're prone to behaving in careless and inappropriate ways. We'll often stop at almost nothing to get into a position where bodily fluids may be exchanged. We don't care who we step on or what kind of trouble we cause, just as long as there's some four-legged frolic involved. All kinds of trouble have resulted from the simple desire to shag someone without the necessary reflection on what that shagging might entail.

So now that we've chanted, let's get started with the discussion, shall we?

Chapter 2

ARE BUDDHISTS ALLOWED TO JACK OFF?

L et's start out by clarifying some of our terms. Although Zen Buddhism is probably the most talked about form of Buddhism among Westerners these days, it also seems to be the least practiced one. Very briefly, Zen is a specific form of Buddhism that developed at the beginning of the Common Era around five hundred years after Gotama* Buddha's death as a reaction to the way Buddhism had strayed from its origin as a meditative practice and become more of a religion. The Zen movement sought to strip away all the inessential rituals, costuming, and other trappings and get back down to basics. This is evident in the name of the sect. "Zen" is the Japanese pronunciation of the Sanskrit word *dhyana*, meaning "meditation."

Not all Buddhism is Zen, however. I don't have the statistics, and as far as I know nobody else does either, but my educated guess, based on what I've seen and read, is that Zen is a fair ways down the list after Soka Gakkai, Pure Land, Tibetan, and Vipassana Buddhism in terms

---

* Or Gautama, if you prefer. His name was not spelled out in Roman letters to begin with, so spellings vary.

of popularity in the West. So if you walk into a random Buddhist center in your town, chances are it might not be a Zen temple — unless you live in Minneapolis–Saint Paul or in the San Francisco Bay Area, where there is either a Zen center or a Starbucks on every corner.

A lot of Americans I meet are surprised to discover that there are often vast differences in practices and teachings among the various schools of Buddhism. But, really, that's like being surprised to discover that Catholics and Baptists have different practices and beliefs, even though they're all Christians. Because of the diversity within Buddhism, and also because I personally tend to have somewhat idiosyncratic views, you may find that the Buddhist places you visit have far different ideas about sexuality than what I am laying out in this book. I only really know Zen, myself, so that's all I'm going to be addressing here. I don't even claim that what I'm saying here goes for all, or even most, Zen people. And, just FYI, we Zen Buddhists tend to be so arrogant that we just call what we believe "Buddhism" without specifying the sect. I'll be doing a little of that, too. Deal with it.

Also, I will use the word *meditation* from time to time to refer to zazen practice. I do this mainly to keep from repeating the same word over and over, as well as to remind those who may not be familiar with the word *zazen* that I am talking about a practice that most people consider a form of meditation.

In these cases I'm using the word *meditation* as a blanket term to cover sitting still in that way that, y'know, like, meditators do and stuff. I'm sorry to get all vague and "teenage" on you here, but let me unpack this a bit, and maybe you'll understand why. According to the dictionary function on the word-processing program I'm using, *meditation* means "emptying the mind of thoughts, or concentration of the mind on just one thing, in order to aid mental or spiritual development, contemplation or relaxation." That's not zazen — which the same dictionary function tells me is "a form of meditation in Zen, practiced sitting in a prescribed position." Actually, *that's* a good definition and a good use of the word *meditation*, just as a rather neutral term for a type of familiar activity.

But most forms of meditation are pretty much what the folks at the software company think they are — methods for emptying the mind or developing concentration aimed at some kind of spiritual goal. Zazen, on the other hand, looks like meditation in that you sit up straight and cross-legged staring at a wall. But there is no goal to the practice. You're not trying to empty your mind of thoughts or concentrate on anything. You allow thought to proceed as it needs to without deliberately adding to the stew. This is, of course, far easier said than done.

Zazen is not a means to any end. It's not a method to get spiritual enlightenment or anything else. It just is what it is. This is a very tricky subject. So rather than attempting to comprehensively describe what zazen actually is right here, I will do so piecemeal throughout the book. I've also added an appendix to try and explain it more succinctly.

At any rate, the foregoing is just a heads-up for you, so we're clear on a couple of things. But let's get started with the discussion about sex. That's what you paid for, after all!

In April 2009 I was giving a talk at a place called Casa Del Popolo in Montreal. I had given a talk there once before, about four years earlier. That one was kind of a tense gig. And a weird one. I'd never been there before, and I'd been told the place was a coffee-house. But when I got there, the audience was drinking beer and wine and smoking cigarettes. This, I gathered, was normal for coffee-houses in Montreal. *Mais sacré bleu!* I had never spoken about Zen in a place where people were getting drunk. I wasn't sure what kind of reaction I'd get in a place like this.

One guy in the back seemed angry about some of the things I said. From up on stage I could see him getting agitated as I spoke. When I opened the talk up to Q & A he was the first to raise his hand. He said, "Are you saying that there's no difference between truth and what is true?" He seemed pretty pissed off about this. But I couldn't quite get the question. This made him even angrier. I thought he was going to rush the stage and slug me.

But he didn't. I answered as best I could — I think I said something about how there is no distinction made in Zen philosophy between Big Ultimate Truth and the small things that are true and factual right now — and I moved on to the next question. After the show the guy lingered, which worried me. But we just chatted for a bit. I got his email address. We emailed back and forth for a while, and then I stopped hearing from him.

But a lot of people who came to the talk in April remembered the guy and the incident at that talk all those years ago. They kept saying stuff to me like, "I wonder if that guy is going to be there again?" I was a little concerned myself. I didn't know if he was a known psycho or something.

Anyway, the event went okay this time. But there was a guy standing by the door with a slightly ornery look in his eye. He looked a little like the guy from a few years ago. Maybe he was the guy. Sure enough, when the Q & A started he was one of the first to raise his hand.

"Are Buddhists allowed to jack off?" he said.

"They're encouraged to!" I replied.

It was a weird question, and I'll get to my full answer in a second. But it was that question, among other things, that inspired me to write a book about Buddhism and sex. Because when I answered that question, I ended up doing what every book I'd seen that addressed the subject of Buddhism and sex did. I regurgitated the history of Buddhist monastic rules regarding sex.

The history of sex in Buddhism in a nutshell goes something like this. The earliest monastic Buddhists were strictly celibate. Buddhists in those days were not allowed to jack off, much less have sex with any person, animal, or celestial being — this last one was something they considered a real possibility, so it had to be addressed. When

Buddhism reached Tibet things changed drastically, to the point where a certain sect began to use sex as a kind of meditation. Then when Buddhism got to China, things became even a bit more varied. Most Chinese monasteries favored celibacy, but there were numerous notable exceptions. Later on, when Buddhism migrated to Japan, the government declared that Buddhist monks could be legally married. Then Buddhism migrated to Europe and America, and everything went crazy.

Or maybe it didn't. Maybe we're finally coming to terms with something those other folks never really dealt with. The dude's question is significant and concerns me and, I assume, you as well. As I said, there are better books to read if you want to know the history of how Buddhism has dealt with sex. But I don't know of any books that address the question of how contemporary Buddhists deal with it.

In trying to come to terms with the true Buddhist way of sexuality, I'm much more interested in how Western Buddhists of the twenty-first century approach sex than in what the ancients did. This might strike some readers as odd. We're used to the idea that the best way to understand what a religion really stipulates about some subject is to go back to its earliest texts and discover what the founders of the religion in question said about it. If we want to know the proper Christian attitude toward sex, we consult the Bible, particularly the words of Christ himself. If we want to know how a good Muslim should deal with sex, we just open up the Qu'ran and see what Muhammad had to say on the subject. So if we want to know how Buddhists should view matters of sexual interaction, the best way would be to find out what Buddha himself had to say, right?

Well, no, actually. Buddha himself said in the Kalama Sutra,

Rely not on the teacher, but on the teaching. Rely not on the words of the teaching, but on the spirit of the words. Rely not on theory, but on experience. Do not believe in anything simply because you have heard it. Do not believe in traditions because they have been handed down for many generations. Do not believe anything because it is spoken and rumored by many. Do not believe in anything because it is written in your religious books. Do not believe in anything merely on the authority of your teachers and elders. But after observation and analysis, when you find that anything agrees with reason and is conducive to the good and the benefit of one and all, then accept it and live up to it.

Thus Buddha himself left us with completely different criteria for determining what is and what is not real Buddhism from those of any religion. If we accept Buddha's words about his philosophy, it obviously won't do to just look at history, even the most ancient strata. It also won't do to accept at face value what has been said by great Buddhist teachers, or even by lousy Buddhist teachers like me.

If we want to know how to behave adequately and morally in terms of sex we can't rely on solutions provided for other cultures and other times.

The specific matter of whether Buddhists were allowed to jack off was actually very important to me when I first started this Zen thing. I was a freshman in college and dating a woman who described herself as a born-again Christian. It's a very long story. Don't ask. Anyhow, she had strong opinions about pretty much everything, including masturbation. She didn't necessarily think of it as sinful, though that was probably in the back of her mind. But she did think it was a form of cheating.

Her opinion was based on the famous quote from the Bible that to lust in your heart is the same as committing adultery. As far as I was concerned, even though I didn't really believe in God in the sense of believing in a gigantic white man on a throne up in heaven who judges our actions, I still thought that maybe somewhere out there was a cosmic scale by which morality was measured. What I mean by this is that I thought maybe there was some absolute measure of right and wrong action, and I supposed that the Bible might possibly be a source of information about that absolute scale of right and wrong. So maybe masturbation *was* the same as sexual infidelity.

My parents, as far as I know, were the very model of sexual fidelity. They'd been together since high school and stayed together right up until my mom died in 2007. If they ever cheated on each other, I did not know and do not need or even want to know. But in all the time they were together I never even heard a rumor that either one was unfaithful. So the idea of sexual fidelity was very important to me. If the Bible was right, then I was in big trouble! But then I started to wonder: What if there were other sources of information about what was right and what was wrong?

I was attracted to Buddhism for a whole lot of reasons. One of the things I hoped to find was some way of determining the real nature and content of this absolute scale of right and wrong that I believed might exist.

I discovered that the question of what is and is not acceptable sexually in Buddhism is actually a small part of a much bigger matter. It's about morality, what Buddhists call "right action." In Western culture, many of our questions about moral action involve sex. We Western people tend to take for granted that our decisions about sexual action are all rather weighty moral matters. We believe this to such a degree that we even question whether or not even our *thoughts* about sex are moral issues.

But in Asian cultures traditionally far less attention has been paid to sex as a matter of morality. Which is not to say it's all free love and orgies over there. But the Asian attitude toward sex has always been much freer — or at least lighter — than the Western one. Buddhism, being an Asian import, has a relationship to sex that is completely unlike the ones found in Christianity, Judaism, or Islam.

The key aspect that makes the Buddhist attitude toward sex utterly different is that the concept of sin does not exist in Buddhism.

I will be saying this again and again in this book, to the point where you might get fed up with hearing it. But it really is the key issue.

As Westerners, our belief in sin is so deep that we tend to think of it as a real and substantial thing, even if we are not devoutly religious. Even if we don't necessarily believe in sin ourselves, the belief in sin is so deeply ingrained in our culture that we cannot hope to escape it. Our belief in sin runs so deep that even when we learn that Buddhism does not have this concept, we try to look for it anyway. It's not that we forget what we've been told. It's just that we take it so much for granted that sin actually exists that we keep returning to the same idea over and over without meaning to.

I say this because I do it myself, and it's weird that I should since I was raised pretty much without religion. My family wasn't anti-religious or atheistic. They just didn't really give a crap one way or the other. I was raised to believe that it was up to me to believe or not believe whatever I wanted. I had no religious indoctrination or training at all when I was a child. So when I see that even I react to a lot of what I find in Buddhism with a very deep belief in the real existence of sin, I can only imagine what people from more religious backgrounds have to struggle with.

Furthermore, in Western culture we've been steeped in the religious view that sex itself is a sin. Whether it's good sex or bad, consensual or nonconsensual, within the bonds of holy matrimony or outside it — what they used to call "in sin" — the act of sex itself is seen as a sinful activity. It's hard to know just why this is. As far as I'm aware the Bible doesn't call sex in and of itself a sin.

It doesn't really matter how we got the idea as a culture that sex is sinful. Maybe we got it from the fact that lust is called sinful in the Bible, and it's difficult to have sex without at least a little bit of lust. At least, I've never managed it! What really matters is that most of us in this culture have the belief, however deeply buried it may be, that sex = sin.

But getting back to the preliminary stuff I wanted to say before we dig into these questions, I also have to let you know that even if you searched the entire world you could not possibly find anyone *less* qualified than me to write a book about Buddhism and sex.

The image that most people have of the ideal Buddhist master in regards to sex is that of a person so enlightened and self-controlled that thoughts of sex rarely arise in his* chaste and unsullied mind. On those rare occasions when such thoughts do arise, he redirects his spiritual sight to more lofty concerns, and the impure impulses pass away like an erection at 4:00 a.m. when you channel-surf from a phone sex ad to a commercial for "Sweatin' to the Oldies."**

That's not me. At all.

At heart I'm kind of a horndog. This may be one reason why Gene Simmons of KISS has always been kind of a hero to me. He's far less of a hero to me now than he was when I was a teenager, but I still like him. Gene was a rock star who did not smoke, drink, or do drugs, activities that hold no interest for me either. But Gene was, and by all accounts remains to this day, a sex maniac. While lead guitarist Ace Frehley and drummer Peter Criss destroyed their minds and bodies with booze and pharmaceuticals, Gene indulged instead in nookie, racking up a reported four thousand sexual conquests of various shapes and sizes. Apparently he would fuck anything with two holes. One of Gene's band mates said of him, "You've heard of the Beast Master? Gene is the Beast Fucker!"

This I could relate to. It's exactly how I imagine I'd have been, had any of my rock bands become successful — though I'd like to believe I would have been a bit more selective and avoided the beasts. If I'd had a chance for a life of sex, drugs, and rock and roll, I would have indulged heavily in the sex — and in the rock and roll, of course. But I doubt I'd ever have been a druggie.

---

* Or her, but you know that Buddhist teachers could be any gender, so I won't keep saying that each time I use a male pronoun.

** I stole this line from a blog at http://ratebeer.com/ when I was searching for metaphors for things that disappear quickly.

Sex has always been my main vice, my main temptation. I've kept it in check by getting involved in long-term monogamous relationships in which my sex drive could be reined in. But even so I've lived my life bass-ackward. I spent my twenties and thirties in domesticated monogamy, and it's only been since I entered my forties that I found myself cut loose, not by my own choice,* and free to indulge sexually the way most people get over doing by the time they are out of their twenties.

So what you will be reading, if you choose to keep reading this book, will be the product of my own struggle to come to terms with sex and how to deal with it as a Buddhist teacher.

Sex and spirituality are odd bedfellows. Most spiritual practices are not very sex positive. And a few are a bit too sex positive, to the point of being a little creepy. Or a lot creepy.

But Buddhism is not a form of spirituality. This may surprise you since you probably found this book in the spirituality section of your local Book Barn. So maybe we should get that out of the way right now.

The history of philosophy throughout the world has been a struggle between two basic fundamental systems — idealism and materialism. Spirituality is a kind of idealism. It takes the view that the spiritual world, the world of ideas, imagination, and mental formations, is the true reality. Matter is regarded as secondary at best or sometimes even as nonexistent. We are spirits trapped inside bodies made of gross matter — and some bodies are a lot grosser than others — and the way to happiness, according to the idealists, is to get free of this material world and its miseries.

In many Eastern philosophies we are told, "I am not this body. I am the spiritual soul within." These days, what people in the West often regard as "Buddhism" is really just a mash-up of a couple dozen

---

* I wrote a lot about my split-up with my wife in my previous book, *Zen Wrapped in Karma Dipped in Chocolate*, so I won't go into it here.

Eastern philosophical traditions. So people often think this is the Buddhist belief as well. But the idea that we are souls trapped in bodies is not at all a Buddhist viewpoint.

Materialists, on the other hand, see matter as primary and spirit either as nonexistent or, at least, as negligible. What we perceive as our soul, we are told, is only the workings of a highly complex biological machine. We're all just animals. The Marxists tried to find a rational way to deal with this by distributing material wealth fairly so that everyone could have the best chance at a good life. Or at least that's what they said they were doing! The more radical materialists assert that the only way to be happy is to get as much money, sex, and power as possible for yourself and screw the other guy. There is no soul. There is no afterlife. There is no God. There is no reason to be moral, they say, because the material world does not operate according to those terms.

Buddha explored both these ideas and found them lacking. He was born a prince and spent the first part of his life dedicated to the practical study of materialism. He had everything he could possibly want — money, hot babes, power. We'll get into the hot babes bit a little deeper* later on in the book.

But these things didn't make him happy. So he set off in the opposite direction to see if happiness could be found there. He dedicated himself to various spiritual practices, such as fasting, and achieved their highest goals. He got a massive spiritual high, but in the process he nearly destroyed his body. That wasn't what he wanted either. It wasn't until he rejected both extremes and found the Middle Way that he began to teach the philosophy that now bears his name.

Buddhism starts from the basic premise that neither materialism nor idealism is correct. We are not immaterial spirits trapped in material bodies, nor are we mere permutations of essentially dead matter

---

* Heh, heh! I said, "Get into hot babes deeper!"

who only imagine we have a spiritual side. The Heart Sutra says, "Form is Emptiness, Emptiness is Form." In other words, matter is the immaterial, the immaterial is matter. With apologies to Sting, we are not spirits in the material world. Rather, the experiential, internal, subjective, spiritual side of our day-to-day existence and the hard, external, objective, material world we inhabit are manifestations of one underlying reality that is neither spirit nor matter.

This is a very radical idea. Even today, 2,500 years after Siddhartha Gotama first put forth this notion, few people can accept it. Even those who call themselves Buddhists all too often believe that Buddhism is a form of spirituality.

While it's not spirituality, Buddhism is not materialism either. Buddhism is realism. There's a tendency for contemporary people to assume that realism is the same as materialism. When they use the word *reality* it most often refers to the material world as explained to us by science. But that's not how Buddhists think of "reality." The materialistic point of view is also just a concept. It is not reality, and it is not realism.

Now, matter itself is obviously real. If you have any doubts just drop a big rock on your foot to check. But the trouble is that our understanding of matter may not be accurate. Most of us believe that matter exists first, and because of the existence of matter sense stimulation occurs. Both idealists and materialists tend to conceive of it this way. The book in front of you is made of matter and it's real. So is your forehead. If you smack your forehead real hard with the book, your head will hurt. The subjective experience of pain is the result of the objective collision of material forehead with material book.

Buddhist philosophers like Dogen, Nagarjuna, and Buddha himself turn this around and place sense stimulation first. They say that it is because our senses are stimulated in certain ways that we then assume matter exists. It is a completely different way of conceptualizing the world from what we're used to.

Science happens to be a very good way to look at the material side of reality, so we need to accept science.* But Dogen, the thirteenth-century Buddhist monk who founded the school of Buddhism in which I study and practice, said that the universe in all directions is just a tiny fragment of reality.

That doesn't mean that the material world is here and that somewhere out in the vastness of space is another even bigger universe made of something else. Dogen was talking about our day-to-day experience. The material component of our experience forms just one small part of our reality.

Furthermore, we never experience mind separate from body, and vice versa. The idea that one side is true, while the other is false, doesn't fit our real experience.

We constantly swing back and forth between materialism and idealism. When materialism doesn't satisfy, we try idealism. When idealism lets us down, we swing back to materialism. As a culture we can see this happening right now. A century ago it seemed like materialism might one day solve all of humankind's problems. But in spite of the fact that most of the poorest among us enjoy wealth and comfort our ancestors couldn't have dreamed of, materialism has failed to fulfill many of our most basic needs. Science created the flush toilet and sliced bread, but it also created the atomic bomb and a host of other horrors. So, as a culture, we have started to drift back toward spirituality in the hopes that a more spiritual approach might solve our troubles and bring us the fulfillment we seek. What we've forgotten is that we pursued spirituality for thousands of years before we got started on the materialism kick. Spirituality already let us down. It didn't fulfill our basic needs and wants. That's why we became so materialistic in the first place.

A lot of people look to Buddhism as a spiritual answer to their

---

* I mean legit science, of course. Lots of stuff calls itself "science" these days. But most of us know the difference between the reliable stuff and the crackpot junk. Or maybe we don't, since so many people bought The Secret.

materialistic woes. But if Buddhism is just another form of spirituality, it's as worthless as any other religion. We need something different. And Buddhism is something very, very different.

Every religion, philosophy, addiction, and any other method for
dealing with what life throws at us that I've ever encountered says,
"You feel unfulfilled? Okay. Try this. It will fulfill you." Materialism
works for a time. But after you buy something the thrill of buying it
vanishes, and you want to buy something else. Spirituality can give
you a great big high. But there's always a comedown.

Buddhism doesn't promise to fulfill our desires. Instead it says,
"You feel unfulfilled? That's okay. That's normal. Everybody feels
unfulfilled. You will always feel unfulfilled. There is no problem with
feeling unfulfilled. In fact, if you learn to see it the right way, that
very lack of fulfillment is the greatest thing you can ever experience."
This is the realistic outlook.

Because of this notion that the truth is neither spirit nor matter,
when we get into sexuality, Buddhism does not proceed from the
same standpoint that spiritual religions do. Much of the hatred and
fear of sexuality found in religions stems from the idea that sex is a
thing of the body and that the body must be denied so that the spirit
may be elevated. In Buddhism there is no notion that the body is
made of inferior matter while the spirit flies free within.

My teacher Gudo Nishijima uses the phrase *dimensionally different* to talk about the way Buddhism is radically unlike other religions. By "dimensionally different" he means that the Buddhist view
is so unlike the religious view that comparisons become almost
absurd. It's as if they exist in different dimensions. This is certainly
true of the Buddhist take on sexuality.

One of the most important aspects of Buddhist practice is the
idea of moderation, the Middle Way. While most of us can usually
see the logic of practicing moderation in most things, we tend to put
sex into a special category where extreme reactions of all kinds are
not only acceptable but almost inevitable. We're either way too hung

up on getting sex or way too hung up on avoiding it. Either our sex drive is too great and we try desperately to control it, or it's too little and we start popping Viagra or taking hormones. What's the deal with that stuff anyway? Does everyone's sex life now have to measure up to some kind of *Penthouse Letters*–inspired fantasy? They make that stuff up, you know . . .

On the other side, religions tend to advocate various ideals of sexual purity. And this often leads to trouble. Whether it's Roman Catholic priests fondling choirboys or Indian gurus bedding movie stars, it seems like the religious world is rocked every couple of years by some kind of sex scandal. The Buddhist world has had a few sex scandals, too, including some involving a few well-known American Zen masters.

It's easy to see why this is so. Religious leaders are always presented as something better than ordinary people. True believers see these people as manifestations of the divine, as the living embodiment of some kind of ideal.

But what are ideals, really? They don't actually exist outside our brains. When we project our expectations about what a divine being ought to be onto real people, what else can we hope for besides disappointment? Of course, it doesn't help matters that so many people are perfectly willing to be thought of as manifestations of the divine. Still, the worshippers of such people deserve as much blame for their disappointment as do those whom they worship. Without any followers, people who think they're God's messengers are just delusional. But when they've got crowds of worshippers around them, look out!

Ideals are always matters of mind. And in the pure world of mind, unsullied as it is by messy things like bodies with wee-wees and pee-pees attached, there is no sex. So divine beings should not boink. When we discover that the folks we considered divine are in fact boinking away like mad, our dreams are shattered. In fact, it is precisely because these people are trying to live up to an impossible ideal that they so often turn sex crazy. It's an unbalanced way to live, and nature has a way of balancing things out by tipping the scales in the opposite direction. I'm not saying that celibacy and chastity are in and of themselves impossible. But it isn't just celibacy or chastity we expect from our representatives of the divine, is it? It's *purity*.

And that's where we get into real trouble. Because purity is very hard to pin down. What is it, anyway? "Purebred" dogs and horses do not exist in nature. They are artificially bred by human beings. "Pure" water is water filtered by human-made machines. So what about pure desires? Could all purity be a human concept, never to be found in nature?

People who are "into Zen" often tend to misunderstand the point of Buddhism to be the destruction of all desire, including the desire to get one's rocks off. But this religious attitude toward sexual purity just replaces society's extreme views on the matter with another set of equally extreme views. The real problem — the fact that we permit ourselves to act so extremely with regard to anything at all — remains unaddressed. To view sex as a vile act that the pure of heart dare not even dream of is in its own way just as unbalanced as spending all your time, energy, and cash trying to get some hot man-meat or some tender yoni.*

To practice the Middle Way means applying that view to all areas of your life, without exception. You can't establish real balance if you hold certain areas of experience apart and say it's okay to go to extremes as long as it has to do with sex, or with skeeball, or with whatever it is you're obsessed with. Constantly moving from one extreme to the other is what got your brain and body into the mess they're in right now. How can you expect to get at the root cause of your troubles by doing the very thing that caused the troubles in the first place?

Not being a total sex freak doesn't mean you have to swing the

---

* Or both, if you're so inclined.

completely opposite direction and try to live your life as a sexless robot. Deal with the sexual desires you have in the most reasonable way you can.

When you're jacking off, just jack off. When you're not, just don't.

Chapter 3

ALL SEX IS SUFFERING

Sex and the Four Noble Truths

The Four Noble Truths are the foundation of Buddhist philosophy. They were, in fact, the topic of Buddha's first public discourse. Buddha had given up his life as a prince, in which he had access to all the best things life had to offer, including a bevy of hot babes whose only purpose was to provide him with pleasure. Rejecting this lifestyle, he next dwelt in the forest as a naked ascetic, enduring tremendous physical hardships in order to enhance his spirit by denying his fleshly body. But this, too, proved as fruitless as a hedonistic life of physical pleasure had in his quest to find real happiness. Finally he embarked on the Middle Way, bringing both body and spirit in equal measure to his pursuit of the ultimate truth. He first expressed the understanding he had found in the Middle Way as the Four Noble Truths.

These truths are among the most widely quoted aspects of Buddhist philosophy. They're also among the most widely misunderstood aspects of Buddhist philosophy. The standard translation of the Four Noble Truths goes like this:

1. All life is suffering.
2. The cause of suffering is desire.
3. To cut off desire is to end suffering.
4. Following the Noble Eightfold Path is the way to cut off desire.

The Noble Eightfold Path, by the way, consists of right view, right intention, right speech, right action, right livelihood, right effort, right mindfulness, and right concentration.

It's easy to relate this version of the Four Noble Truths to sex.

All sex is suffering — in some sense, anyway. When Buddhists talk about this version of the Four Noble Truths, the first thing that happens is someone says, "Well *my* whole life isn't suffering! In fact, lots of things in my life are pretty great!"

That's a very good point. This translation is one of the reasons Buddhism was originally described by Western scholars as a kind of radical pessimism. But real Buddhism isn't pessimistic at all. This translation, which has become standard even in Japan, where they have access to the original, is also one of the reasons my own teacher, Nishijima Roshi, initially thought Buddhism made no sense at all. But before I go into that, I want to stick with the usual version of the Noble Truths because that's the one most people are familiar with.

The way this seeming contradiction inherent in the first Noble Truth is usually explained is that even when things seem to be going great in life, there's still an undercurrent of suffering. For example, say you're a hetero guy, and you're having the hottest sex in your entire life with — let's just up the ante here — the two most desirable and delicious twenty-year-old women you've ever had the privilege of meeting, let alone getting to bed down with. Even at that very moment there is suffering because you know it has to end. This is the way it is with anything pleasant in life. It's always transitory.

To get into the sexual side of Noble Truth number two, the reason sex is suffering is desire. In the case cited above, you desire not to have the sex ever end. Or, more commonly, you desire sex when you're not having it, and you suffer until your desire is met. And then you suffer while your desire is being met because you know you're going to end up back where you started at some point. You can't have sex all the time, so after it's done you'll be left with desire and no sex to fulfill it.

As for Noble Truth number three, if you could cut off your desire for sex, you'd end your suffering over it. But who wants to do that?

Noble Truth number four, the Eightfold Path, is ripe for erotic reinterpretation — especially the stuff about right action and right effort. And let's not forget right speech, as in having all the best pickup lines. But I'll leave the rest up to you.

Nishijima Roshi's version of the Four Noble Truths is a bit different. To his way of thinking, all life is certainly not suffering. Lots of things in life are pretty great. Lots of other things are kind of so-so, but certainly not what anyone would call suffering. Yet since he could see the great logic in the rest of Buddhism, he studied this matter in depth and came to the conclusion that the usual way of phrasing the Four Noble Truths is wrong. Or at least it interprets them from a mistaken point of view.

So he looks at the first Noble Truth as the truth of idealism. When looked at idealistically, nothing is ever as good as your ideas about it, so you suffer. Even sex with those cute little coeds I talked about earlier would, if you could actually manage it in real life, have all kinds of pitfalls you never considered in your fantasies. Maybe one of them would get jealous and walk out in the middle. Nothing real is ever quite as good as the things you can dream up.

The second Noble Truth is materialism. Desire implies the accumulation of things. This works both in the standard sense of the desire to accumulate more sexual experience and more stuff, and in the more scientific view that all material objects are the accumulation of smaller particles.

In Nishijima's interpretation, the third Noble Truth refers to action in the present moment rather than to the cutting off of desire. It's completely impossible to be free from all desire. You'd die if you stopped desiring air, water, and food. So what this Truth really refers to, according to Nishijima, is the way in which real action is the coming together of the material and idealistic (or spiritual) sides of life. In the moment of real action, body and mind work together as one.

The ancient Buddhist philosopher Nagarjuna stated that action itself was the fundamental aspect of the universe. To him, human beings were not creatures with the ability to act. Rather, action itself manifested as human beings and as the entire universe. Pretty freaky idea, eh? But when you get deeply into it, this outlook actually makes a lot more sense than the standard view of things. I'll leave it to you to do a few decades of zazen and see what I mean.

The final Noble Truth is reality itself. This world here and now is where the foregoing three Noble Truths really happen. The realistic way to live a better life is to follow the Noble Eightfold Path. In other words, it's more practical to live an ethical life because it will make you happier.

This version of the Four Noble Truths also relates to sexuality. In the idealistic phase, sex is a beautiful dream, shared romance, fantastic pleasure, and all the rest. In the materialistic phase, sex is sweating bodies rubbing together. It's base and mechanical, the action of two animals in the throes of trying to reproduce — or at least in the throes of using their reproductive organs to experience physical pleasure. In the phase of action, sex has a spiritual or idealistic component and a material or physical component. These cannot be separated, or what you'd have wouldn't really be sex. The mental component alone would be masturbation, and the physical component alone with no conscious involvement whatsoever just wouldn't be any fun at all. In the moment of having sex, body and mind function as a single entity, and you lose all sense of separation between the two. Finally, in the realistic phase, sex is exactly what it is, beyond any attempt to explain or comprehend it.

Chapter 4

You Celibate, I'll Buy a Bit!

H is Holiness the Dalai Lama made all the papers not long ago by saying celibacy is good. Must've been a slow news day.

What he actually said — in English without a translator, hence the cutely weird grammar — was, "Sexual pleasure, sexual desire, actually, I think is short-period satisfaction, and often that leads to more complication. Naturally as a human being . . . some kind of desire for sex comes, but then you use human intelligence to make comprehension that those couples always full of trouble. And in some cases there is suicide, murder cases." As for celibacy he said, "We miss something, but at the same time, compare whole life, it's better, more independence, more freedom. Too much attachment towards your children, towards your partner [is] one of the obstacle or hindrance of peace of mind."*

He's correct, of course. Sex is complicated. Abstaining from it relieves you of those complications. Since having sex isn't strictly a

---

* From a story reported by the American Free Press, November 28, 2008.

necessity — meaning you, as an individual, *can* live without it — it makes perfect rational sense simply to drop it. So before we start talking about sex let's talk a little about celibacy, shall we?

In the Zen sect, of which the Dalai Lama is not a member, there are ten precepts one must agree to adhere to if one wants to be accepted into the order as a monk or layperson. I've put this list in every one of my books so far. But for those who haven't read the others,* here is the list: 1) Not to kill 2) Not to steal 3) Not to misuse sexuality 4) Not to lie 5) Not to cloud the mind with intoxicants 6) Not to criticize others 7) Not to be proud of oneself and slander others 8) Not to covet 9) Not to give way to anger and 10) Not to slander Buddha, Buddhist teachings, or the Buddhist community.

The last five precepts are different in other sects of Buddhism, but the first five are common to pretty much every active Buddhist order. In early Buddhism the list of rules for monks to obey was much, much longer. The precepts originated when monks would come up to Buddha and ask him if this or that activity was acceptable for a Buddhist monk. His answers formed the basis of a list of rules called the *vinaya*, which was the moral code for Buddhist monks.

When Buddha died he told his students that they should keep the major rules of the *vinaya* but that they could ignore the less important ones. Unfortunately he never specified which rules were important and which were not. I'm convinced this was not an oversight on his part or due to his being so ill with the diarrhea that ended up killing him that he couldn't come up with a specific list. He did this deliberately. Buddhism is all about finding your own way, not imitating the ways of others or even the ways of Buddha himself.

The monks who carried on after Buddha's death ignored their master's advice and tried to keep all the rules. There are still some sects today that attempt to follow the entire *vinaya*, though there

---

* And you shouldn't need to in order to follow this book. But I could sure use the cash if you do decide to buy them!

aren't many Buddhists like that anymore. What happened more often was that different groups of Buddhists picked out those rules among the *vinaya* regulations that they considered important.

As a result, different Buddhist sects have different rules. Some have eight precepts instead of ten. In some versions you're supposed to refrain from eating after noon, attending entertainment spectacles, and sleeping in high or wide beds. Then there are six *other* precepts you take in the Zen initiation that I don't even want to go into here.* There are a few other versions out there. Since I don't know all the variations, I'm going to stick with the Zen rules. You can find other, more scholarly writers on the subject if comparing and contrasting the various lists is your idea of fun.

One rule that every Buddhist sect I know of has maintained as a major rule is "Do not misuse sexuality." Their notions of what does and does not constitute misuse of sexuality vary wildly. But they're pretty much all in agreement that sexuality is something that should not be misused. For many Buddhists, celibacy appears to be the ultimate way to avoid misusing sexuality. You can't possibly misuse sex if you never have it. Right? Well, maybe.

The Dalai Lama represents one of the schools that believe the best way to avoid misusing sexuality is to avoid sex altogether. I happen to come from the Japanese Soto Zen sect, which allows monks and nuns to marry. And not just each other! Suffice it to say, no vow of celibacy is required to be a Zen monk. Because if it were, brother, I never woulda become a monk!

What it means to misuse sexuality differs from culture to culture and changes over time. What went for ancient people in the Far East isn't always workable in our culture. According to Clifford Bishop's book *Sex and Spirituality*, "In 13th century Cambodia, the

---

* If you must know, they are the Three Devotions: 1) Devotion to Buddha 2) Devotion to dharma and 3) Devotion to the sangha and the Three Universal Precepts (meaning they aren't limited to just Buddhists), which are: 1) To observe social rules 2) To observe the rules of morality and 3) To work for the salvation of all beings.

daughter of a wealthy family was deflowered between the ages of seven and nine by a Buddhist priest." The priest received gifts of wine, cloth, and silver for performing this service, which was considered a distasteful thing that nonetheless had to be done by someone. Our contemporary Western views of what constitutes the misuse of sexuality are quite different.*

But as to the question of celibacy being the ultimate and eternally foolproof way to avoid misusing sexuality, my response is, if only things were that easy! As Shunryu Suzuki, author of the classic book *Zen Mind, Beginner's Mind*, once said, "Sex. Problem. No sex. Problem."

Sex is such a knotty subject** in so many ways. Religions always try and come up with a single formula for dealing with sex that will work for all people in all situations — from holy matrimony to pious abstinence. The Hare Krishnas, to cite just one example, try to mix the two, allowing sex but only for the procreation of Krishna-conscious children and only after the couple chants for a few hours first to ensure that the dirty deed is sufficiently pure. I don't see that ever becoming a widespread practice. In any case, no matter what religion or philosophy you follow, no one will ever come up with one formula for dealing with sex that will satisfy everybody.

Buddhism never really got into regulating people's sexual behavior the way Christianity and other spiritual religions often do. Apart from the vaguely defined idea of not misusing sexuality the few specific regulations concerning sexual behavior in Buddhism have always applied only to the clergy, never to laypeople. Laypeople, as the term suggests, were free to get laid however much they wanted, in or out of wedlock, in homo or hetero couples, whatever

---

*   As they should be, by the way!
**   And a naughty one, too, sometimes! (Or a literally knotty one if you're into that!)

they enjoyed. Oh, there have been Buddhist leaders who have made pronouncements to laypeople regarding what is and isn't acceptable sexually. But there has never been widespread agreement on these specifics, nor has there been widespread condemnation of certain specific acts, such as homosexual ones, for example, as there has been within Christianity, Islam, and other spiritual religions.

Let's talk a little more about the meaning of the precept "Do not misuse sexuality" and what that means to us now.

I think we can all agree that sexuality can be misused. The most obvious examples would be rape and child molestation, which are never acceptable behavior under any circumstances. But beyond that there are millions of variations in the ways human beings relate to one another, and to themselves, sexually. An activity that would clearly be a misuse of sexuality under one set of circumstances might not under different conditions.

My teacher rephrases the third precept as "Do not desire too much" rather than "Do not misuse sexuality." Bodhidharma, the fifth-century Buddhist monk traditionally cited as the founder of the Zen school, said, "There is nothing to grasp. Not giving rise to attachment is the precept of not misusing sexuality."

I am saving the matter of attachment for later in the book since it is a very complex issue. For now we'll just look at the precept itself.

Even in its common form the precept is deliberately vague. We can assume that the people who created it had already seen the damage done by religious leaders who tried to create hard-and-fast* rules for sexual behavior that could be applied universally. So they simply acknowledged that sexuality could be misused, that its misuse leads to trouble, and that Buddhist practitioners would be better off if they vowed not to misuse it. Just what constituted misuse was left up to individual interpretation.

---

* Heh, heh, I said, "hard-and-fast."

Or not. Even Buddhists sometimes aren't as smart as they ought to be. As I mentioned before, an early school of Buddhism tried to work out exactly what did and did not constitute misuse of sexuality, at least for monks and nuns, if not necessarily for the general population. Among the huge and detailed list of rules they made up, my favorite one says that it's not misuse of sexuality if a woman has sex with a monk while he's sleeping and he doesn't realize what's going on. You just *know* there's a story behind that one! I'm sure some douche-nozzle priest used that as an excuse — *I was asleep the whole time! I swear!* — and it made its way into the books.

Some of the other *vinaya* rules on sex include:

- Monks are not allowed to rub their bodies against each other when bathing.
- A monk shall not castrate himself. Apparently, one of Buddha's monks did, and Buddha said, "When one thing wanted cutting off, this foolish fellow has cut off another!"*
- It is a greater offense to have sex with a rotten corpse than with a fresh one.
- Having vaginal sex with an iguana is a greater offense than sticking your weenie up the trunk of an elephant.**

These days Zen centers and other Buddhist monasteries in the West are often coed and have no celibacy requirement, which creates a set of problems that Buddha never had to address — that people who live in these centers often become romantically involved. Needless to say, the *vinaya* does not address this possibility at all!

---

*   *Vinaya*, pt. III, 77.

** I swear I did not make this up! I got it out of that book I told you about earlier, *The Red Thread* by Bernard Faure. By the way, these last two rules, and similar ones, probably do not indicate that these types of offenses actually occurred, but that the compilers of the *vinaya* were obsessive people who wanted to cover every conceivable possibility. At least I'd like to think so!

The San Francisco Zen Center (SFZC) is an interesting case in point. Although I've never lived there and am not part of their lineage, I have spent a good deal of time there and know a number of people at the place. It's fascinating to see how they approach the problem.

SFZC has had some rather infamous problems in the past with regard to the sexual activities of its members and its leadership. The book *Shoes Outside the Door: Desire, Devotion, and Excess at San Francisco Zen Center* by Michael Downing recounts these in gory detail. In a nutshell, the leader of the center had an affair with a student or possibly a few students, got ousted, and everyone went bonkers.

Plus, the Zen Center came of age in the late sixties and swingin' seventies, in San Francisco, of all places. Free love, Eastern religions, and communes were all the rage. So it was inevitable that certain members of the organization tended to regard SFZC as, at least potentially, yet another swingin', free love, Eastern religious commune.

The problems this created led the Zen Center to enact a number of policies intended to make life in the community run more smoothly. One of the advisors in developing the center's current policies was the famous Vietnamese Zen monk, Thich Nhat Hanh, author of every third book on Buddhism on the shelves of the store where you bought this one. He created his own version of the precepts, one of which went:

> Do not mistreat your body. Learn to handle it with respect. Do not look on your body as only an instrument. Preserve vital energies (sexual, breath, spirit) for the realization of the Way. Sexual expression should not happen without love and commitment. In sexual relationships, be aware of future suffering it may cause others. To preserve the happiness of others, respect the rights and commitments of others. Be fully aware of

the responsibility of bringing new lives into the world. Meditate on the world into which you are bringing new beings.*

Respecting his views on the matter, the folks at the San Francisco Zen Center thought Mr. Hanh might be able to help them out with formulating a policy to deal with their coed monastic practice. After much discussion and debate, in which Thich Nhat Hanh and many others were involved, the Zen Center eventually adopted its own variation on the Third Precept as part of a code of ethics for members living communally at the center:

> A disciple of Buddha does not misuse sexuality but rather cultivates and encourages open and honest relationships. The Zen Center sangha recognizes that sexuality is as much a part of the field of practice as any other aspect of our daily lives. Acknowledging and honoring our sexuality is part of creating an environment where conscious, mindful and compassionate relationships can be cultivated. Special care must be taken when people of unequal status or authority enter into a sexual relationship. In particular, there are two forms of relationships which can lead to great harm and confusion. Therefore both are considered a misuse of sexuality within our community.**

The first type of sexual relationship that is considered forever and always to be misuse is one between an adult and a child. Take that, thirteenth-century Cambodian Buddhists!*** The second kind is teacher-student sexual relationships. But there is a loophole. According to Stephanie Kaza in her article "Finding Safe Harbor: Buddhist Sexual Ethics in America," "Zen Center recommends a

---

* From *Interbeing: Fourteen Guidelines for Engaged Buddhism.*
** From *The Ten Essential Precepts*, available at www.sfzc.org.
***Although I'm joking about the vast differences in what is considered "misuse of sexuality" among different cultures and time periods, pedophilia is never funny. We'll address its terrible repercussions later.

six-month neutral period after ending a teaching relationship and beginning a sexually active peer relationship. Further, they recommend that anyone in a formal religious leadership role with 'clear advantages of influence in relationship to others' should discuss the appropriateness of their potential relationship with a practice leader."*

When I went to stay at the Tassajara Zen Mountain Monastery, run by the San Francisco Zen Center, I received a list of rules all residents are expected to abide by. A few of them are as follows (the capitalization in what follows is theirs, by the way):

A ZEN STUDENT EMBRACES AND SUSTAINS AWARENESS AND ACCOUNTABILITY IN SEXUAL CONDUCT:

- By adhering to the SIX-MONTH RULE: that is, refraining from beginning a new sexual relationship, at any time, in which either person has not practiced at Tassajara for at least six months, or in which either person is under eighteen years of age. (Not following this rule may result in being asked to leave the monastery and not being accepted to practice periods.)
- By refraining from contact with a person who repeatedly requests no contact.
- By speaking to the Director if we believe that this policy has been violated in an effort to seek resolution and reestablish harmony.
- By becoming aware of how sexual energy is communicated through speech, and nonverbally through touch, eye contact, body language, and attitude.
- By refraining from engaging in noncommitted sexual relationships.

---

* From "Finding Safe Harbor: Buddhist Sexual Ethics in America," *Buddhist-Christian Studies* 24 (2004): 23-35.

- If considering a relationship with someone at Tassajara, by speaking to a practice leader first about it.

There are a few more rules, like that Zen students can't bathe nude in the creek where the guests often do and so on. But the most interesting one to me is that you cannot enter a relationship with someone at any of the Zen Center's three communities (City Center, Green Gulch, and Tassajara) unless you've both been residents there for at least six months. And that when you do enter into a relationship, you need to have a meeting with the center's administration about it. This is a fascinating and, I think, clever way to try and emulate the spirit of Buddha's original celibate flock in India 2,500 years ago in a way the people of twenty-first-century San Francisco can accept.

The thing about discussing the relationship with the administration is, I have been told, not as draconian as it sounds. The committee, they tell me, is not there to determine if your relationship is permissible. They are there to help you deal with the unique problems posed by trying to date a fellow member of a very tightly knit religious community that shares the same living space. And while I understand SFZC's unique situation and their ways of dealing with it, and while I have no argument with their methodology, I have to say that I myself could never submit to this. I just have a very hard time believing such a committee would take absolutely no interest in determining who gets to sleep with whom.*

In any case, as I said earlier, whether you're in a monastic situation or living in the wider community, celibacy would seem like the ultimate solution to the problem of misusing sex. How can you misuse it if you never do it?

---

* Having said that, though, I want to be very clear again that I am not condemning the way they handle things. It's probably the only way to do it, given their situation. I'm just saying that I personally would not submit to it. Maybe this is one of the reasons why I am clearly unsuited to monastic life and have never spent any extended periods as a monastery resident.

Unfortunately, it's much easier to take a vow of celibacy than it is to keep it. I think about this every time I hear about yet another supposedly celibate religious figure getting caught with a choirboy. It seems pretty likely to me that if some of those guys just got it on with some willing lass of an appropriate age, or maybe with one of their fellow clergymen if they were so inclined, one less child would be traumatized for life.

My first Zen teacher once told me he sometimes thought that the best way to avoid misusing sexuality is to just go ahead and fuck. If you're so hot and bothered that your condition is starting to become a danger to others, and there's someone willing to, um, help you remedy that, then maybe fucking is the most efficient way not to misuse sexuality.

As for me, my opinion of what constitutes the misuse of sexuality is illustrated by something I saw when I took a look at the infamous Gene Simmons sex tape that's been making the rounds on the Interwebs for a while.

If you haven't seen it, basically, Gene Simmons, the demonic bass player of the heavy-metal band KISS, and a childhood hero of mine, has what looks like the worst sex on Earth with a pretty Australian model. He barely touches or acknowledges her. At one point he tries to kiss her, and she turns her head.* He appears to be using her as little more than a receptacle for his sperm. I'd have to say the activities depicted in the tape seem to me to be a very clear case of the misuse of sexuality.

Don't get me wrong, I love Gene Simmons, and I'll be a KISS fan till I die. And it's really not for me to comment on Gene's personal life. But I will anyway, because it's fun. That video is just sad. I mean, the guy moistens his lady friend up by licking his fingers and then rubbing them on her. What is that world-famous seven-inch tongue for? If I had a tongue like that you better believe I'd put it to

---

* Ouch!

good use every chance I got! Plus, he is chewing gum throughout the proceedings.

Look. If you don't like or at least trust a girl enough to get your face up in there and use that famous tongue, if she won't kiss you, and if you're so blasé about the whole thing you can't even spit out your gum, then what is the point of fucking at all?

As I mentioned earlier, Nishijima Roshi has rephrased the precept that usually goes "Do not misuse sexuality" as "Do not desire too much." I wouldn't put forth what I'm about to say as *the* definition of misuse of sex. But one clear indication that you're desiring too much is when you fuck someone even though you aren't even that into it. This doesn't just go for sex, either. It goes for pretty much any time you do something just because you think it's supposed to be fun or because it was fun the last time you did it, even though you really don't care for it now. In cases like that you're not even acting on your true desire anymore. You're just acting on what you think you *ought* to desire. I can only say this because I've done it.

I have often found myself doing something just because it seemed like it was fun, then finding out it wasn't fun. A lot of these times I've found myself following through on an activity mainly because it had been fun before and *dammit, it was gonna be fun now*. Or because society had designated it as one of the fun things people did. I'm sure everybody's done that.

Getting back to celibacy, though — what about true celibacy? What about someone who doesn't just *say* they don't have sex but who really and truly does not have sex of any kind? Remember that even masturbation was forbidden in those early Buddhist sects I mentioned. Good for them, I say. If they can manage it. I don't think I could, personally. My head would get so filled up with thoughts of fucking that I'd be a menace to society. If you get so sex obsessed you can't think straight, what good are you to anyone?

One of the biggest complaints people have about Zen is that it's too self-centered, that it doesn't spend a whole lot of time addressing how you can do good works for the world, only about how you can do good for yourself.

Damn straight it does! That's the point. The idea in Zen is that the best way to truly do good for the world at large is to get yourself together. It's like when you're on an airplane. They tell you that if you're traveling with children and there's a loss of cabin pressure, you need to put on your own oxygen mask before helping your child. The reason is that if you are not breathing properly you will be in no state to help your child. It is critical to look after yourself first, or there's a good chance both you and your kid will bite it.

So in terms of sexuality, if your celibacy starts to interfere with your mental processes, it may be better to break your vows in a manner that is rational and morally right than to keep the vow and be a nutcase whose nuttiness makes everyone he or she encounters nutty.

Still, maybe there are people who have tremendous self-control, who can keep a vow of celibacy and remain perfectly sane. And if there are and that's what they want to do, I say go for it. But I doubt anyone with that much self-control needs my permission or even cares about my opinion anyway.

I think true celibacy can be a terrific way of making a person more self-sufficient and balanced. The times in my life when I've been celibate by choice, it's always been very nice to have that particular burden taken off my shoulders. My friend Daigan Gaither, a gay Zen monk at the San Francisco Zen Center who has from time to time taken temporary vows of celibacy, put it to me like this:

> There are two ways to look at celibacy. One is celibacy as denial. To say I can't think about it, I can't have it, I can't look at it, oh, my God get it away from me. Or there's celibacy that says I'm still a sexual being, I'm just choosing not to engage in this behavior. I still have these thoughts and have to work with this stuff. This is just a choice about how I behave. When I was celibate I started looking at what I found attractive. What do you find attractive when you're horny, or when you're lonely?

You notice all this stuff when you're choosing not to engage in it. The fact of not engaging in it allows you the space to just look at it and see it for what it actually is.

The drive to sex is fueled by one of the worst feelings ever, which is loneliness. That's the most difficult emotion of all. There are nights where it manifests for me as physical pain, even though I live communally in the Zen Center. Loneliness has more to do with my own connection to myself than how many people are around. When I've allowed myself to get harried and lose touch with my practice, allowed myself to reify the sense of self, that's when I get lonely.

When I don't have zazen practice the baseball bats come out. I start beating myself up. I feel lonely, therefore I must be a piece of crap, blah, blah. But when I practice it's just seeing that there is loneliness. What else is there?

Whether you're gay or straight, loneliness is a killer. We all got socialized to believe we're either the victim or the bad guy. So you look at every situation asking, "Am I the victim here or am I the bad guy?" Zazen practice lets us sift through this and say, "that's the crap, that's the story you tell yourself, all of that stuff."*

On the other side of celibacy you've got stuff like polyamory. I first became aware of the word *polyamory* when I started getting asked about it by polyamorous people who seemed to want my Buddhist master blessing on their lifestyle.

So among other works, I read *The Ethical Slut: A Practical Guide to Polyamory, Open Relationships & Other Adventures*, by Dossie Easton and Janet W. Hardy, one of the most popular and respected books on polyamory, and discussed polyamory with people who practice it.** For those who've never come across the word before,

---

* From an interview with Mr. Gaither, January 27, 2010.
** See my interview with porn star Nina Hartley later in this book for evidence.

polyamory refers to a lifestyle in which a person chooses to forgo both monogamy and celibacy and has sex with a number of people. Sometimes it's a fixed number, like a threesome or a specific circle of people. Sometimes it's completely open. There are hundreds of variations.

As the title *The Ethical Slut* suggests, polyamory is intended to be something like what used to be called "slutting around," only with a code of ethics. There is supposed to be open communication, benevolence, trust, freedom from jealousy, and lots of other nice stuff.

This all sounds fine. But then again, lots of things sound fine... on paper. I enjoyed *The Ethical Slut* and found a lot of the ideas in it both good and useful. I agree with the authors' stance that monogamy is not the only viable type of sexual relationship, that the traditional responses to jealousy are learned behaviors, not natural instincts,* that loving someone doesn't mean you have the right to control that person's behavior, and so on. But I also felt the authors were far too idealistic. They even use the word *utopia* from time to time to describe the ideal polyamorous lifestyle — their concluding chapter is titled "A Slut Utopia" — but they don't appear to understand that the word *utopia* refers to something that is a beautiful idea on paper but ultimately impractical when actually carried out in the real world.

My biggest argument with that highly influential book is this. The authors write about the problems of polyamory, such as jealousy, the lack of acceptance by society, and so forth, and then they offer a number of possible solutions. But the one solution they never discuss is abandoning polyamory. While I'll agree that the lifestyle they advocate sounds really terrific, and there may even be people out there who can make it work, it is definitely not for everyone.

---

* Although I think that jealousy itself — as opposed to the way we *respond* to jealousy — may be a very deeply rooted, almost instinctual thing.

I'm fully convinced that human beings are basically pair-bonding animals.* It takes a very long time to raise a human child to maturity, far longer than any other animal. Though it's certainly possible for one parent to do this alone, it is much easier with a pair. Therefore evolution favors strong pair-bonding instincts.

You and I are alive today owing to a very long tradition of pair-bonding human beings, even if our own parents got divorced or never knew each other. You cannot simply decide to undo this kind of hard-wired conditioning just 'cuz it feels cool. I'm not saying it can't happen. I'm saying it can't happen simply because you decided you want to be that way.

Evolution doesn't only happen on the physical level to individual organisms. Societies evolve as well. So we are all parts of a society that has evolved in a particular way, and this way happened to favor pair bonding very strongly. Societies can and do change, as do biological organisms. But, just like biological evolution, radical social changes do not occur rapidly or painlessly. So if you decide to buck several hundred thousand years of social evolution, you need to expect some difficulties.

In Buddhism we say that inside and outside are essentially the same. This means that you and the society you live in are intimately connected. Even if your views are completely at odds with the prevailing views of the society you live in, that society is still part of you. Simply making a conscious decision to live in a different way from what your society considers normal is not enough. You may find that you "believe" certain things on a very deep subconscious level even while consciously rejecting them. It's odd to use the word *believe* to describe something that happens unconsciously. But it's been my experience that I hold a whole lot of beliefs that I am not at all conscious of, and I am absolutely certain this is not unique to me alone.

---

* Don't get your panties in a twist. I will also discuss whether or not pair bonding and monogamy are the same thing later. I don't think they necessarily are.

If you're going to try polyamory or some other similar alternative sexual lifestyle — and I'm not saying you should not try them, that's entirely up to you — you need to know what you're up against. This is not trivial stuff, either externally or internally. It's deep, deep conditioning far beyond the level of conscious thought.

Then there's the matter of attachment. We'll get deeply into the Buddhist idea of attachment soon. But in this context I just want to say that none of us can go through life without any attachments at all. And you're *always* going to form some level of attachment to anyone you share bodily fluids with. A woman I once shared fluids with told me that she felt that when she let a man enter her body sexually she often felt like a bit of his karma entered her as well. By karma, she was referring to his history, the chain of cause and effect that made him who he is. This, she felt, became part of her, too, on some level. I think this is true and that it also works the same way for men and, I'm certain, in same-sex couples and other groupings as well. There is always entanglement, whether or not you are willing to admit it.

Buddhists do not view human beings as discrete, unconnected units who are able to move about the playing board of life like the little plastic shoe or the little plastic hat on a Monopoly board. Instead we see individual human beings as something like the visible crests of waves. The ocean manifests itself as waves that can be seen as discrete units. We might even be able to name the waves the way we name people and pets and planets, if we really wanted to. But the waves are made up of nothing more than the ocean of which they are part, and when they're done being waves they become undifferentiated parts of the ocean again. In the Buddhist understanding of things, individual human beings are no more apart from each other than waves are apart from the ocean. The interaction between the waves goes miles deeper than just the way they might superficially splash up against each other at the very top of the ocean.

Sex without some kind of attachment, however minor it might be, seems to me a lot like the Loch Ness Monster. It would be really cool if it existed. And every once in a while you get tantalizing hints that it might. But whenever you examine the evidence objectively, it falls to pieces. Still, every time someone comes out with a new photo purporting to be the real Nessie, I'm right there. Some fantasies are very hard to give up on. And I'll admit it, every so often I've fallen for the belief that sex without any attachment at all might exist as well. I'll probably fall for it a few more times before I kick the bucket. But that's because I'm stupid.

Just because you *think* you're so cool that you won't have any notions of commitment or betrayal or jealousy or any of the rest of that stuff doesn't mean your partner(s) won't. Or even that *you* won't. Thinking is only a teeny, tiny part of what goes on in the mind/body. The entanglement I'm talking about here happens at a level far deeper than thought can ever hope to reach. You may not even be consciously aware of what's happening. But you can at least be consciously aware that it *is* happening and operate from that standpoint. This is a very sticky proposition in more ways than one.

Still, I have no interest in trying to convince anyone to live the way I think is best. And anyway, you might actually be surprised at what I think is best. But that really doesn't matter, which is why I'm not saying. In any event, what you do is your own business.

Yet to some extent the way other people conduct their sex lives does affect me. And the way I conduct my sex life affects you as well. It affects all of us. The fewer people there are running around all stressed out about their sex lives, the better things are for everyone. They won't be so busy figuring out their social calendar that they crash their cars into the guardrails and stop up traffic for hours. They won't be so sexually repressed that they strap bombs to themselves and attack hotels in Mumbai. Stuff like that. So to that extent, I'd like to see more people paying more attention to how they manage themselves sexually. Then when they interact with me they'll be a little more chilled out.

I suspect this is at the deepest root of all religious restrictions about sex all over the world. Ancient people were just looking for ways to manage this new thing they were developing called "society." They knew sexual interaction created complications. The day after caveman Og did the nasty with caveman Ugum's woman, they started throwing rocks at each other, and all hell broke loose in the village. Something needed to be done, so the chief made a rule. All the moralizing and threats of burning in hell just got tacked on later as extra incentive for the more suggestible to do what seemed likely to keep things civilized.

The Dalai Lama admits that abstaining from sex means missing out on certain aspects of life. He seems content in the idea that these things aren't really worth much anyway. You might feel differently. Maybe it's not just wild nights of unbridled passion you're after. Maybe you want marriage and family and all that nice stuff. That's fine. I'm not so sure the Dalai Lama's solution is quite as neat as he thinks it is anyhow. I've hung around enough monks to know that there are plenty of cases where all the emotional and attachment-related bullshit they escape by not having families just ends up getting transferred onto the surrogate family of fellow monks they live with. Like I said, there's no easy answer to any of this that'll work out for everybody every time.

Anyhow, in the end it doesn't matter what the Dalai Lama thinks, and it certainly matters even less what I think. It comes down to what's most important for you. I would only say that I've found that what's most important to most people is to live as stable a life as possible. If you understand that you want that, then sex has to be handled carefully. It pushes a whole lot of buttons, whether or not you want to admit that. Pay attention, and be willing to accept things you don't really want to accept. This is the advice I give myself all the time.

Chapter 5

[SEXUAL ANGLES ON BUDDHISM]
SAVING ALL BEINGS...FROM MY DICK!
Sex and the Bodhisattva Vow

A bodhisattva is someone on the path to Buddhahood who vows to hold off on entering nirvana until she or he has saved every other being in the universe from suffering and distress. It's a really noble ideal, although I always figured Nirvana broke up when Kurt Cobain died.*

This idea took hold in Northern India around the time of Christ. It led to the revitalization of Buddhism because it provided laypeople with something they could aspire to. Popular understanding at the time had it that only monks and nuns could become enlightened. But anyone could live a moral life and become a bodhisattva. I'm ignoring a lot of fascinating historical and mythological details here. But you can find those in better books than this one.**

---

* Them Crooked Vultures, though, is a very cool band.

** In fact, you can find a bit more detail than this in my own first book, *Hardcore Zen*. Though if you really want to know, I suggest consulting a thorough history of Buddhism. *Buddhist Religions: A Historical Introduction* by Richard H. Robinson, Willard L. Johnson, and Thanissaro Bhikkhu is my personal favorite, although it's very expensive. *A Concise History of Buddhism* by Andrew Skilton is also very good, and a lot cheaper. For a look at the history of Buddhism in the West, *How the Swans Came to the Lake* by Rick Fields is very good, though I wish someone would do an updated edition.

In any case, a bodhisattva makes four vows, which are repeated in many Zen temples as a daily ritual. They go like this:

1. Beings are numberless; I vow to save them.
2. Delusions are inexhaustible; I vow to end them.
3. Dharma gates are boundless; I vow to enter them.
4. Buddha's way is unsurpassable; I vow to become it.

Let's just deal with the first vow here. How exactly *does* one go about saving all those numberless beings? Well, for one thing, you'll notice that all four vows first acknowledge the impossibility of accomplishing the things one is about to vow to do before one actually vows to do that impossible thing.

Rob Robbins, a guy who often came to the Saturday morning zazen meetings I had when I lived in Santa Monica, once said that he understood the first bodhisattva vow as "I vow to save all beings ...from myself." I think this is an excellent way of looking at it. It's ridiculous to imagine you're gonna turn into some kind of spiritual Superman who can go out and save everybody everywhere with his super-Buddha powers.

The matter of the bodhisattva vows and how to keep them is a topic of endless discussion and writing among Buddhist types. But since we're talking about sex in this book, let's talk specifically about how they relate to sex. This is very legitimate, even in terms of orthodox Buddhism, since one of the main things that differentiated the Buddhist clergy from the laypeople for whom these vows were originally intended was that laypeople could get laid.

The bodhisattva vows are mainly about compassion. We can't save everyone, we can't get rid of all our delusions, we can't enter all those dharma gates, whatever the heck they are,* and we can't become the Way of Buddha. But we vow to do those things anyway. We vow to do our best, even in the full knowledge that we will fail.

In terms of sexuality this mostly means vowing not to be an

---

* That's why they call 'em laypeople!

asshole, vowing to respect other people, and vowing to live ethically, no matter what lifestyle we choose. This doesn't mean that we have to lead our sex lives according to some arbitrary system that society has decided is moral. But it does mean that we have do whatever — or whomever — we do in a way that causes as little harm as possible.

You can't rescue everybody, but you can make efforts to save them from yourself. That's the one place where you can really be effective. Not by saving them from whatever has caused damage in the past or may harm them in the future, but by making an effort not to be the cause of more damage right now. Of course, this, too, is impossible. Just by being alive you cause some level of damage.

This doesn't mean you ought to hide out in the corner afraid to make a move lest you harm someone. Sometimes the action you think would be harmful might actually be necessary and welcome. Yelling at a little kid when she's about to step out into traffic might "harm her" by making her cry, but it might also save her life. Life is full of situations like that, and they're usually far subtler. Often the most loving thing to do also hurts. Just be very, very careful when dealing with those kinds of situations!

This is where intuition comes in handy. It's hard to know the right thing to do just by thinking a situation through. But Buddhists have a long-standing tradition of believing that at some level we always know what the best course of action is in any given situation. We just have to be quiet enough to let that course of action present itself to us. And we need the confidence to act when life shows us what we need to do. Not to sound like a broken record, but zazen can help a whole lot with both.

I'd like to step slightly sideways here and talk about another aspect of "saving all beings" as it relates to sex. If, for example, you're romantically involved with someone who has been psychologically damaged by sex in the past — through sexual abuse in childhood, for example — you might have the urge to try and save that person. Don't.

You heard me right. I'm saying screw the bodhisattva vow.

Or at least screw that interpretation of it.

This kind of approach is almost always seen by the person you're trying to help as demeaning and disrespectful. This goes way beyond cases of abuse. I have a bit of experience with this. Once upon a time I thought it was my duty to be Super-Buddha Man and rescue someone I loved from her past, owing partly to my misinterpretation of the bodhisattva vows. It was an unqualified disaster.

Sex abuse notwithstanding, ultimately you can't ever save anybody from anything but you. You can't save them, but you can listen. Sometimes that's all someone really wants. The urge to rescue someone who has had a difficult time with sexuality may seem noble. But it's incredibly arrogant to assume that you're somehow better than another person, which is what you have to assume when you try and effect such a rescue.

Chapter 6

ATTACHED TO NONATTACHMENT

In a previous chapter I mentioned that Bodhidharma, the fifth-century Buddhist monk traditionally cited as the founder of the Zen school, said, "There is nothing to grasp. Not giving rise to attachment is the precept of not misusing sexuality."

This brings up a key area of concern when speaking of Buddhism and sexuality, so let's talk about attachment.

I got an email recently, and it said:

> I was given your book *Sit Down and Shut Up!* and love it. I am married with three beautiful daughters, I feel I follow the Buddhist philosophy, and I have read many books about Buddhism but always had one question. I think I understand that I have to give up attachments to end any suffering but...
>
> Can you be married and a parent, yet not have any attachments? Does a family fall into the category of "an attachment"? I try to detach myself from things, but at the same time I feel like my family should have a nice house and the typical American life. I feel I can give up everything, but I don't think I could give up my family. Hopefully you have time to answer this, if not, that's cool. I will just keep doing what I'm doing.

I get a lot of variations on this question of how to cultivate "nonattachment." Here's another example:

> I've been wrestling with two attachments I can't seem to let go: reading and running. My problem is, while trying to free myself from attachment, I vacillate between donating my books and ceasing exercise and buying more books to learn about Zen Buddhism and on a different track, running (which I love for its meditative and liberating nature) but also having to do yoga, lift, blah blah blah to make sure I'm balanced. I'm having trouble finding a middle ground, and was interested in what you thought. They are healthy endeavors, it just seems that I'm allowing myself to become too attached to them."*

The idea of nonattachment has to be one of the most misunderstood ideas in all Buddhist philosophy. It's kind of odd I would be asked about cultivating nonattachment since I personally never talk or write about cultivating nonattachment, and none of my teachers was particularly concerned with the matter. As I said, in Western pop culture the words *Buddhism* and *Zen* have come to represent a gigantic blancmange of unrelated Eastern philosophies and religions. In some circles it's seen as dangerous sectarianism even to suggest there may be essential and irreconcilable differences between the teachings propounded by the various yogis and gurus and Eastern meditation masters of all shapes and sizes that have washed up on our shores over the past fifty years. But there are.

Also this idea that good Buddhists shouldn't be attached to their families may stem from the story of Buddha himself leaving his wife and kid to go on his quest for true balance. We'll get to that stuff more deeply a bit later. Suffice it to say it was a very different society he

---

* There's nothing wrong with buying books — as long as they're my books! But seriously, authors need to eat, and buying books and magazines is a way to help them earn a living. And for those of you who don't believe in wasting paper on books and magazines, I think that's very noble. But you still need to pay writers for their work! Once we get it together to pay writers for the work they do online, I'll go paperless. Until then I still buy books and magazines.

lived in, and there was a long-established social tradition that dealt with families when one of the parents went on such a quest.

Be that as it may, while the idea of nonattachment is present in Zen philosophy, the idea of *cultivating nonattachment* is not part of Zen practice. There is a difference. Nonattachment is not something you can cultivate. In fact, Zen is never about cultivating anything. It's about seeing what's already there and moving on from that. Nor is Buddhist nonattachment the same as the psychological condition we call detachment. Certain confused people read about this idea of nonattachment and believe it means adopting an attitude whereby a person strives to be an island unto him- or herself, loving nothing, caring about nothing, and generally just not giving a shit about much at all.

The Zen Buddhist idea of "nonattachment" is not about running away from your family or ceasing to read or exercise. And the goal of Zen practice is not to turn us all into unfeeling robots or clones of Mr. Spock from *Star Trek*. Though with all the confusion about what "nonattachment" means I completely understand why I'm getting questions like this. I used to ask the same kinds of questions myself. But Buddhist nonattachment has nothing to do with the belief that we should all be completely aloof from everything in life, including things that are good for us and things we really ought to care about.

The notion that we should cultivate this kind of warped version of nonattachment is extremely dangerous. It's one of those beliefs that cult leaders use to dominate a community. We all form attachments to those close to us. When we're told to cut ties with family and friends and with mainstream society and to give up activities that are good for us and that we enjoy, we naturally form ties with the community and its leader and take up doing the things that they want us to do. Attachments follow, but the community generally characterizes the attachments they support as something else. It's a very slippery slope. Even when the community and its leader start off relatively cool, the kind of power that results from this corrupts quickly and thoroughly. Unfortunately, it's a very common scenario.

The aloof, don't-give-a-shit attitude cultivated by far too many who proudly label themselves Buddhists is one of those things that people who dislike Buddhism always use to trash it. And rightly so, because it's a crap idea! Unfortunately for those who use this idea to trash Buddhism, it isn't Buddhism at all. It's a kind of psychosis — what the psychiatric community calls sociopathy. That's not what Buddhist practice is intended to bring about.

In fact, this bizarre misunderstanding of nonattachment runs completely counter to the Buddhist worldview. It's utterly impossible for anyone to be unattached in that way. What we call self and what we call nonself are one and the same. Our real attachments to everyone and everything we encounter run so deep and so strong that we couldn't possibly break them, no matter how hard we tried. We are fundamentally attached to everything. And of course you're going to form even deeper attachments to the people and things most closely related to you, such as your family, friends, and home. Don't sweat it.

Dogen, who wrote extensively about Zen, wrote about not being attached to self and not being attached to views. Nonattachment to self and views is something entirely different from detachment and the don't-give-a-shit attitude. This kind of nonattachment means not trying to force yourself to be one single solid unchangeable thing forever and ever world without end amen. What you call your "self" is constantly in a state of flux, mutating at every moment. But most of us fight that. We try to establish a fixed and unchanging self and lock it in place. We waste all kinds of energy defining and defending this fiction we've worked hard to create. Stop doing that, and you're free to use all that energy in far more constructive and beneficial ways.

True nonattachment is understanding that you are fundamentally attached to everything and, through that understanding, dropping your attachment to the view that you are detached from that which you encounter.

At the same time, real nonattachment means not clinging to things or people. It means dropping the idea that if you don't have this or if you can't get that, your life will be a catastrophe. Sex and romance are biggies here. The idea that we would be okay if only we had that special someone is an illusion. It turns our focus away from our real situation and on to things that could be *if only*. By the same token the idea that if we lost that someone we think we "have" everything would turn to shit is another way to redirect ourselves from what is onto what could be. It's a game the ego plays to try and prove its existence. But the less we cling to people — and to things — the better our relationships to them become.

You never really own anything. Even your material possessions will not be yours after you die. In terms of people, you have relationships to them. But those relationships always change. It's important not to be too attached to the form a relationship may have had in the past. But it's also important to do your best to make that relationship as good as it can possibly be right now.

In his most famous quotation about attachment, Dogen said, "Flowers, though we may be attached to them, still fall while weeds, though we may hate them, still flourish."*

We are constantly confronted with things we love and become

---

* And just FYI, Dogen never actually used the word *attachment* since he didn't write in English. He actually used the word 愛惜, pronounced "aiseki." This is usually translated as "fondness" or, I admit, "attachment." But it's interesting to note that the Chinese characters used to spell the word mean "love" and "pity." So although the translation is essentially correct, it's important always to understand that words in one language at one time may have far different shades of meaning and connotations than even their correct translations into another language. Further still, it's important to try and get at the meaning behind the words rather than fixating on the words themselves. Even the Japanese words Dogen chose were just imperfect stand-ins for how he actually felt. It's the same for anyone else who ever wrote anything in any language.

attached to and things we hate and wish we didn't have to deal with. Dogen acknowledged this fact and advised us to take a realistic view of it.

So how does this play out in real life? How might the practice of zazen affect your attachments? *Will* it turn you into Mr. Spock or make you into one of those glassy-eyed "spiritual" robots?

Nah. As far as your attachment to the things you ought to be attached to is concerned, the worst that Buddhist practice is going to do is to make you a little less emotionally frantic about that stuff. When my mom died in early 2007 at age sixty-five of a lingering disease, I didn't sit around calmly going, "I have no grief for, lo, as a Buddhist master I am serene and unattached." I cried. Hard. But at the same time I didn't hang on to my grief as tightly as I might have had I not done zazen for so many years.

Let's take grief as a case in point that we can apply to the rest of what we might call emotional attachments. The initial wave of grief you feel at the loss of someone you love just happens. No need to dwell on how or why. It's just there. How it got there doesn't matter.

And you react; you cry or feel sullen or respond in whatever way your cultural upbringing has conditioned you to respond. After that, though, is where things get complicated. The habit of attaching to emotions and incorporating them into the sense of self is so strong that we'll grab on hard to even the most unpleasant feelings that come along. In fact, "bad" feelings are often much better at reinforcing our sense of self than "good" feelings. We hang on for dear life to these emotions, lest our sense of who we are should collapse. We very literally feel like we'll die if we don't. Habits like this have us abusing our bodies and minds in ways that lead to all kinds of trouble. But they're not necessary. You won't vanish if you stop reinforcing your image of who you are at every moment.

You can't instantly undo habits this deep. You shouldn't even try. But once you become aware of them you find that you always have a clear choice whether or not to respond habitually. Not responding habitually doesn't mean you become cold, robotic, and "nonattached" in the way that a lot of people seem to envision nonattachment. It just means you don't push your body/mind more than it needs to be pushed.

Anyway, the fact of the matter is that we all have attachments. We love our families, our kitty cats, our favorite breakfast cereals, and all the rest. You can't be a real human being without having some attachments.

If you can recognize your attachments, that in itself is very good. Most people never do. It's useful to see your attachments for what they are, just thoughts inside your head. The lighter your attachments are, the easier your life will be, because nothing stays one way forever, so whatever you're attached to will change someday and eventually be gone. The real goal of Zen is to find a way of life that's easy and undramatic. Strong attachments lead to upset and drama.

I sometimes think the way people try and practice "nonattachment" by being detached and robotic is a way of trying to numb themselves so that the day they lose their mom and their kitty and the store runs out of Corn Chex they'll be all cool and "nonattached" about it. But it won't work. They'll still feel exactly what they feel, no matter how hard they try to suppress it.

After making zazen practice part of your life for a while, you will still love all the people you loved before. You may even hate the same people you hated before. Even hate doesn't have to be a terrible thing when you don't latch onto it and call it your "self." It arises and fades away like any other emotion, and there's no need to act on it. We'll get into the balance of love and hate in a little bit. In any case, the "attachments" those guys who wrote me those emails had remain fully intact. You still love your family and your friends and your kitty cat, too.

So don't get all attached to the idea of nonattachment. Okay?

Chapter 7

OUCH! MIND WHERE YOU PUT THAT THING!
Sex and Mindfulness

I hate the word *mindfulness*.

I'm sorry. But I'm just sick to death of hearing it. After the word *attachment*, *mindfulness* has got to be the single most overused word in all of pop culture Buddhism. The use of the word in English these days comes mostly from the Theravada school (predominant in Sri Lanka and most of Southeastern Asia). Zen people generally don't do mindfulness exercises or mindfulness meditations or most of the other activities that have become associated with the word. So I'm honestly not so familiar with what this mindfulness stuff is all about.

In fact, a lot of Zen folks, including my teacher, are highly critical of the contemporary pop culture idea of mindfulness. When you say, "I am mindful of (fill in the blank)," you are already creating separation between you and your activities. It's a very idealistic attitude. This is the kind of separation we're trying to uproot through our Zen practice.

In any case, I'm not quite sure what most people in the West these days mean when they say "mindfulness." Near as I can tell, the general population uses the word to mean something like "thinking really hard about stuff." Or at best it's sometimes a synonym for paying attention to what you're doing. But if that's what you mean, why not just say "paying attention"?

But let's just say that mindfulness means a state in which one is fully present — and not just paying attention to what's going on but doing so without thinking a whole lot about it. Let's say it refers not just to the activities of the brain but to the entire body and being. And let's take it even further and say that mindfulness doesn't refer just to what you as an individual do, but to a condition that includes the entire universe. If we take the word *mindfulness* to be something like that, then I can get behind it.*

If we define the word *mindfulness* like that, then sex may often be the very best place to experience mindfulness. In fact, the only time lots of people are ever fully present in the moment, doing exactly what they're doing right now, not hoping to be somewhere else or to achieve something apart from whatever it is that's actually happening, is when they're getting it on.

That's a sad state of affairs. But I think it's the way things are. It explains why sex is such a key issue for most people. The one time when they come fully into themselves is when they're coming fully into someone else.** The fact that sex is so important to you as a

---

* In the *Shobogenzo* chapter titled "Thirty-seven Elements of Bodhi," Dogen says this about mindfulness: "There is mindfulness that exists in moments of owning one's body, and there is mindfulness that exists in moments of having no mind. There is conscious mindfulness, and there is mindfulness in which there is no body. The very life-root of all the people on Earth is 'mindfulness as a root.' The very life-root of all the buddhas in the ten directions is 'mindfulness as a root.' There can be many people in one state of mindfulness and many states of mindfulness in one person. At the same time, there are people who have mindfulness and there are people who do not have mindfulness. People do not always have mindfulness, and mindfulness is not necessarily connected with people. Even so, through the skillful maintenance of this 'mindfulness as a root,' the virtue of perfect realization exists." I'm not gonna even try to interpret this. I'm just providing it FYI.

** I'm sorry for that pun. I truly am.

mindful experience is, I would assume, why lots of you bought this book.*

So can we use the mindfulness we find in sex to inform the rest of our lives? Can we learn from the state of body/mind established in sex to become more fully present in all activities? Can a Buddhist who is already committed to trying to be as mindful as possible in all situations use sex as a kind of mindfulness practice?

My answer to all the above is maybe. But probably not. Of course theoretically it's possible to do these things. But it requires that you give up something you might not want to give up. It requires that you put aside the view that sex is something apart from the rest of your life. Were we to give the kind of attention to *all* our activities that most of us give to sex, our lives would become entirely different. We would no longer be the people we imagine ourselves to be. Because much of what you imagine yourself to be is wrapped up in differentiating the activities you really like — such as sex — from the ones you find boring.

Also, the idea of using sex to establish mindfulness would bring a degree of separation to the act of sex that would ultimately make sex less mindful than it would be had you not made that effort.

True mindfulness is when you let go of the idea of mindfulness and just do whatever it is you happen to be doing. Trying to be mindful seems to me to defeat its own purpose.

So where does that leave us? In an earlier book I concluded a similar rant by saying something like, "When you're fucking, just fuck. When you're not, just don't." And that's still really all I can say about the matter, when you get right down to it.

Yet I'm well aware that this is easier said than done. It takes a lot of practice to unlearn umpteen millennia of human conditioning. This is where zazen is helpful. You sit there very quietly, and very still and allow yourself to be exactly as you are. Then, each time

---

* Thank you.

you get up and reenter the world you do so a little bit quieter and with a little bit more stability.

Of course, you could also try and do this with sex. But it's much more difficult. Sex tends to be far too exciting and stressful for most of us to find a calm center. Sure, we're fully present most of the time we're fucking and sucking. But we're also a bit too distracted by all the beautiful sights and smells and sensations to find a peaceful center of that sensual cyclone.

Zazen, on the other hand, is kind of the opposite of sex in that it's really, really boring. And, honestly speaking, most of our lives are pretty boring. So if you want to learn how to be fully present for most of what goes on, it's better to try and do so by concentrating on a really boring activity rather than on a really exciting one.

So I would say that you *can* use your knowledge of the full engagement of mind and body that you find in sex as a way of understanding what a life of full engagement in all activities is like. It's like being just as engaged in washing the dishes or cleaning out the cat box or waiting for a bus as you are when you're getting it on hot and heavy with the object of your fondest desire.

Still, to find that kind of engagement in all things, I think it's better to deal with something a bit less exciting than sex. To find the way of being fully engaged in doing the dishes, you might want to try becoming fully engaged in something way more boring than doing dishes. This is why zazen is so desperately dull. Try it sometime and see for yourself.

Chapter 8

IS ORGASM THE HIGHEST FORM OF MEDITATION?

When I was in San Francisco a few months back, a guy I know took me to this place where they teach something they call "Orgasmic Meditation." I didn't actually get a chance to see how it works — dang! But the woman who invented the technique explained it. A girl lies down with her pants off. A guy kneels beside her. He diddles her until she comes. Then they call it meditation.

Okay. According to them there's more to it than just that. They say, "Orgasmic Meditation (O.M.) is a technique that develops mindfulness, concentration, connection, and insight in the arena of human sexuality. Orgasmic Meditation can facilitate greater physical and mental health, deeper intimacy, and for some, a method for spiritual aims." It's grammatically weird, but that's how they put it.*

A method for spiritual aims, eh? That might just be the crux of the problem right there. Remember what I said about spirituality and aims? Zen is neither about spirituality nor about trying to get into some predetermined state.

---

* From the FAQ on their website, www.onetaste.us.

Anyway, while I talked with the folks who ran the place I was distracted by dozens of extraordinarily pretty girls going back in the meditation room for sessions. I won't lie to you. I woulda gone in there in a heartbeat if they'd have invited me. Hey! It's research! But they didn't invite me. So I have nothing to report from back there.*

I did, however, get a guided tour of the dorms. Apparently most members of the group live communally in what was once a rather sleazy downtown hotel. The person who invited me to meet the leader of the organization took me up to show me his room. The members of the group are each assigned a roommate, usually of the opposite sex, with whom they share a teeny, tiny room with barely space for a single bed, which they also share. Mmm-hmm.

As we walked around the dorms we began to hear moaning coming from one of the rooms. The door was wide open, but I demurely turned away. My host said, "It's an O.M. session. They usually don't do them in the dorms." It was two women; the moaner was being diddled while the diddler talked her through the process using much the tone of voice and words used by people doing guided meditations.**

Maybe I'm not the most sexually free person in the entire world. I mean, I believe very strongly in sexual freedom as a rule for people in general. Consenting adults should be allowed to do whatever they want. But me, I'm a bit conservative about some things. Loud sex with the doors open is a little much for me — even when you call it meditation.

Whether or not this technique is a form of meditation, I can't

---

* Seriously, though, if I had gone back it would have been with an open mind. But I would have made no secret that my dick was going along for the ride as well. I got the feeling that men were subtly encouraged to attend the proceedings as if seeing a lot of pantsless women moaning in orgasm did nothing for them sexually. I can't pretend like that. Still, I was honestly curious to see how this stuff worked out as meditation.

** By the way, I'm not a fan of guided meditation. Meditation should never be guided.

say. Remember, friends, that in my view zazen isn't really a form of meditation as such. In some ways what they do sounds like it could be fun, though perhaps not fun for me personally. But in any case, it doesn't sound a bit like Buddhism. Let me tell you why.

As I briefly touched on* earlier, the idea that sexual activity is a way to establish a deepened meditative state has been around for a very long time. It's part of what is called Tantra, a system that has made its way into both Hinduism and Buddhism. Tantra itself is not necessarily sexual. Equating Tantra with sex is an unfortunate mistake made by a lot of Westerners. A whole lot of tantric practices have nothing to do with sex. But the ancient sex-based systems that appear in certain forms of Buddhism and Hinduism come out of the tantric tradition. So the confusion of terms is not all that hard to understand.

The word *Tantra* actually means "continuum." Its origins are attributed by its followers to Gotama Buddha — the historical Buddha of circa 500 BC. But it appears to date from several hundred years later. According to the definition of *tantra* found in *The Shambhala Dictionary of Buddhism and Zen*, "this tradition [is] strongly oriented toward human experiential potential [and] describes spiritual development in terms of the categories ground, path and fruition." Whatever that means! You tell me. Anyhow, it includes a number of practices, but even *The Shambhala Dictionary of Buddhism and Zen* admits that it "finds its strongest expression in a multi-layered sexual symbology. Transcendence of the masculine principle and the feminine principle through the union of the two is given as the key characteristic of the supreme yoga Tantra."

According to the all-knowing Wikipedia, which is the very best place to go when searching for answers about Buddhism,** "When

---

* Heh, heh, I said, "touched on."

** This is sarcasm. But so many people use the darned thing as their main source of info that I'm using quotes from it to illustrate general understanding about certain things. Plus, I'm too damned lazy to look this up in a more reliable source.

enacted as enjoined by the tantras, the [sexual] ritual culminates in a sublime experience of infinite awareness, by both participants." Uh-huh. I'm sure it does. I have a couch right over here where we can try it out if you like . . .

I don't know a whole lot about tantric sexual meditation — obviously. But there are a million books and websites out there all about it if you want to study up on it for yourself. However, I can tell you why I remain unconvinced that sex is a viable path to the Absolute. Sex is just too easy to abuse, and it's too emotionally charged an activity for most people to maintain equilibrium while engaged in it.

Anyway, by now whatever may have once existed of serious tantric sexual rituals has devolved into pure debauchery. Okay, maybe — *maybe* — there are a few monks and nuns on a mountain in Tibet who do the practice seriously. But let's get real here. You aren't gonna find them on the Internet or in the back pages of the local free paper, or even in the ads section of your favorite Buddhist magazine. And they have not opened a center conveniently located in San Francisco that you can join as long as you look hot enough.*
Reading a bunch of books about this or about any other practice is not the same thing as learning it for real through a genuine tradition handed down face-to-face from master to disciple over thousands of years. The folks who wrote the modern books on the subject probably don't have a clue about the real practice. They've just translated a lot of other books, most of them probably also by people who did not actually do the practice. Even if you go back to the most ancient sources you have to recall that there were windbag scholars who wrote about things they didn't really have any firsthand knowledge of even then!

I've never seen a single person advocating tantric sexual meditation who didn't strike me as mainly just wanting to get his or her

---

* I only spent a couple hours at the O.M. center, but there was not a single person in the place who was not delicious looking.

rocks off. And while those Orgasmic Meditation folks in San Francisco didn't seem quite as overtly sleazy as the average bearded tantric sex dude walking down the Venice Beach boardwalk in a flowing robe with a hash pipe in one hand and a paperback copy of the *Kama Sutra* in the other, there was still something that seemed very clearly *off* about the whole business.

True tantric sex practices were extremely complex rituals that required years of training before they were to be attempted. The practices themselves were shrouded in secrecy so as to prevent those uninitiated into the deeper truths from trying them out at home. Nowadays some folks just read a book about 'em, jump right in bed to test 'em out, and then start mouthing off about how spiritual it all was.

That being said, the balanced state of body and mind that occurs through zazen practice can also occur spontaneously in other situations. As a musician I used to find it when playing onstage. All consciousness of myself and the outside world would vanish, to be replaced by a fluid state of action alone, in which thought and feeling ceased to be important and in which the sense of self and other utterly dissolved. Athletes often experience moments like this. So do artists of various kinds. So do many people involved in a whole range of activities to which they have fully devoted themselves. And so, quite often, do lovers engaged in sex.

In fact, I'd hazard to guess that there may be a lot of people who have no meditative or artistic practice, whose lives are a drab and ordinary routine dictated by society, for whom perhaps the one time when they are ever fully engaged in the present moment is while fucking.

And I do admit that fucking can be a powerful, even spiritual, thing. This is why the ancient Buddhists made such a big deal of it in the precepts. You can get into some really deep stuff during sex.

But as I said, my problem with sex as meditation is that, as a method, it's much too prone to abuse and danger. It's very easy for someone in the position of "spiritual master" to present himself as a tantric adept and con some young lady into participating in a bogus "holy ritual." Cases of this abound, including one supposed "Zen master" in Los Angeles* who claimed that his spiritually charged sexual energy was too great to be contained by one person and therefore he needed to have sex with two or more women at a time.**

Sex can be a lot of things. It can be fun. It can even be recreational. It need not be heavy and need not lead to emotional commitments. But that's not the kind of sex we're talking about when we're talking about sex being used as a way to access higher levels of consciousness or "sublime experiences of infinite awareness."

That kind of sex is very heavy stuff. You cannot get into those levels of awareness unless you're prepared to get into some very deep stuff within yourself and within the person with whom you're engaging in your "meditation." It is absolutely a necessary part of the territory. So sexual meditation, if it's to be engaged in at all, needs to be handled with a lot of finesse. It's not the kind of thing an amateur ought to attempt. And you sure as hell cannot expect to have such an experience with somebody you just met that day at an Orgasmic Meditation class.

In terms of the dangers one might encounter on this path, remember, you're talking about a shared experience between two people (at least). Emotions and other such reactions are bound to run high. Even if the orgasmic meditative experience is euphoric, there is always a comedown. And the comedown will also be a shared experience.

Much of what we're talking about here involves trying to reach so-called bliss states. So I should say something here about those states as they relate to Zen practice in general, even apart from sex. Unlike a lot of meditative practices, Zen is not focused on achieving states of bliss — orgasmic or otherwise. But while Zen practice is

---

* Where else?

** I'm not even making this up!

not geared toward moving you into bliss states, it can carry you through those states.

States of bliss occur when you try to turn off everything else that's going on at a given moment and focus only on bliss. You're going, "Oh, wow! Bliss! Far out!" But bliss is just one aspect of any given experience. It's impossible to really turn off everything else. Everything else is still going on. You're just focused on one aspect of the experience. And that's an unstable position to be in. Eventually it's going to fall apart. It has to.

And when it falls apart it's actually worse than not having had it at all because it's like any other kind of high. When you get high on something — including "spiritual bliss" — there is always going to be a low. The comedown is your body/mind returning to balance, or to the closest thing to balance that it knows. If you desperately crave bliss while your body/mind needs balance, you are bound to label the changeover as "feeling bad," when in fact it is actually the best thing that can happen.

Zen practice is about not getting high on anything and in so doing getting high on absolutely everything. We then find that everything we encounter — bliss or nonbliss — possesses a tremendous depth and beauty that we usually miss.

The idea of orgasmic meditation is very attractive because it's one of those great "something-for-nothing" games people like to play. It's like one of those ads that tell you that you can earn $75,000 just by sitting at home watching TV or whatever. But there are plenty of suckers who fall for pitches like that, too.

Orgasmic meditation is the very opposite of Zen practice because it focuses on one aspect of life — the moment of orgasm — and says that this one specific category of experience is the way to salvation and realization. But that kind of focus just leads you to turn away from life instead of toward it. It encourages you to miss the so-called mundane aspects of existence while constantly thinking about the joys of getting your rocks off.

You can't get your rocks off 24/7. Not even if you're a porn star. You've got to take out the trash. You've got to go see your mom's display at the county flower show. You've got to talk to your boss with the bad breath about getting a new bulletin board for the break room. There's doing the dishes and mowing the lawn and figuring out your taxes and all the other stuff a person needs to do to live.

By focusing on just one thing, whether it's orgasm or so-called states of bliss or whatever it might be, you train yourself to turn away from most of your life. And that's a damned shame. Because you were put on this Earth to live that life. In a very real sense you chose to live because you wanted to experience life — all of it, not just the pleasant aspects but the unpleasant and the tedious, as well as the just plain boring. When you miss out on those things you're really doing yourself a terrible disservice.

Zen practice includes everything. Not just having orgasms but cleaning out the cat box and raking the leaves and all the rest. You begin and end your day with your zazen practice. But you do the practice for the sake of your entire day. It's a way to learn how not to run away from the rest of your life.

Chapter 9

HOW HAVE I COME TO THIS?

From orgasm as meditation, let's move on to the subject of writing about meditation in a forum where people go mainly to have orgasms. See, I used to write a monthly column about Zen for the alt.porn website Suicide Girls, an Internet forum whose main selling point is photographs of naked women, usually punk rock or goth girls with lots of tattoos and body piercings. This created a certain amount of controversy among Buddhists who thought that I, as a monk, shouldn't be associating with pornographers. Here's a typical email from one of these folks:

> Why are you writing for Suicide Girls? Seriously, why? I
> think there are real repercussions to a respected Zen
> teacher writing for a soft-porn website. Please give us an
> explanation; is it your idea of skillful means, or what?
> Someone is getting rich by pandering to base desires, and
> you seem to be endorsing it through Zen. I don't under-
> stand how you came to this. Who cares how many tattoos
> or piercings they have? It is still Internet porn; they just do
> a better job than most sites of making people feel okay

about it. Your presence on the site, I'm sure, will help to justify many a lonely night in front of the computer screen. If I may be so presumptuous as to offer a blog title for you: "Get your hand off your cock and touch your thumb tips lightly!"

I expected a lot of this kind of reaction when I started writing for the website. One guy did compare my writing for Suicide Girls to what it would've been like if Shunryu Suzuki had written for *Hustler* in the seventies. I think that's kind of stretching things. But I actually received a lot more support than condemnation.

In any case, though, I think it's important to explain clearly why I chose to write for that website as well as why I chose to write this book you're reading right now. I think what I'm going to say speaks to the basic attitude toward sex within Zen as a whole.

When Helen Jupiter from Suicide Girls first asked me to write for the website, I was surprised. I thought SG was just photos of naked girls. I didn't know there were articles on it at all.

But I checked it out and found it had a lot of intelligently written columns and interviews. Seeing that, I thought, okay, I can write for this. I was a little worried, however. But not because there are photos of naked girls on the site. I was worried I might not be allowed to say what I wanted. I've had problems before with people who ask me to write for them and then demand significant changes to match their view of what they thought a Buddhist teacher ought to say.

When I first started writing professionally I compromised to a certain extent. I made up my mind that I would never allow anything I absolutely did not agree with to be published under my name. However, if I couldn't get an editor to understand what I wanted to say about a particular topic, I would leave that topic unaddressed and sort of write around it. I spoke to Helen at length about this and felt I would not have any real problems with censorship at Suicide Girls, so I agreed.

But then I thought about what impact it might have on my lineage.

So I asked my teacher, Gudo Nishijima Roshi, what he thought of my writing for the Suicide Girls website. I sent him a link and the password they'd given me when I agreed to start writing for them so that he could see what it really was. I'll leave what he said exactly as he expressed it in the email he wrote me shortly thereafter. Excuse the slightly idiosyncratic English. He said, "I think that it is very good decision for you to accept such a job. I do not find any kind of moral problem in them [the pictures on SG], however, I found only whether they are beautiful, or not. I think that we are usually influenced by old-fashioned religious criteria, but on the basis of Buddhism, there seems to exist a kind of criterion that what is moral is always beautiful, and what is beautiful is usually moral. Even though my idea is not so affirmative to me yet, I think that there are some kind of criteria to identify morals and beauty in Buddhism." What he means by "my idea is not so affirmative to me yet" is that he is using this as a provisional theory but has not drawn any final conclusions about the matter. Once I knew Nishijima Roshi was okay with it I figured whatever anyone else had to say didn't matter all that much.

But as for SG getting rich pandering to base desires, I have to admit it's true. But lots of people get rich pandering to base desires. And lots of us wouldn't have jobs at all if it weren't for people who get rich pandering to base desires. When something sells, it indicates a need for human beings to explore a particular aspect of their collective consciousness.

In and of itself, this is neither good nor bad. Sometimes we need to open up to stuff. Our prehistoric ancestors had to see each other naked all the time. This caused some problems, especially when human beings started gathering together in larger groups. In the animal world an exposed penis is generally an indication either that the exposer wants to fuck or that he wants to fight. Our upright posture, coupled with the fact that our genitalia is absurdly large and visible compared to those of other primates, caused us to send inappropriate signals constantly.

In fact, human beings are a real anomaly in a lot of ways that have to do with sex. Compared to other primates we have giant penises, massive boobs, and gargantuan butts. Human females conceal their ovulation to the point where even they themselves do not know exactly when they're fertile. In the rest of the animal kingdom, signals such as enlarged breasts, bums, and weenies occur only during the times when conception is most likely to occur. Yet humans have evolved so much that we're able to have sex all the time! This is the state in which we come into the world. We are born as incredibly sexual creatures, compared to just about any other animal we know of.

Our ancient ancestors knew that something had to be done to tone this down. So we started wearing clothes, and being covered up came to be seen as natural. But it isn't really. So perhaps we need to get used to seeing each other naked again, and maybe the widespread availability of pornography is part of that process. This is just a little pet theory of mine. Of course, most porn shows only naked women, so it's a bit off balance. But I saw *Watchmen* and *Forgetting Sarah Marshall*, and I think nude men are making inroads in popular entertainment.

In any case, when it comes to base desires I have a lot more problems with some of the base desires I see being pandered to in spiritual publications than the ones pandered to at Suicide Girls. When I see ads for instant enlightenment seminars and meditation machines, ads that pander to our base desires for big experiences that will elevate our status,* I wonder if everything I might say in such a forum will be taken as an endorsement of that kind of garbage. At least at SG, I can be reasonably certain that most readers don't think I'm pushing naked boobies — not that I have any problem with naked boobies. It's just that there's no instant association with the rest of

---

* Hey, kids! Be the first one in your meditation class to have a genuine certified Enlightenment Experience!

what SG sells, the way there would be with any of the scams that choose to call themselves "spiritual" if I, as a so-called spiritual leader, were to write for a publication devoted to spirituality.

As to whether I am "justifying many a lonely night in front of a computer screen," this, I think, is a serious question. It tends to imply that Buddhism takes the puritanical outlook that masturbation, and by extension sex in general, is sinful. I think a lot of people are confused on this issue. Here is where I start belaboring the point I brought up earlier about sin. But I really believe it is crucial to understand it.

As I said earlier, in Western culture we've been steeped in the religious view that sex is a sin. So whenever we hear about other religions, we tend to assume that they must think of sex as sinful, too. It's almost a given. And whether or not we think of all sex as a sin, the Bible is very clear that lustful fantasies are sinful, and it's hard to masturbate without any of those! So the idea of a religious teacher justifying masturbation seems outrageous. This begs the question of whether or not Buddhism is actually even a religion. As I've said before, I don't think it is. But since Buddhism is classified as one of the "major world religions," the opinions of myself and the many others who don't regard Buddhism as a religion may be irrelevant in this case.

Now, I don't really know if my writing truly justifies masturbation anyway. As if anyone is waiting for justification from me in order to masturbate! It's not like I can give or withhold such permission and expect anyone to give a shit. In any case, I don't really care either way.

Masturbation is just something people do. There are a lot of theories out there as to why. Animals only seem to masturbate when kept in captivity. So in a sense it may not be strictly "natural." By this I'm not saying that it goes against the laws of nature, only that it may be an outgrowth of an urban lifestyle and may not be present except when animals live in confinement. It could be one of those things that only occur when animals, like us, are placed in artificial shelters and removed from the natural world, which we humans have done to ourselves. Then again, given the highly sexualized nature of our species, we may need masturbation more than other animals do just to keep everything in balance.

But I'm no expert in such things. So don't take it from me! In any case, as far as Buddhism is concerned there is no sin in masturbation since there is no concept of sin to begin with. Personally I think masturbation is probably one of the least entangling ways of relieving sexual tension. It's something you can do if you know you're in a highly sexual frame of mind and want to avoid imposing that on others. So I think it's probably a very good activity for monks, especially those who have taken vows of celibacy.

As I said, though, the earliest Buddhists didn't feel this way, and they forbade masturbation among monks. To be frank, this prohibition just seems wrong to me. It seems like a way to create more tension and anxiety, not less. But it's impossible to know what things were like in India 2,500 years ago. Maybe it was necessary to have this rule but not as important to actually enforce it. That is to say, maybe it was better to project the image of rigid sexual purity to the outside world while allowing some flexibility in actual practice. This is just my hunch. Bear in mind, though, that the only historical records we have are of what people *said* they did, not what they actually did. I tend to assume that in practice the prohibition on masturbation wasn't really enforced except when someone blatantly disregarded it or when someone's masturbation became a problem to others.

Now, as far as photos of naked women are concerned, depictions of naked people have been a part of human artistic expression — including Buddhist art — as long as humans have been expressing themselves artistically. Deal with it, already. If you masturbate to art, does that mean it's no longer art? I don't think so. But, of course, you're free to decide that as you like.

American society is still strongly influenced by Puritan ideas of morality. When Buddhism was first introduced to this country, it was interpreted through these ideas. A long-standing misunderstanding of Buddhism that we've already looked at a little bit is that Buddha's formula for achieving peace of mind was the destruction of all desire. For people raised in a Christian society, one of the worst of all desires is the desire to get one's rocks off.

We take it for granted that sexual desire is a terrible thing. But other societies don't see it that way. In Japan, for example, sex is much more open. One of my favorite TV shows when I lived there was a cartoon called *Crayon Shin-chan*, all about a horny little five-year-old who likes to look at dirty books and tries to peep up his mom's friends' dresses. It's a children's show in Japan, but when it was imported to the United States it was prefaced with a warning before each episode that it was not intended for children. In fact, it was intended for children, just not *American* children!

So our Western notions about what is and is not appropriate in terms of sexual expression should not be taken as universal. So many little things I encountered when I lived in Japan brought up hidden pockets of Puritanism I never even thought were part of my psychological makeup — like *Crayon Shin-chan*, or the fact that sexy videos could be found on the bottom shelves at the video store where kids could see them, or how among the people I knew, having sex with someone recreationally seemed to bring up no feelings of guilt or shame whatsoever. Jeez! These people even felt okay getting stark naked in front of each other and sharing a bath!

Even though the average Japanese person probably knows far fewer facts about Buddhism than the average reader of a book like this one, it is still a culture as steeped in Buddhist philosophy as American culture is steeped in Puritanism. The ideas about sex that Japanese people take for granted are deeply conditioned by Japanese-style Buddhism and, as such, are vastly different from our Judeo-Christian views.

But getting back to desire, when you examine it clearly, the idea that you should destroy all desire becomes absurd. The human race

wouldn't exist without the desire for sex. But this hasn't stopped lots
of people from engaging in a futile struggle to produce some magi-
cally altered mental state in which they want nothing. It ain't gonna
happen. The real trick is to see all your thoughts — desire being just
one type of thought — for what they really are. How about your
desire for a Buddhist teacher who doesn't write articles for soft-porn
websites? Where does that come from?

I felt really good about writing for SG, and I was sorry to see it
end owing to someone in management's deciding that saving money
by cutting all their columnists was a good thing to do. I mean, when
I joined the team they were trying hard to make the public see them
as something more than just a site where you go to look at naked
goth chicks. And for a time they were truly cutting-edge in a lot of
ways other than the fact that you could see girls with blue Mohawks
rubbing their boobs all over each other. I'm still grateful to have had
the opportunity to write for them, and I'm glad they let me keep my
free subscription. I hope to be able to write for them again.

I liked doing that monthly column because writing for SG made
it possible for me to be more what I think a Buddhist teacher ought
to be. See, I'm the kind of person who wants to do the opposite of
whatever most other people are doing in a given situation. Even
when I played hardcore punk, I wore hippie-style clothes and refused
to cut my hair because I liked seeing how supposedly "noncon-
formist" punks got so upset at somebody who didn't conform to *their*
punk society.

If I'm in a room full of pompous wannabe Buddhists all trying
to be pure of heart and mind, I just want to rip my clothes off, plug
my Stratocaster into a stack of Marshalls, and blow the fake-ass
beatific smiles off their faces. All that soft-soap lovey-dovey good-
vibes shit makes me gag. But when I was on Suicide Girls with all the
punk rock nutcases and tattooed women, I got to be the guy who
advocated quiet and equilibrium. Cool.

I've long felt that the reason Buddhism has been relegated to the junk heap of hippie-philosophies-that-didn't-work-in-the-sixties-so-why-bother-with-them-now is that it's been presented so exceedingly poorly, mainly by people who don't have a clue what it is anyway. It's not about some kind of mystical serenity available only to those rare beings among us who have freed themselves from their base desires. Buddhism is for everyone. It's for what you are and who you are right now, warts and tattoos and naked pictures saved on your hard drive for those lonely nights and all.

But let's get into this a little deeper and talk about the relationship of Zen to pornography. Read on, read on ...

Chapter 10

ZEN AND PORN

To continue our discussion from the last chapter, here's another email I got regarding my work as a columnist for the Suicide Girls website:

Hi Brad,

Some pieces of yours I've been reading lately make it seem like you advocate porn. In your book *Sit Down and Shut Up!* you indicate that, as humans, we all have desires, which is true of course and can't be denied. I found that refreshing to read in a Zen context. You go on to say that we shouldn't try to kill desire, but rather to desire less.

So, my question: if one of the premises of Zen practice is that we should desire less, how is porn — which, by definition, stokes desires that usually can't and in some cases shouldn't be fulfilled — consistent with Zen practice?

I can see how someone steeped in Zen might approach porn and sex in a different way than the average person, but I don't see that porn would have any good effect on either Zen or non-Zen people. It's like beer or Cheetos. Sure, it might not hurt you in small quantities, but it certainly doesn't help anyone. I agree with Nina Hartley that Americans are screwed up with regard to sex.[*] I just don't think that exposure to more sex, in an impersonal way — even in a frank and honest nonpersonal way — is really going to help people. And I feel like the manifest content of your current writings might give people new to Zen the impression that they can be totally into porn and still practice Zen consistently. You yourself have said that Zen isn't "anything goes," but your writings lately seem to speak otherwise. I realize that you are reaching out to a community that might otherwise hear nothing of Zen, and that is definitely valuable, but in speaking their language, does the Zen still come across? Please help me understand.

Best,
Elizabeth

What I'm presenting here isn't an exact transcript of my reply, but it's based on that. So here goes.

A lot of issues are raised in this email. But as for my writing giving people "new to Zen the impression that they can be totally into porn and still practice Zen consistently," I don't know if I'm giving that impression or not. I'm not trying to. Yet I'm not necessarily trying *not* to. If you see the difference. I don't really consider it any of my business whether or not people who read my stuff are "into porn."

Let's agree, though, that there is a condition we might call "being into porn." There must be as many degrees of this condition as there are of the condition of being into anything, including Buddhism, from

---

[*] Sometime before I got this email I'd published an interview I did with porn star Nina Hartley on Suicide Girls. A longer and more detailed version of that interview appears later in this book.

casual fans to people who are truly obsessive, or even addicted. So let's assume we're talking about people who are very deeply into porn to the point that it consumes much of their time, money, and energy. I don't know whether someone actually could be so deeply into porn and still practice Zen consistently. Maybe they could. Maybe not. I tend to think it would have some effect on their practice, as would anything they might be obsessed with.

Certainly a lot of people who consider themselves not to be new to Zen think a person who is into porn at any level cannot possibly practice Zen, and they are happy to point this out to anyone who will listen. However, most Zen teachers I know of, and in fact, most Buddhist teachers of any style I'm aware of, don't seem too fussed about the issue of pornography one way or the other. There aren't a lot of Buddhist sermons denouncing the evils of porn.

An interviewer once asked Bob Dylan if he was worried that young people might misinterpret his songs as advocating the use of drugs. Dylan replied, "That's not my problem."

I agree with Bob. I can't be too worried about people misinterpreting my writings as a call to gorge themselves on smut. The moment you say anything publicly, someone will completely misconstrue it and then blame you for having told them to do whatever it is that gets them in trouble. This goes for anything you say about any subject in any tone of voice or with any string of words in any language. Charles Manson blamed the Beatles' *White Album* for his actions. The guy who killed John Lennon said it was because he read *Catcher in the Rye*. Communication is tough. And people — especially Americans — like to be able to blame their troubles on others.

But for what it's worth, I tend to doubt that you can be a total porn glutton and keep a very good Zen practice going. Any kind of obsession is going to get in the way of practice, whether it's with porn or with food or even with Buddhism itself. The obsession is the bigger problem, not the object of the obsession. The object can be anything at all. But with consistent and, more important, constant practice these kinds of obsessions tend to work themselves out anyway.

As for porn stoking desires that cannot and probably should not be fulfilled, that is certainly true. But pornographers are rank amateurs compared to the folks who make mainstream TV shows, movies, and commercials when it comes to stoking desires that can't and probably shouldn't be fulfilled. Pornographers just flash you some tits (or cock or whatever) and, if you're in the mood, you take the bait and enjoy the images until such time as you've, um, come to desire them less. The folks who make TV shows, movies, and commercials know how to get you wanting the stuff they're selling any time you switch the idiot box on. Mainstream TV shows have millions of people convinced that if they aren't living the kinds of lives they see on screen something must be terribly wrong. I'm pretty sure most consumers of porn don't feel unfulfilled if their real lives aren't like an X-rated video. Most of us are well aware that real life doesn't work like that, that pizza delivery boys don't often find themselves gang-fucked by sorority girls, and that astronauts don't often end up on planets ruled by women who have never seen a man before and who have captured them to repopulate their world. Again, I'm not denying that porn does stoke desires,* but I think much greater dangers are lurking in mainstream media.

Also, maybe my approach to porn is not like other people's. I don't know. Because for me, when I look at, say, one of my fave Suicide Girls photo shoots, I don't ever think, "Damn! If only I could fuck her I'd be fulfilled!" I know I'm not likely to ever get my mitts on Aspen's or Sash's or James's** or Bee's shapely ass. And that's fine. I can still enjoy pictures of them. I'm not so sure every guy feels that way, though. Some may mistakenly believe they'd be better off if they could have real rather than virtual sex with the girls whose

---

* And gives you desire to stroke — haw!
** She's a girl, not that there'd be anything wrong with it if she weren't.

photos they look at, and they may suffer for having such delusions. But you know what? People have lots of delusions. Most of them cause far more suffering than that one.

Sure, you would probably be better off if you stayed away from viewing such material entirely. Dogen certainly thought so and cautioned his monks against viewing pornography. But we live in different times, and most of my readers are not monastery-bound Buddhist monks. And I have to say that I personally do sometimes look at dirty pictures.

I also think that although the sex portrayed in porn is totally unrealistic, ironically enough people's attitudes toward sex seem to be far more realistic and healthier in cultures that allow porn than in cultures that suppress it. This is just my "eyeball" assessment, arrived at through personal observation rather than any kind of scientific analysis. But it appears to me that in societies like ours, where porn is allowed, there is greater equality for women, lower incidence of institutionalized sexual violence, a greater tolerance for people of nonstandard sexual orientation, and so on than there is in societies where porn is forbidden, such as in most of the Middle East. I strongly suspect that open access to pornography plays some role in this process. I don't really think the availability of porn *causes* people to be more rational about sex. But I think the two factors occur together and shouldn't be arbitrarily separated.

There is a difference between fantasy and reality. Most of us know that, at least to some extent. Porn is fantasy, as are almost all forms of entertainment — including, to a certain degree, the book you're reading now. In Buddhist terms a whole lot of what we perceive as reality is an elaborate fantasy created by our brains as a stand-in for reality itself. In fact, we could say that all our perceptions are fantasies in that they are never actually reality itself but an interpretation of reality. But that's getting very deep.

For now, let's stick to the more obvious distinctions between fantasy and reality. Any addictive fantasy is problematic. And porn, being such a strong stimulus, can become quite addictive for some. Trying to escape real life into a seemingly better fantasy world will always bite you on the ass in the end. You can never escape reality. It's important to always be aware of that.

Through my work with Suicide Girls I've become acquainted with people in the sex industry. People used to ask me, "What if it were your daughter/wife/girlfriend in those pictures?" My answer in the past was that it wasn't my daughter, wife, or girlfriend in those pictures, so I couldn't say. I'm not a big fan of "what-if" scenarios. They're fun in science fiction and may have some value when making contingency plans, but generally they mostly just cause the brain to start spinning out fantasies. These days, though, some of the women on Suicide Girls are friends of mine, as are some other people in the sex trade. And while Suicide Girls isn't really hardcore porn by today's standards, it's certainly erotic nudity. I admit I sometimes get a funny feeling when I see someone I know naked on the Internet.

And it's not just "that kind" of a funny feeling either. I find myself sometimes worrying about them and how their decision to "go pink" might affect their lives. But their decision to pose for those pictures is theirs, not mine. So it's really none of my business. I agree with my ninety-year-old Zen teacher who said that the photos were beautiful and that beauty is an expression of truth.

Still, certain difficulties come with posing naked in public. I always hope that my friends who do that kind of work can handle the inevitable pressures that come with it. Doing this work shouldn't be taken lightly. I think that a lot of people who produce pornography encourage their models to think of it as no big deal, and a lot of those models find themselves in a very bad way when they discover that some people do consider it a very big deal indeed. There are all kinds of repercussions when family members, friends, potential employers, and others see those pictures. It's hard for me to look at any piece of pornography these days in a detached way without considering the lives of the people I'm seeing.*

But that's my own take on it. I don't know if it's "right," nor would I want to try and somehow universally mandate that attitude, even if I could. Still, Elizabeth, who wrote me that email, is correct. Buddhism is not an "anything-goes" philosophy. Yet it's not as if there is or ever could be a list of rules that would apply to everyone in every situation for all time.

If you're too goddamned horny to think straight, then perhaps the best way to avoid misusing sex is to log on to Suicide Girls, or whatever site you enjoy, masturbate furiously, be done with it, and then go out into the world more mellow, less sex crazed, and less likely to misuse sex in a far more damaging way.

Desiring less is one aim of Zen practice, but achieving some mythical state of desirelessness is not. Ain't no such thang! No one is ever free from all desire. But through our practice our desires gradually become less compelling. We also start to see the consequences of those desires, and we start to avoid fulfilling those desires that cause us problems.

---

* Some feel that merely to view porn is to participate in its creation and in the exploitation of women. And to a Buddhist, this is true, but in ways most of those who use this argument wouldn't begin to suspect. Because to a Buddhist, to be against pornography is also to participate in its creation. To be a human being who lives on a planet where porn exists is also to participate in its creation. It's much the same as the way many Buddhists view eating meat. According to the ancient Indian Buddhists, one should not deliberately take the life of an animal or cause it to be killed for one's own dining pleasure. Yet if a Buddhist monk is offered meat that the monk knows has not been specifically killed for her or him, the monk is expected to accept and eat it. So yes, to view porn, as far as I'm concerned, is to partake in a very small way in its creation. But then again, to live in the United States is to partake in the creation of nuclear weapons, and in the existence of slavery in our past, and in the popularity of bad emo music, and so on and on and on. The participation of the viewer is a very minor thing.

All desire is essentially empty in the Buddhist sense. By that I mean that desire is what it is. The various ideas we have about desire and about what we ought to do either to satisfy or to rid ourselves of desires are also empty. They're just ideas. I'll go into this idea of emptiness in the next chapter.

The desire for sex is a very basic human condition. Without that desire none of us would be alive. Pornography has been with us since human beings first learned to communicate their desires to each other through art and language. It's not going away. In fact, we can expect it to become more and more open in the future. As Zen practitioners we need to learn to live in a world in which pornography is open and available. Whether or not we consume it is up to each individual. It's certainly not up to me to decide for anyone.

Other issues regarding pornography are far trickier, though. There are certainly very good reasons for some people to be opposed to the very existence of pornography. It's often exploitative of women. It objectifies them. It's often connected with organized crime. It sometimes glorifies violence. The list goes on and on.

Yet in the end I have to come out mostly — but not entirely — in favor of the existence of porn. There are bad things about it that need to be fixed. But I don't think that means we should eliminate it altogether. I think the acceptance of pornography is a sign that civilization is moving toward a more balanced state. It may not be pornography itself that moves society forward in a positive way. In fact, it's hard to imagine it does. But openness to porn seems to come hand in hand with openness in general. I think it would be more useful to work at making porn better and less exploitative than it is to waste time trying to eliminate it altogether.

To sum it all up, in our earliest history, sex and nudity were not hidden. People were naked, and they copulated in front of each other. With the development of civilization, these things had to be kept in check for the sake of maintaining a peaceful society. But the suppression of sex and human nudity created its own set of problems. To deal with those problems, modern societies have been gradually allowing more openness about these issues.

The openness of sexuality these days is a sign that we're finally ready to face up to the whole of what life is.

Chapter 11

FILLING THE VOID —
IF YOU KNOW WHAT I MEAN!

Sex and Emptiness

Words like *emptiness* and *the void* crop up with almost equal regularity when people talk about sex or Buddhism. They have very different meanings, depending on which of these subject matters is being addressed. But there is some common ground.

The Buddhist notion of emptiness has been largely misunderstood in the West for about as long as Buddhism has been studied here. When scholars first came across Sanskrit words like *sunyata* and *nirvana*, they didn't know quite what to make of them. *Sunyata* seemed to refer to "emptiness" or "the void," and *nirvana* literally meant "extinction," deriving from a word originally meaning "to put out a fire."

Yet these two depressing-sounding ideas were held up as ideals in Buddhism. And to Western scholars at the time, that was just plain weird. At first these scholars were convinced that Buddhism must be something akin to nihilism. And yet the practicing Buddhists they encountered were so damned happy compared to the nihilists back home who were always so dour and miserable. Something was definitely amiss!

Actually, though, the Buddhist notion of emptiness refers to the world as it is when emptied of our preconceived notions, opinions, desires, and all the rest of the baggage we bring to any situation we encounter. In more recent times several Buddhist thinkers have substituted the phrase "as-it-is-ness" for emptiness. Awkward as that is, it's a lot closer to what Buddhists mean when they talk about *sunyata* or *nirvana*.

When words like *emptiness* and *the void* come up in terms of sex, they're usually referring to a condition that the speaker seeks to fix with sex. We feel alone, unloved, unfulfilled, and we want someone to plug up the empty void in our lives with...well, with *something,** though we rarely have even the vaguest clue what that something might be. We think that if only we found that special someone, this aching sense of being incomplete would disappear and we would at long last be happy and whole.

Most of us who are in any way conversant with current ideas in psychology are well aware, at least intellectually, that we can never really be fulfilled by another person. But even if we know this in our heads, most of us still have a strong tendency to act as if we can or we should be fulfilled by other people, or by possessions or experiences.

For Buddhists the big stumbling block here is enlightenment. We, the few, the proud, the meditators, may be ready to accept that no significant other will fulfill us or that no amount of material possessions will ever satisfy. But a lot of us Buddhists still labor under the mistaken belief that there is an experience called enlightenment that will fulfill us once and for all, forever and ever. And we will live happily ever after.

Sorry to burst your bubble. Not even total and complete enlightenment will fulfill you. It didn't work for Buddha, and it ain't gonna work for you, no matter what the guy running the get-enlightenment-quick seminars tells you!

---

* Heh-heh-heh...

In perhaps his most famous piece of writing, *Genjo Koan*, or "The Realized Universe," Dogen says, "When the Dharma has not yet satisfied the body and mind we feel already replete with Dharma. When the Dharma fills the body and mind we feel one side to be lacking."* In other words, the lack of fulfillment we feel is natural and normal. That's true enlightenment. It's when we feel fulfilled that we're deluded.

By doing zazen practice we gradually begin to loosen our grip on the idea that we ought to be fulfilled. We begin to see that our normal condition of feeling that something is missing in our lives isn't really such a terrible thing. It's just a feeling. No more and no less. We no longer desperately seek to shove something into that void.** We can let it be just as it is and accept that it's all right. It may be that we are here on this Earth to experience the awe and beauty of feeling forever incomplete.

If we can accept this lack of fulfillment as our natural condition, we can be totally free. We can accept good and bad equally. We can accept loneliness, and we can accept love. We no longer feel that things ought to be different from how they actually are. At the same time we do not complacently accept things that actually do need to be changed. We can understand that it is often our duty to change a situation.

In *Each Moment Is the Universe*, Dainin Katagiri Roshi says the reason we can't ever be satisfied is that we live in the constant stream of time. Time is change. We want change. We couldn't exist without it. And yet we have the delusion that we don't want change, that we want someone or something to create within us a feeling of permanent satisfaction. But not only will this never happen, we don't really even want it to happen! Can you imagine how dull life would be if we felt constantly fulfilled?

---

* From *Shobogenzo*, vol. 1, translated by Gudo Nishijima and Chodo Cross (Windbell Publications, 1994, and Numata Center for Buddhist Translation and Research, 2007).
** Heh-heh-heh...

The thing is, though, you can't just intellectually understand this. Western philosophy as well as pop culture "common sense" often seem to say that it's enough to get a handle on these things with your head. It's not. Merely getting the idea of something doesn't equate with truly accepting that idea.

This is why Buddhism is a philosophy of action. It's a philosophy that you don't just study with your head. You study it with your whole body. In zazen practice we come face-to-face with real emptiness and real lack of fulfillment without flinching or running away. By doing this again and again and again we gradually begin to truly understand these concepts not just with our minds, but with our bodies as well.

Then the void is no longer a scary place we need to avoid. It's our natural and comfortable condition.

Chapter 12

WOMEN, EVOLUTION, AND BUDDHISM

In spite of some people thinking I should not be writing for Suicide Girls, I was very pleasantly surprised to see two articles by R. Elisabeth Cornwell, an assistant professor of research at the University of Colorado at Colorado Springs, in the news section of the website. The articles were titled "The Evolution of Religion" and "Why Women Are Bound to Religion: An Evolutionary Perspective." I started wondering if Suicide Girls could end up becoming a journal of serious discourse on religious matters. Alas, that was not to be. Too bad.

In any case, in "The Evolution of Religion," Cornwell says that our ability to imagine the thoughts of others enhanced our survival as social creatures and was promoted through natural selection: "As our ancestors developed a sensitivity to the thoughts of others as an aid to second-guessing their outward and visible behavior, they would have started to see an intelligent creative force wherever they looked. An individual watching another chip away at a flint would attribute to him a purpose similar to his own when he created a tool.

So too would he assume that lightning, rain, the sun, the stars, the moon must have had some sort of purposeful creative force behind them. Here lie the very deepest roots of our religious beliefs."

There can be no doubt that spiritual religions began, in part, for this reason. This is why Buddhism is not a religion in the usual sense. It has no creator deity and no belief in spiritual forces that control nature. At the same time, though, Buddhism does not deny a spiritual aspect to nature. It takes the view that because we human beings have a spiritual aspect to our own natures, it is reasonable to assume that all creation — sentient and insentient beings included — possesses a similar spiritual dimension. I suppose in a way that this is the same sort of process, but it's a much more rational version. We aren't trying to second-guess the rest of nature or to read its mind. Yet we acknowledge that it makes sense to believe nature has a spiritual dimension. Through the practice of zazen, we allow our thoughts to become quieter and can thus directly experience a little of the spiritual dimension of things outside ourselves.

Buddhism does not, however, take the view that this spiritual dimension is in any way higher or more pure than the material aspects of our makeup. I've said it before and I'll say it again because it's important: Buddhism says that both the spiritual and the material sides of our nature are manifestations of one underlying reality that is neither spirit nor matter.

The evolution of religion is a fascinating subject. But it's Cornwell's other article that interests me more in terms of what the book you're reading now is all about.

In "Why Women Are Bound to Religion," Cornwell says,

> Religion has both revered and reviled women, exalting their fertility and fearing their sexuality. While religions throughout history have mutated, gone extinct, and propagated — the position of women within their ever expanding reach has usually fared poorly. Yet, women are far more likely to be

religious, attend religious services, and inculcate their children with their beliefs. Why are women so willing to give in to religious dogma and subject themselves to the degradations often inflicted upon them? This is a fascinating question, and is especially perplexing when you consider the great strides toward equality women have gained in the West. Yet, without women passing on faith, belief, and dogma, religion could not survive through the generations.

There can be no doubt that women generally have been extremely poorly treated by religion and yet continue nonetheless to propagate the very beliefs responsible for their often sorry position in society. You hear a lot of talk about primitive matriarchal religions in which women fared far better than in our current patriarchal religions. But most of those religions are so ancient and so thoroughly dead that what we can say about them is mainly conjecture. So we really don't know if this was true. But we do know for sure that the powerful patriarchal religions of the modern world have mostly treated women like shit.

Except for Buddhism.

You knew I'd say that, didn't you? But it happens to be true. Historically Buddhism has been much better to women than any of the other major religions.* This is not to say that Buddhism has never been used as an excuse to treat women poorly. There are certainly many examples of times when certain Buddhists have treated women just as badly as have adherents to any other religion. And I will be talking about those. But in doing this stuff these Buddhists have gone against the explicit directions of the founder of their faith.

Buddha's first order of monks was an all-boys club with a big "No Girls Allowed" sign on the door. But there was a group of women, including Buddha's stepmom (his mom had died giving birth to him,

---

* For the sake of this discussion I'll lump Buddhism in with religions, although I really don't believe it is one.

and he was raised by an aunt) and the wife he ditched when he first went on his quest for the truth,* who hung out with the monks, listened to Buddha's lectures, and practiced the meditation he taught. One day Buddha's stepmom went to Buddha on behalf of these women and asked that they be admitted to the order. Buddha said, "Forget it."

But a little while later, Buddha's chief attendant, his cousin Ananda, asked Buddha, "Are women less intelligent than men?" Buddha said no, women were just as intelligent as men. Ananda said, "Are women less capable of reaching enlightenment than men?" Buddha said no, women were just as capable as men of reaching enlightenment. Having thus backed him into a corner Ananda went for the kill and asked, "Then why don't you allow them to join the order?"

Buddha had to admit that his initial decision had been wrong. So he opened the order to women. But he was a realist. The reason he'd barred women from entering the order in the first place was that he knew India in his time was a male-dominated society and would look very much askance at a religious order that allowed women to join its clergy. Plenty of people were already bitching at him for a lot of the radical stuff he'd done, like speaking out against ritual animal slaughter and questioning the authenticity of ancient scriptures. So he made up a list of special rules women had to follow that were much stricter than the ones men had to observe. There were 250 rules for monks and 348 for nuns.

According to Rev. Patti Nakai in her article "Women in Buddhism,"** many of the rules for nuns were based on the ancient Indian belief that women existed to please men and make babies. Of

---

* Yes it's true, Buddha left his wife. But he didn't exactly dump her in a roach-infested tenement with four screaming babies. Buddha was a prince at the time and knew his wife would be very well cared for while he was gone. There was a tradition in India of householders leaving home on spiritual quests, and there were, and still are, customs and legal regulations in place to deal with such cases. And please note that later on his wife, too, entered the Buddhist order. I'll be addressing this stuff in a later chapter.

** It's on livingdharma.org.

course this is true, but they left out cleaning toilets and cooking.* These early Buddhists therefore tended to regard all women as sex-crazed hussies. A large number of the rules were intended to help the nuns avoid any behavior that might possibly be taken as sexually suggestive. Because the nuns were often harassed by the general populace, there were also rules saying that monks should escort them from place to place, thus giving rise to the unfortunate misunderstanding that women were incapable of acting on their own.

A number of ancient passages from the *vinaya* rule books seem geared toward helping male monks curb their desire for women by depicting them as disgusting creatures. This also had unfortunate repercussions. Lots of folks reading these passages in later times misunderstood their intent. Rather than using them as ways to help curb their sexual appetites, they used them as a justification for their own petty, chauvinistic, sexist attitudes.

Although he had decided to allow women into the order, Buddha predicted his order of monks and nuns would eventually fail because of this decision. He was wrong there, as we all know today.

Or maybe we don't all know that today. As I write this book there's a major controversy brewing in the Theravada school of Buddhism. *Theravada* means "the Way of the Elders." Much like Zen, it was a school of Buddhism that sought to bring the philosophy back down to the basics of what Buddha actually taught and focus on meditation practice rather than on ritual and systems of belief.

The most essential — though certainly not the only — difference between Zen and Theravada is that Zen accepts what are called the Mahayana or "Great Vehicle" sutras as authentic. Actually I should rephrase that. It doesn't necessarily accept all the Mahayana sutras as authentic. But it doesn't consider them all to be inauthentic, as does Theravada. It's from this essential difference that most of the other differences between the two schools have sprung.

---

* I'm joking! Jeez!

The thing about the Mahayana sutras is that they were composed after Buddha's death, but many of them were written in the style of the older Buddhist sutras and often contain words that are attributed directly to Buddha. Historically speaking, though, Buddha clearly could not have actually said any of these things. In the view of Zen and other Mahayana schools this doesn't really matter. If the words themselves are true, the sutras are authentic, no matter who said them. The Theravada school doesn't see it that way and rejects all the Mahayana sutras as inauthentic, regardless of their content.

What this means in terms of the position of women in the Theravada school is that the adherents of that school only go by what is said about women in the oldest Buddhist sutras, which they consider to be more authentic since they represent something at least close to what Buddha himself probably actually said. I'm leaving aside for now the massive disputes over whether even the oldest Buddhist sutras were revised and added to before they came to us in the form we have them now. But we don't need to go into all of that here. What's important to this discussion is that these early works are, as we have seen, the most sexist of all Buddhist writings.

What you also need to know in order to follow this is that even though Buddha did establish an order of female monks, the order he personally established died out in the eleventh century. So, to the Theravada way of thinking, there is now no authentic order of female Buddhist monks, nor can there ever be since Buddha is no longer around to establish it. Therefore women cannot be ordained in the Theravada order.

Like Zen, Theravada has also made inroads into the West beginning in the twentieth century. The idea that women could not be ordained has never sat too well with many, perhaps even most, of the Western practitioners in the school.

On October 22, 2009, one Australian-born teacher in the Theravada tradition, a man by the name of Ajahn Brahm, bucked the system and ordained four female monks. The Thailand-based home office of his particular order did not like this one little bit. They voted to expel Ajahn Brahm and his group from their sangha.

By the time you read this, I expect the matter will either have been resolved or have changed significantly. So I'm not going to go into the specifics. To my way of thinking the whole thing is a no-brainer. If I personally started practicing in a Buddhist lineage that I later came to find out ordained men but not women as monks and teachers I'd just leave. End of story. Because that's sexist bullshit, and I don't want to be part of a sexist bullshit organization.

I'm sure there are lots of very valuable teachings within the Theravada order, and I know a lot of people have gained a whole lot through their association with it. It's not the teachings I am questioning here. It's the politics. There are plenty of other ways to get into the teachings and practices of Buddhism without joining an organization that has ridiculous chauvinist policies.

So why doesn't everyone in this order just get up and leave? It's because there is a lot at stake. Just to give one specific example, when this controversy first erupted, some very wealthy Thai people who regularly financially supported the Western branches of the lineage withdrew their financial support. Without that money, these centers will have a very hard time remaining in operation. The message is clear. The financial supporters are saying either you support absurd and outdated sexual bigotry or you don't get money and you can't run your centers.

I don't claim I have the answer to this problem. Fortunately plenty of Buddhist organizations do not practice bullshit sexism. The ones who do practice sexism are clearly in the minority, even though some of these organizations are quite large and powerful. Dogen Zenji, the founder of the Buddhist order in which I was ordained, was one of the people who called sexist Buddhism bullshit. And he did it eight hundred years ago.

Dogen wrote a piece called "Prostrating to the Attainment of the Marrow" (*Raihai Toku*ʐ*ui* in Japanese). You can read it in volume one of the Nishijima/Cross translation of his masterwork, *Shobo-genzo*.

In this chapter Dogen says,

Nowadays* extremely stupid people look at women without having corrected the prejudice that women are objects of sexual greed. Disciples of the Buddha must not be like this. If whatever may become the object of sexual greed is to be hated, do not all men deserve to be hated too? As regards the causes and conditions of becoming tainted, a man can be the object, a woman can be the object, what is neither man nor woman can be the object, and dreams and fantasies, flowers in space, can also be the object. There have been impure acts done with a reflection on water as an object, and there have been impure acts done with the sun in the sky as an object.

I can vouch for that last bit about the possibility of anything at all being the object of an "impure act." I used to work in a group home for mentally handicapped adults. We had one guy there who had a thing for shoes. You didn't dare take yours off when he was around, lest you find a sticky present inside when you put them back on!

Dogen says, "If we hate whatever might become the object of sexual greed, all men and women will hate each other, and we will never have any chance to attain salvation." I always think of this when I hear people talking about the supposedly great virtue in the way some religions force women to cover their bodies, lest men become sexually greedy. If we follow that logic, then an oil magnate who owns a flashy Cadillac ought to drive around with it covered in a burlap sack to keep those who can't afford such cars from suffering the sin of envy. We've all got our own specific objects of greed, and it's up to us to deal with that. It's not up to other people to shield us from temptation.

---

* "Nowadays," in this case, being the year 1240.

Dogen goes on to say, "Even in China, there was a stupid monk who made the following vow: *'Through every life, in every age, I shall never look at a woman.'* Upon what morality is this vow based? What wrong is there in a woman? What virtue is there in a man? Among bad people there are men who are bad people. Among good people there are women who are good people." He cites numerous famous female Buddhist masters whose understanding far surpassed that of most men, saying that a man who took a vow like this would never get a chance to learn from them. He then derides the then-current Japanese custom of not allowing women to visit certain temples, saying that it makes no sense to exclude anyone from having the opportunity to experience the Buddhist Way.

So Dogen didn't regard women as inferior to men the way many religious people of his day, and today, did and still do. But what about the benefits sexist religions have to offer women? There must be some, or they wouldn't be so popular with women. In her article on women and religion Cornwell says, "In order for women to abandon religion and its securities, there needs to be something tangible to replace the support that it offers." The tangible support and other benefits that religions offer are something that both women and men need — though we may not need religion itself to obtain these benefits.

One of the greatest marks of Buddha's true genius was that he didn't throw the baby out with the bathwater. He realized religion and spirituality were pretty fucked up. But he also understood the very important role they play in human society. As Cornwell points out in her article on the evolution of religion, religion serves a need much, much deeper than anything the intellect can ever hope to reach.

This is why atheism, as rational and sensible as it is, will never be an adequate substitute for religion. It's like trying to substitute actual eating with a superbly argued essay on food. It's an intellect-based solution for a problem that has nothing at all to do with the intellect.

I understand that a lot of people consider Buddhism a form of atheism. In a sense it is, in that it does not have a god in the usual sense of the word. We don't have a deity figure. We don't have a creation myth. We don't fear reprisals from some cosmic grandpa if we fail to worship him properly.

Yet we do believe in the universe. And in many ways the universe itself is like God. Or perhaps it would be better to simply say that the universe *is* God. The universe in Buddhist terms is not dead matter or a cosmic void. It is a living, intelligent thing that we all partake in. The universe manifests itself as us.

If God is a big ol' white dude in the sky who smites sinners and rewards football players, then I'm an atheist. If God exists outside the universe, I'm an atheist. If God cares more for one religion than another, I'm an atheist. And if God believes that women are inferior to men, I'm an atheist.

On the other hand, God is too apparent for me to deny his* existence. I guess by *God* I mean the aspects of this universe that cannot be explained away easily. There's a kind of benevolence here. Sometimes it's tough love. But it's always love. Or maybe *compassion* is a better word.

I don't worship God as an old man on a throne beyond the orbit of Jupiter, but I do worship the universe. The universe is more than dead matter. It's more than insubstantial spirit.

Atheism too often degenerates into something like religion. When I posted some of my objections to atheism on Suicide Girls, the atheists there went after me almost like the Christians did when John Lennon said the Beatles were more popular than Jesus. It was very upsetting to them, perhaps even threatening, that someone might question their nonbelief in God. But if the very concept of someone believing in the existence of God is frightening to you, you're back in the same boat as the religions you despise who fear those who don't believe in God.

---

* I'm being conventional here by using a male pronoun. God is genderless.

Buddhism did away with deities and belief systems but not with ritual and practice. Buddhist temples, though they aren't, strictly speaking, "religious temples," look like religious temples, and the things you do in Buddhist temples seem like the things you do in religious temples. You chant and you prostrate yourself in front of statues, there are people in funny clothes inside, there are rules to be followed, there is a supportive community of fellow adherents, and all the rest. Thus the deep need we all feel to belong to that kind of a community and to perform those rituals is satisfied. Yet there is no pretense that some big guy with a beard who lives up in the sky will smite you if you fail to do these things or reward you if you get all the steps just right. It's all up to you.

People are often puzzled by the fact that Buddhists don't believe in a deity that needs to be worshipped and yet, in practice, they often seem to be worshipping a deity. I myself resisted this kind of activity for a very long time. But when I tried doing those rituals, I could clearly see the reasons for them. It's impossible to articulate. There's just a tremendous sense of rightness to this kind of activity. Try it sometime and see for yourself.

You have to handle this sort of thing very carefully, though, or it will turn into something dangerous. This is why I do it, but only a little bit. And it's why I also refuse to practice the rituals to the point where I get to be any good at them. It's kind of an absurd truism in American Zen that the rituals performed in most temples are done kind of badly. I was once at the Tassajara Zen Mountain Center when a certain ritual ended up as a train wreck of wrongly chanted sutras and missed steps. Leslie James, who was leading the practice that day, said, "That's all right. It shouldn't be too perfect."

In spite of the fact that I write books about Zen for a living, I'm trying very hard not to be a shill for Buddhism here. If you can find another philosophy that does all these things, by all means go for it. Or if Buddhism's just not for you, that's fine, too.

Although technically I am a Buddhist monk, I'm also a bit of a reluctant Buddhist. I'm a Buddhist because I have to admit that Buddhism really is the best thing on offer. I tried the rest and went with the best. But I don't really self-identify as "a Buddhist" unless I'm specifically called on to do so.*

The Buddhist attitude toward women is one of the things that sold me on the practice early on. I had seen how other religions treated their female followers and was frankly pretty disgusted by the whole thing. Buddhism was clearly different. Its attitude was far more sensible. Ms. Cornwell's points are well taken but may not apply to Buddhism.

Equality is important. But this doesn't mean we can ignore the differences between men and women.** In terms of sex and in terms of society, things will always be unequal in some areas. Next I'd like to tell you about a time I went to a strip joint and how it affected the way I, as a Buddhist, view some of these matters.

---

* Such as when I write a book on Zen or a column about Buddhism on a soft-porn website.
** Vive la différence, I say!

Chapter 13

GETTING NAKED

While Buddhism, or at least Zen Buddhism, tries to treat women and men equally, certain roles in non-Buddhist society are mainly open to one sex or the other. One such role is that of the professional stripper. Oh, sure, there are the Chippendales Boys and things like that. But we all know that's not quite the same thing. There are far, far fewer men in the stripping business, and the social implications for them are completely different from what they are for women. I got in some hot water not long ago because I wrote a piece for Suicide Girls about going to strip clubs. It's not something I do a lot — in fact, I've been to strip clubs a grand total of six times in my life. But it's not something I have any particular moral qualms about doing. I just happen not to like it very much. So I want to talk about that.

But first, there's an old Zen story that goes like this. A Zen master walks by a butcher shop. He overhears a customer saying to the butcher, "Please give me some fresh pork." The butcher gently sets his cleaver down on the counter, places his palms together in front of his chest in the manner of a Buddhist monk, and says, in a respectful tone, "Sir, do you see any pork in this shop that is not fresh?" The passing Zen master, hearing the butcher's sincerity and graciousness, had a deep insight into the truth.

This is a kind of Zen story called a koan, which means "public case." Some people will tell you that koans are absurd and illogical stories meant to enable people to see beyond logic. But I disagree. All the koans are perfectly logical. It's just that their logic is often at odds with what most people call "common sense." For reasons unknown to me this particular koan seems to baffle some people a whole lot more than many of the others. But it's really very simple.

Back in those days in China, where the story takes place, as well as throughout Buddhist Asia, the general populace considered butchers to be a particularly low form of life because they made their living by violating the first Buddhist precept, the one about not killing. It was pretty hypocritical of folks to look askance at butchers, since these self-righteous "Buddhists" still went to their shops to buy meat and get leather for their shoes. In Japan this view of butchers persists in a weirdly modified form to the present day. Butchers are no longer seen as lowlifes. But those in the *burakumin* caste are still looked down on since traditionally they worked as butchers. Prejudice is a weird business.

So in any story from that time in which a Buddhist monk is paired with a butcher, it was expected that the monk would represent all that was true and holy and right, while the butcher would stand for ignorance and sin.* In this story, though, a butcher enlightens a monk by sincerely fulfilling his station in life, doing that most un-Buddhist of jobs with a Buddhist sense of wholehearted commitment. He has transformed his scorned humble work into Buddhist practice.

These days we don't look down on butchers. But we do look

* Yes, yes. I know I said there's no sin in Buddhism. But wherever you go there's the idea of serious wrongdoing.

down on lots of other people for the work they do — like people who work in the sex trade — especially if they happen to be female people.

Years ago I lived at a place called "the Clubhouse," a rat hole in Akron that I shared with several other broke musicians. Nick, the drummer for my band Dimentia 13, who lived upstairs, had a girlfriend named Candy, a stunningly beautiful woman — she looked just like a young Teri Garr* — who was a stripper. Nick really hated what Candy did for a living and constantly gave her a hard time about it.

Now, there are lots of perfectly legitimate reasons for Nick not wanting his girlfriend to be a stripper. And there are plenty of reasons any woman might want to think very hard before taking such a job. Strip clubs tend to be sleazy places run by sleazy people and frequented by sleazebag customers. Many women in the business have been driven there through economic desperation, drug addiction, physical abuse, and a whole host of other unsavory factors. Strip clubs are generally run by men who care nothing for the women who work for them, who exploit and abuse them. Stripping is not a job I'd recommend.

But this is what Candy did, and when she and I spoke about it she was adamant that it was her choice to do that type of work. She didn't feel abused or exploited, and she didn't plan to do the job for very long. For her it was an easy way to make a bit of extra cash to pay for college. Plus, she kind of enjoyed it.

It's not that I can't understand Nick's attitude toward Candy's job. I once dated a woman who worked as the receptionist at a BDSM** dungeon. That in itself didn't bother me. But the management constantly encouraged my girlfriend to "work the floor" as a

---

* Look her up, kids.
** Bondage, discipline and domination, submission and sadism, and masochism, for you innocents out there.

professional submissive. It seems you can't just start out as a dominatrix. You have to work your way up to spanking the customers by
allowing them to spank you for the first few months. They call this
activity "play." My girlfriend was a perfect Maggie-Gyllenhaal-in-
Secretary type, and the management knew they could make tons of
money by hiring her out for sessions — the girls take half, and the
house takes half the money paid for each session.

This absolutely infuriated me. I have never been as angry as I
was when I would hear about these conversations. I finally told my
girlfriend that she could do what she wanted. It was not my business
to tell her how to make a living. But, I said, if she ever "played" with
customers or "worked the floor," it was over between us.

This had nothing to do with any disagreement in principle with
what the women who worked at the dungeon did. I have no moral
issue with that sort of work. And, just FYI, I have a whole chapter
about BDSM coming up, so I'm skipping over some stuff here that
we'll get into later. At any rate, it's up to each person to decide for
herself whether this kind of work is right for her. But at the same
time I knew that it would be more than I could stand to see bruises
on my girlfriend's bum caused by strangers who paid her to be a submissive.

I don't want to get too specific about the rest of the reasons for
my objections, because to do so would invade my former girlfriend's
privacy. Suffice it to say that I knew the work involved could bring
a lot of her past issues to the surface in ways that I felt would be
unhealthy. I had interacted with some of the other women where she
worked, and I could see that this kind of thing was going on for them.
If you already have issues with men, then beating them up or letting
them beat you up, even if it's only "play," can exacerbate those issues
more than it helps resolve them.* Enough said, I hope.

---

* Note that I say "can," not "does." I felt that in this specific case, though, the activity definitely would exacerbate the specific issues in question.

But beyond that, the jealousy I felt was something much deeper than rational thought could ever hope to reach. It was like some kind of pure, animal reaction. No matter how hard I tried to defeat it with rationality, it refused to go away. No matter how hard I tried to even it out with zazen practice, it stubbornly remained. I had no choice but to acknowledge and deal with it.

This is important. Just as one should not apply arbitrary moral standards in judging others, you also need to be true to yourself. If you are in a situation that causes you a lot of emotional distress, it is important to be honest with yourself about that fact and to deal with the situation. In this case my principles remained the same and remain the same even now. People should be able to choose for themselves how they earn their living, regardless of what I think of it. And yet I knew that on a personal level I could not accept this particular situation.

By saying "be true to your*self*" I'm getting into a slightly tricky piece of Buddhist philosophy, namely the Buddhist notion of nonself. How can you be true to something that Buddhists think doesn't even exist? I'll discuss that in the next chapter, so let's just move along, ignoring that for the moment.

Anyway, decades ago, when Nick was dating Candy, I thought what she did for a living was kind of cool. Maybe I would have felt differently if she'd been my girlfriend and if I'd known then what I know now about how the stripping business usually works. I honestly don't know. But I want to talk about how I felt at the time, because I think that's also relevant.

I was a professional musician in those days — even though I rarely made much money. As far as I was concerned, Candy was a fellow performer, a fellow artist, even. I mean, we were both doing essentially the same thing in some way, which was going up on a stage in front of lots of people and doing something we enjoyed but that was potentially embarrassing, in order to elicit some kind of reaction from the onlookers.

In my case, as a musician and songwriter, I was trotting out the pure stupidity of my naked psyche for all to gawk at and pairing that with a minimal talent for making interesting sounds come out of a guitar, while Candy just took off her clothes for them. Candy's approach struck me as enviably more straightforward. Bodies or psyches, we were both kinda saying, "Here's what people look like when they're naked. Deal with it."* Candy did it far more directly and with less pretension than most musicians I knew. Plus, she made way more money.

Candy was an intelligent woman who took up her career as a way to finance her education. She wasn't ashamed of her work. It really hurt her that Nick could not appreciate it. We used to talk sometimes, and I knew Candy liked the fact that I was one of the very few people in her life who didn't think less of her for what she did.

So one Tuesday, about eleven in the morning, I was sitting in my room brooding over the fact that the Summit County Board of Mental Retardation had once again failed to call me in. I was a substitute instructor for their sheltered workshops, which meant that if not enough regular instructors called in sick on any given day I did not work. The phone rang, and I rushed to get it. But to my disappointment it was Candy looking for Nick.

I told her Nick was out at his day job doing drywalling. Candy sounded sad about that and said she was at work on her break. We talked a bit, and she asked me if I'd like to come by and see her perform. Gulp! In the first place, I was really surprised that people stripped at eleven in the morning. But apparently her place was open all day and all night. I made excuses. As much as I wanted to see Candy naked, the whole thing sounded incredibly embarrassing and a little bit iffy. I mean, who goes to a titty bar at eleven in the morning on a Tuesday?

---

* Which is pretty much what my books are about, too, when you get right down to it.

But Candy persisted. I said I didn't have much money, and she said she'd leave my name at the door and I could get in for free. I told her I was about to make myself some lunch — probably some delicious Top Ramen, the mainstay of my diet at the time. She said, "We have pizza." Knowing I was vegetarian she even said she'd have the kitchen make me one without any pepperoni or sausage. That would be on the house too. The pizza's what clinched it for me. I was seriously strapped for cash, and free lunch was something I could not refuse. If I had to see Candy's boobs to get it, well then, so be it.

The place turned out to be a nondescript little brick building on a dusty rural back road in the no-man's-land between Akron and Kent. It was one of those places where out front in the gravel parking lot they have a sign with movable type and misspelled words — "Beer, Piza, and Stripers All Day Long" or something. I parked my Chevy Shitbox next to a couple of mud-encrusted Ford pickups and Kawasaki motorcycles and went on in, nervously giving my name to the big guy with the beer gut who guarded the door.

It was a dank little dive reeking of Marlboros and barfed-up Pabst Blue Ribbon with about four or five lonely-looking guys sitting at tiny tables around a little stage with a runway that went back into the dressing room. The speaker system blasted out vaguely suggestive rock tunes — maybe Foreigner's "Hot Blooded" or "Like a Virgin" by Madonna, I can't recall. While these blared away a nice-looking brunette did what looked like an ancient fertility ritual around a pole. She gave me a funny, knowing look like maybe Candy had said something about me to her. I didn't really fit in with the rest of the clientele. When she caught my eye, though, I turned away all embarrassed. I mean, that's what polite people do when there are naked people around, right? It's rude to stare!

My pizza arrived, piping hot, covered in mushrooms and sun-dried tomatoes. It was actually a damned fine pizza, too, which I certainly hadn't expected. The brunette left the stage. I started to applaud but stopped after two claps when no one joined in. The music changed over to something a bit more "punk." I think it was Blondie's "Heart of Glass."

Candy stepped out dressed in a white baby doll nightie and high heels with long white stockings and garters. She gyrated languidly to the music, coyly removing each piece and smiling at me to make sure I saw. When she was down to nothing but a pale pink lace butt-floss panty,* she stepped off the stage, sauntered over to my table, and proceeded to treat me to a thoroughly jaw-dropping lap dance, grinding hard against me with that cute little bum of hers. I tried to slip a dollar into her garter, but she wouldn't have it. At the end of the song she gave me a sly smile and trotted off backstage.

In short order another girl was up on stage taking off her clothes. But I was too dazed to pay any attention. After a few minutes, Candy came out with a robe draped over her shoulders and asked me if I'd enjoyed the show. Without getting too graphic, I'll tell you that during the lap dance she had pushed herself against me with enough force to be able to — er — assess that I had been, indeed, happy to see her.** But I told her yes anyway.

It's been something like seventeen or eighteen years since all this happened, and it remains a treasured memory. I've seen other strippers, but none of them ever interested me very much. That particular dance meant a lot to me because it was Candy and because she was dancing for me. It was personal.

But was what Candy did for a living acceptable by Buddhist standards? Was my going to see her — and thus participating in that work — acceptable? In chapter 3 I told you about the Noble Eightfold Path, which Buddha recommended his students follow. Just to review, the eight folds are right view, right intention, right speech, right action, right livlihood, right effort, right mindfulness, right concentration. People who are into Buddhism worry a lot

---

* No bottomless stripping allowed in Summit County, Ohio.
** It was not a pistol in my pocket!

about whether strippers and other sex workers are engaging in "right livelihood."

This idea of right livelihood seems to cause Buddhists in America more trouble than any of the other folds. I think this has a lot to do with American culture and the emerging phenomenon of American Buddhism. There are two things you could call "American Buddhism." One is Americans who do real Buddhist practice. The other is an emerging consensus among Americans, most of whom will never do so much as five lousy minutes of zazen or any other Buddhist practice in their entire lives, as to what Buddhism is or ought to be. These two American Buddhisms interact and influence each other, of course. But it's this second kind of "American Buddhism" I want to talk about here. I'll keep using the quotation marks around it to emphasize that I'm talking about this consensus-based fiction rather than real practice.

American Buddhists of both types — real practitioners and wannabes who just read a lot about practice but never do it — often spend undue amounts of energy contemplating whether or not the work certain people do is "right livelihood." Note that this is almost always directed outward toward what other people do rather than inward at what they themselves do. The developing pop culture consensus called "American Buddhism" seems to me to tend toward the unstated but nevertheless pervasive view that there are only two jobs that could possibly fit into the category of right livelihood. These are yoga instructor and therapist. This is nonsense, of course.

In early monastic Buddhism just about anything a person could do to earn a living was considered wrong livelihood for monks.* Even receiving donations for teaching meditation was forbidden. But, again, this was a rule aimed at monks who were expected to make a living by begging. These days, though, this system of receiving alms

---

* As I'm sure I've already said, I use the term *monks* to include female monastics as well.

has completely broken down. I once witnessed a Canadian-born monk scarf up a gourmet Indian meal at a fancy restaurant and then get the rest of the people at the table to pay his bill because, he said, "I have vowed never to touch money." His followers had also paid for a skydiving session for him earlier that day. Sounds like a sweet deal, but it's far from the original intention of the vow.

But getting back to whether sex work is "right livelihood": as I've noted before, American culture has been shaped tremendously by the Puritan view of sex and nudity as evil. More than that, it's been shaped by this very notion of evil itself. Neither of these ideas is present in Buddhism. But as Americans we tend to want to force whatever we hear about Buddhism into categories we understand. So when we think of right livelihood, we tend to imagine that its opposite must be evil livelihood. Since our Puritan history leads us to believe that sex and nudity are evil, any kind of livelihood that involves sex and/or nudity in any way must, therefore, be evil.

But to understand what really constitutes right livelihood you have to get rid of this idea of evil. And we have a very hard time doing that. So let's go into what evil is for a bit.

Those who believe in it postulate that there is this substance out there in the universe called "evil." No matter where it goes or what it does, evil is always and forever nasty and awful. We even personify evil into a character we call Satan — who, in addition to being super bad, is a very popular and often extremely sexy choice for a Halloween costume, I might add. We tend to think of evil as a thing that exists before any action is taken to embody it.

But Buddhism doesn't look at the problem like that. There is, however, action that is right and action that is not right. Right action accords with what my teacher calls the Rule of the Universe, while not-right action attempts to go against it. The Rule of the Universe is almost like a fundamental force in physics, except it also applies to morality. The idea of the Rule of the Universe is present, I think, in pretty much all forms of Buddhism, but it's rarely named. Rather, it's

just assumed to be understood. Which is also okay. But I like nam-
ing it.

The Rule of the Universe is very much related to cause and effect.
According to Dogen, Buddhism has always revered the idea of having what he calls "deep belief in cause and effect." We all know from
science that cause and effect is absolute in the physical realm. To Buddhists, cause and effect also operates in the realm of morality.

Going against the Rule of the Universe is kind of like trying to
challenge gravity. You might be able to jump real high, but gravity
always pulls you back down. We all know — even if we don't
acknowledge that we know — that our actions have consequences
and that actions that go against real morality make us feel like shit.
Some of us may be able to numb ourselves to those feelings. But
whatever you do always returns to you. I've never seen it happen
any other way in my own life, and I do not accept that there is anybody to whom this rule does not apply. I know that lots of people
believe there are exceptions. But I don't. Sorry.

The idea of right livelihood doesn't imply there are Buddha-
approved ways of making a living and Buddha-disapproved ways of
making a living. It's more about how you do what you do. To give
you an example, my first Buddhist teacher works part-time at a vet-
erinarian's office, where he administers lethal injections to adorable
little doggies and fluffy little kitty-cats. This would seem, on the surface, to be a clear case of "evil livelihood," especially since it violates the first Buddhist precept, Do not take life.

But Tim's view is that these animals will be put to death whether
or not he does it. As long as he's the one doing it, he can do it in a
way that is compassionate and causes as little pain as possible. Plus,
he goes way beyond the call of duty and tries to find homes for pets
who are sent to him without any compelling reason for being given
a death sentence, even taking a lot of them into his own home. It's a
smelly place, let me tell you! But very, very friendly.

Tim once told me a story about being awakened at three in the morning by a state trooper who had called to say there was an animal-related emergency. The cop asked him to come to the site of an accident on a lonely stretch of road in the Ohio countryside. When Tim got there the trooper led him to a dog that had been hit by a car. The animal was damaged beyond any hope of recovery. Tim said it looked like its body had been nearly torn in half. Yet it was still alive and howling in pain.

Tim got out his kit and injected the dog with a heavy dose of narcotics, along with a chaser that would knock the dog out and eventually stop its heart. As the dog began to lose consciousness it stopped howling and started licking Tim's hand in gratitude. A few seconds later the dog was dead. Sometimes you uphold the true spirit of the Buddhist precepts by breaking them.

Tendo Nyojo, Dogen's teacher, said, "Don't view pornography" and "Don't watch dancing women" when advising Dogen on his practice. But he also said, "Don't watch herds of sheep," "Don't stare at the ocean," and "Don't view big fish." Big fish were a status symbol in ancient China, and viewing them was akin to admiring someone's brand-new Beemer today. There's also an ancient Buddhist precept against watching "grotesque mime." I find all types of mime pretty grotesque myself. What I hear from some American Buddhists regarding matters of sex and nudity kind of reminds me of the church people who warn that in the Bible God condemns homosexuality but who forget to mention the Bible also says you'll go to hell if you eat shrimp or cheeseburgers. What I'm trying to convey here is that if you try and live your life according to a literal interpretation of instructions written in ancient books — even Buddhist books — you'll go nuts. Which may explain a lot of what's happening these days...

What Tendo Nyojo, as well as Buddha and the writers of the Bible, were trying to impart was more a set of examples embodying certain criteria for action. The criteria remain even when the specific examples of how to embody them change. In the twenty-first century in the United States, women who strip or who appear naked on the Internet are hardly a major cause of human suffering. It's socially acceptable to enough people that we really don't need to worry much about those to whom it's not yet acceptable. Those folks had just better get used to it, I say, because it isn't going away any time soon. There's also nothing inherently wrong with looking at naked people. That's absurd.

It could be that in Dogen's day there was such a stigma attached to looking at dancing women and porn that people in general got way overstimulated by them on the rare occasions when they could look at them. So the core advice may have been more along the lines of "Don't deliberately view things that will overstimulate your senses." If watching strippers overstimulates your senses, maybe you shouldn't go to strip clubs. If the act of stripping overstimulates your senses, maybe stripping is not the job for you.

There is no sense in condemning people for the work that they do. How could that possibly help? You have to start from where you are right now.

The examples in the Eightfold Path are deliberately vague because Buddha wanted his students to work them out for themselves according to their own specific situations. That's why he said "right livelihood" rather than providing a nice checklist of jobs he approved or disapproved of.

It's not for me, or any other Buddhist teacher, for that matter, to say whether stripping or any other form of so-called sex work does or does not constitute right livelihood for anyone who chooses to engage in it. I can't possibly judge. I couldn't see myself ever recommending commercial sex work as a good line of business for serious practitioners, because those kinds of jobs, by their very nature, tend to be incredibly overstimulating. But I can't make some kind of general rule because every case is different.

This is because none of the Buddhist precepts is ever to be used as a means for judging the behavior of others, only for judging your own. You don't get to judge what is and is not right for other people. And I'm sorry to break it to you, but it usually doesn't really matter much to them even if you do. Unless you are specifically asked for your opinion it's best not to even waste your energy offering it.

This certainly doesn't mean I think that everything is okeydokey just as it is. Generally speaking, the sex industry is a steaming cesspool of nastiness. It needs to be changed. Drastically changed, and the sooner the better. But the necessary changes are not going to come about until we stop stigmatizing those who work in the industry just because of what they do for a living — especially the women who work in that industry. As for what needs to be done, there are far more qualified people than I already writing about that. I'll leave it to them to make suggestions.

Chapter 14

How Can I Play with Myself If I Don't Have a Self?

Sex and Nonself

Everybody has trouble with the Buddhist concept of nonself. It runs counter to nearly everything we've been taught since the moment we were born. The existence of self is so obvious to most of us that we can't even conceive of questioning it. I think therefore I am, right?

The concept of the real existence of self is so deeply embedded in our language that it's nearly impossible to communicate linguistically what Buddhists mean by the term *nonself*. And this isn't just a problem with English and other Western languages. Japanese has the same difficulty, and so does every other language I know of, including the languages the Buddhist sutras on nonself were originally composed in, like Pali and Sanskrit. It would seem that the idea of self predates even the development of human language.

The basic idea of nonself in Buddhism is not that the something we call "self" or "me" or "I" does not exist. It's that the idea of "self" or "me" or "I" is a mistaken way of understanding something real. This real something is utterly unlike the idea we have of

115

self. Thus it's possible to be true to oneself in the conventional sense that I referred to in the previous chapter, while understanding that there is no real "self" in the sense we generally understand.

Let me try and explain it like this. When you were a small child, your concept of who and what you were was much wider and more inclusive than it is now. You didn't see strict boundaries between you and the people and things you encountered. As you grew older, the bigger people around you, whose ideas you relied on for learning how to survive in the world, told you that this view was mistaken. They told you that you were a much smaller thing and that the connection you thought you felt with the rest of the universe wasn't really there.

Of course they didn't tell you this in so many words. But you learned it anyway. They weren't being malevolent. They were just telling you what they'd learned from grown-ups when they were kids.

Nishijima Roshi likes to say that the practice of zazen brings you back to the state of mind you had as a child. That's been my experience as well. After years of practice I began to recognize something that I had known when I was very, very small but had somehow forgotten. I began to understand that the idea I'd had as a small child that I included everything in the universe was not mistaken after all. But by then I'd also become accustomed to the conventional understanding of myself as a limited thing. That conventional understanding was also useful and, in a sense, also true.

In sex the sense of self often melts away. Romantic writers like to talk about becoming one with your lover. In a really good sexual encounter it's very common to lose sight of where you leave off and where the object of your affection begins. This is a beautiful thing that we know in the moment it's happening is true and real. Afterward, though, we tend to forget the truth of it. We imagine it was an illusion brought on by an overload of hormones and emotion.

But this oneness isn't just something that happens in sex. As a punk rock bass player I have sometimes become so engrossed in the music that the sense that I was something apart from my instrument, something apart from the other members of the band, or indeed something apart from the music itself, vanished completely. This was my own first taste of what I would later discover in Zen practice.

But even though this oneness with all things is a real fact, so is our separation from each other and from the rest of the universe. *I* wear the condom, *you* don't. *My* underwear is gray and has a little hole in the front for my wiener, *yours* is red with reindeer on the butt. I put on *my* clothes and go back to *my* desk afterward and pretend nothing has happened, you get dressed and go back to *yours*. If we make mistakes about these kinds of things we get ourselves into a whole lot of trouble.

We can't get our heads around this contradiction between the reality of oneness and the reality of separation, so we think we have to choose one way or the other. Most folks make the mistake of choosing separation and ignoring oneness. On the other hand, a lot of "spiritual"-type people make the opposite mistake of focusing only on oneness and attempting to ignore separation. According to Gotama Buddha and his pals, both these points of view are mistaken and incomplete. Either view will get you into trouble because it discounts a huge amount of what you actually know deep down to be true.

The fact that we can't hold the concept of oneness and the concept of separation in our heads simultaneously is not a failing that we must seek to overcome. It's just the way our brains are built. It's their job to differentiate things from each other. If they were to stop doing that, we wouldn't be able to function at all.

Yet there is a state beyond thinking in which we can embrace this contradiction. This state is not something far away. It's very near and very familiar. We've just learned how to ignore it. When we unlearn our habits of ignoring this state, it becomes abundantly clear and nearly impossible to ignore.

Chapter 15

Paying for It

In summer 2009 I was invited to Frankfurt, Germany, to lead a three-day Zen retreat. I arrived a few days early so that I'd have a chance to get over jetlag before the retreat began. My hosts, knowing my love for all things connected to the Beatles, arranged to take me out for a night in Hamburg, a few hours' drive to the north. While in Hamburg, a very nice guy named Eberhard took me on a tour of the Reepabahn district, the place where the Beatles first became popular.*

Aside from its numerous rock clubs the Reepabahn is most famous as Hamburg's red-light district. Eberhard took me for a walk over by the area's police station, where prostitutes hang out on the street accosting every male who passes, offering nights of pleasure. It was fun to chat with them. I was impressed with their abilities in

---

* For those who don't know your Beatles history, before the group became popular in England or even had a recording contract, they were a hit in Hamburg. They played in some of the city's sleaziest music clubs, often rocking out for six hours a night. John Lennon later said that it was in Hamburg that the Beatles truly learned the art of rock and roll.

English. I suppose they must get a lot of foreign customers. But I really wasn't interested in hiring anyone for the evening.

I'm not sure I could make use of the services of a prostitute, even if I wanted to. The reasons I've never gone to a prostitute don't have much to do with the idea that it would be immoral of me to do so. We'll get to my opinions on the morality of prostitution in a bit. I just don't feel like I could get it up for anyone who was having sex with me only because I was paying for it. That's not the least bit erotic to me. Whatever I feel about the morality of prostitution doesn't even enter into the question because I simply don't have any desire to go there.

Historically, Buddhism has taken an absolutely different view on the matter of prostitution from the view held by most Western religions. While Jesus consorted with prostitutes, his latter-day followers have never taken such a liberated view of the profession. Most Western religions clearly condemn prostitution as absolutely immoral, and consequently it's illegal throughout most of Europe and the Americas.

In the most ancient Buddhist scriptures, a few different words are used for prostitutes. One of these words, *vesiyā*, means "harlot" and refers to a streetwalking prostitute or a brothel girl. A *gaṇikā*, on the other hand, is a more highly paid and socially respected courtesan. Generally, if a woman enters the profession because of real economic need or is forced into it, she is regarded in these ancient scriptures as more or less karmically blameless, whereas if she got into the business out of vanity or greed she is held to be guilty of violating the precepts regarding right livelihood and the misuse of sexuality. So lowly streetwalkers were actually held in slightly higher regard by the ancient Buddhist sages than were classy courtesans.

But again, we need to remember that most Buddhists do not regard even these ancient scriptures the way most religions regard their gospels. Whatever opinions are to be found in them are the words of human beings, not the holy writ of God. As such, we can choose to accept or reject them as we see fit.

In any case, for Buddhists, even the ancient ones, it's never really been a question of whether buying or selling sex is moral. It is generally regarded to be unwholesome behavior. But this isn't exactly the same as calling it immoral. The differences are very slight. In the end, what is unwholesome is, by Buddhist standards, also immoral. But to call it unwholesome is a comparatively gentle way of saying it's not good for you and it's kind of gross, while calling it immoral seems far more judgmental. But for Buddhists, anything you do that harms yourself is also a kind of violation of the moral Rule of the Universe. So in Buddhist terms this semantic difference amounts to saying something more like, "You really shouldn't do that, you know" rather than saying, "You must not ever do that."

In one famous episode, Buddha was invited to lunch by the courtesan Ambapali. A group of princes approached him a while later with an invitation to dine with them the same day, but Buddha declined, saying he'd already promised Ambapali he would do lunch with her. Buddha was impressed with Ambapali's beauty, and he said so, but he also praised her steadfast character. Later on Ambapali donated a mango grove for the monks to use for their meditation, and Buddha accepted her gift with gratitude. The Buddha also allowed many former prostitutes to enter the order of nuns.

In Japan, Zen monks have always been famous for their dalliances with ladies of the evening. Ikkyu is the most celebrated of the many Zen monks who had a taste for commercial sex workers. This fifteenth-century monk, who referred to himself as Crazy Cloud, composed numerous poems in praise of the girls who worked at the brothels he frequented. One of my favorites is entitled "Sipping the Sexual Fluids of a Beautiful Woman." Ikkyu is one of the most popular and beloved figures in Japanese classical literature. Even today they make animated cartoon shows about his exploits.

Another medieval monk, Sengai, was also famous for composing poetry in praise of pleasure girls, often comparing them to Kanon, the bodhisattva of compassion, for their compassionate acts of quieting the turbulent minds of monks disturbed by bodily desires.

It's an open secret that some Zen monks, even today, spend their days off in the company of hookers. The image of a monk in a brothel poorly disguised with a wig to cover his shaved head is a standard scene in lots of Japanese comedies.

But does this mean that prostitution is okay as far as Zen Buddhists are concerned? Not really. But it does mean that, as with most issues, Zen philosophy offers no hard-and-fast rules about prostitution. It's up to each individual to decide how she or he wants to deal with the matter and to act accordingly. For all of Ikkyu's popularity, he is still regarded as a rogue, and his exploits are not held up as ideals to be imitated by other monks. Yet, just as important, he is also not seen as a heretic or regarded as an example of a monk gone bad. Ikkyu was just Ikkyu. His transgressions — if we can even call them that — don't dim the fact that he was capable of great insight and valuable Buddhist wisdom.

Today in most countries where Buddhism is the religion of choice, prostitution is illegal, yet these laws often go unenforced. Thailand is the most famous example, with its well-known sex tourism. But in Japan, too, prostitution is practiced fairly openly, even though it's technically against the law. So-called soap lands are a common sight in most cities. These are bathhouses where girls can be hired to... uh... *wash* paying customers with their soapy bodies. There's also the phenomenon of *enjo-kosai*, or "paid dating," wherein high school girls charge horny businessmen big money for a couple of hours in a love hotel so that they can go out and buy expensive fashion accessories. This was finally made illegal in the nineties, though rumor has it the custom has not disappeared entirely.

Even so, I don't know how important it is to be concerned with what medieval Buddhists thought of prostitution or what the various laws are in supposedly Buddhist countries. This stuff is interesting, which is why I've brought it up. But it's up to each one of us to decide how we feel about this issue.

Ultimately, what I think of prostitution really doesn't matter much because I'm not a prostitute, nor have I ever been the customer of one. It's hard for me to envision any circumstances in which I might want to pay for some nookie.

When I was in Hamburg it occurred to me that I might try out one of the cuties who were offering their services just so I'd have something more concrete to write about. But, like I said, I just couldn't see myself getting into the actual action. So that was that.

There are lots of good reasons you probably ought not to be a prostitute or the customer of one. There are loads of gross diseases out there. It's dangerous to get involved in what is almost always illegal activity, since breaking the law removes you from a lot of the protection society offers to its law-abiding citizens. The list goes on and on, and I'm sure you can find a better source than me to tell you these things.

In Buddhist terms I feel like prostitution is a potentially unbalanced and destabilizing activity, for both the prostitute and the customer. It's a bit too exciting and overstimulating for everyone involved — though perhaps less so for the prostitutes, though the drama involved in the work probably compensates in stimulation for the boredom of the sex. To paraphrase and misquote Lou Reed, it's easy to lose your head while you're giving head (or getting it) — especially when there's money involved. If your concern is establishing the balanced state Buddhist practice offers, it seems to me you'd be better off avoiding this particular area of human interaction. This is another of my reasons for avoiding it.

That's not how all male Buddhist monks feel about the matter, by the way. When I was in Canada I was told a story by the people who ran the temple where I gave a talk. It seems that a few months before my visit they'd invited an Asian monk from another lineage to speak there. During the course of this monk's stay it became known that he was spending the money he received in donations for his talks on ladies of the evening. It was decided that the leader of the Canadian temple should speak to him about this. So he confronted the monk, who freely admitted to how he was spending his earnings. "Prostitutes make me happy!" he said.

I can understand his view. It's very simple and straightforward. He goes to prostitutes because they make him happy. End of story. He doesn't concern himself with any of the larger issues involved. To some folks in our society the mere fact that he doesn't worry about these issues would certainly seem evil in itself. But, really, why should he worry? It's not his business to single-handedly reform the world sex trade.

So is prostitution an example of right livelihood or not? My friend and fellow writer of books on Buddhism and punk, Noah Levine, said in his book *Against the Stream*, "Working in the sex industry as a stripper, prostitute, or purveyor of Internet porn* is perhaps a more subtle form of wrong livelihood. Sexuality is natural and sex for sale is an ancient profession, but, again, if we look deeply, it is not hard to see that the lust that motivates such an industry has negative effects on both the workers and the customers. At the very least, participation in the sex industry is dependent for profit on lust and attachment, the very causes of suffering and dissatisfaction for people."

Noah's view makes sense, and I'm glad he said what he did. It's just that I'm not as certain as he is about lust and attachment. I don't even know what the word *attachment* means in this context. It sounds good sitting there where it does at the end of that paragraph. But I'm not sure I get what that word is meant to indicate. Maybe he's saying that you get so attached to your sexual desires that you feel you must act on them. If so, then okay, I can see that. But it's still kind of vague. On the other hand, though, lust is surely involved in the sex trade. So I can talk about that more clearly.

---

* I guess I'm included in that last category.

Yet lust is involved in nearly every form of livelihood I can think of. Just to give one example, if you work for a company that makes any kind of product, the advertising of that product is always geared toward inciting the lust to possess it. Is sexual lust worse than lust for a shiny new car or the world's most delicious candy? Maybe it is and maybe it isn't.

Sexual lust is surely a hotter issue for most people than candy lust or car lust, and that's one of many reasons I feel that sex work is probably not the best way for a Buddhist practitioner to earn a living. Yet — apologies to Noah — I still don't think it's my position to say categorically that sex work is "wrong livelihood." The Buddha never set out a categorized list of what was and was not right livelihood, and prostitution certainly *did* exist in his time. He never condemned prostitutes for the way they earned their living, and I think that's a good example to follow. In cases where a life of prostitution causes a lot of stress and imbalance it may not be right livelihood. And it's difficult for me to see the lifestyle of a prostitute *not* causing a lot of stress and imbalance.

That being said, I don't see any reason why prostitution should be illegal. If someone wants to pay for it and if someone else is willing to provide that kind of service for money why should society forbid it? I still don't think it's a good idea from either side of the equation. But there are lots and lots of activities that aren't very good ideas but are not illegal. It makes more sense to do what they do in Nevada and elsewhere and make prostitution legal but highly regulated. If people are going to do it anyway — and they are — then society should acknowledge this fact and deal with it sensibly. In countries such as the Netherlands, where prostitution is legal, the women who do the work aren't at the mercy of violent pimps, have regular health checkups, and so forth. So it's better for the workers, too, if the work is legal.

In any case, if you're already involved in prostitution, either as a customer or a service worker, or have been involved with it in the past, this is not a stumbling block to Buddhist practice. I once knew a woman in Japan who worked as a bar hostess. In Japan, bar hostesses are paid to entertain men at nightclubs, and often this entertainment includes sex. This woman never told me whether she went that far with it, and I didn't ask. But she did request me not to tell our mutual teacher about what she did for a living. So I didn't.

I'm not sure how our teacher would have reacted. But if someone who wanted to practice with me did that kind of thing for a living, I wouldn't have any real problem with it. If you come to sit zazen with me, all I care about is what goes on in the zendo. What you do elsewhere isn't my concern, unless you want to talk with me about it. If you want to talk about it, I might give you my opinion on the matter, and it might not be what you want to hear.

I can't tell you what I'd say to someone who wanted my advice about making a living selling sex because it hasn't happened, at least not yet. I certainly wouldn't categorically bar someone from practicing with me for those reasons. Nor would I give that person a hard time about her way of life. It's not up to me to make those decisions for someone else.

I'd probably just try and assess how her way of making a living was affecting her physical and mental condition and respond accordingly — as I would do with anyone who asked me about their work, whatever it was. I don't think it helps anyone to make grand sweeping judgments about how other people earn their money. That's their business, not mine. Maybe that sounds wishy-washy, and perhaps it is. But I really don't hold any strong opinions on the matter as a general rule.

Speaking of which, while I was working on this book I came across a person who used to work as a stripper and who now works in an industry some believe to be a kind of prostitution, namely hardcore pornography. Yet she has taken the Buddhist precepts and feels that she upholds them in her work. I had a talk with her that I'd like to share with you.

Chapter 16

The Real Porno Buddhist*

If you came of age during the video-porn boom of the eighties, I
don't need to explain to you who Nina Hartley is. And not just if
you're a guy, either. Since she was openly bisexual and not just performing her girl-on-girl scenes for the cash, she had a far greater
female following than most porn stars. But in case you weren't plea-
suring yourself to her work, Nina Hartley was one of the biggest
actresses in X-rated film throughout the 1980s, appearing in more
than four hundred dirty movies, beginning with *Educating Nina* in
1984. Unlike most porn actresses, Nina didn't spend a couple of years
in the industry only to vanish off the face of the Earth. She stuck
with it and these days puts out a series of how-to videos covering
subjects as diverse as how to organize the perfect orgy and how to
take it up the bum.

I spent many a lonely night with Nina Hartley's videos in my
twenties. But that's not why I wanted to interview her. My interest

---

* This is a reference to my previous book, in which I mentioned how I'd been nick-
named "the Porno Buddhist" when I started writing for Suicide Girls.

in her was piqued when a friend lent me her book *Nina Hartley's Guide to Total Sex* and pointed out that on page one she mentions being raised in a Zen Buddhist monastery. How many porn stars can you talk Zen with? Furthermore, I found out she was married in a Zen center with one of the biggest names in the Buddhist business officiating. Once I knew that, I had to meet her. So I used my Suicide Girls connections to break the ice, and an interview was set up. Here's what we talked about.

BW: Your wedding was performed by Mel Weitsman of the Berkeley Zen Center in a Zen ceremony. Part of that ceremony involves taking the Buddhist precepts, one of which is "Do not misuse sexuality." What does not misusing sexuality mean to you?

NH: For me, not misusing sexuality means not to misuse the power of sex to engage in behavior that is harmful to self or others: inappropriate partners, unsafe behavior, sex for the wrong reasons, such as to numb feelings, to escape, or to hurt others. Sex should be to share love, compassion, and support and to experience pleasure with an available partner. It means not to use sexuality to hurt another person by leading them on, to help somebody cheat, just because you think they're hot and you want them but they're not in an open relationship, to do it in order to hurt their feelings, or to get them to fall in love with you.

BW: There are lots of ways you can misuse sexuality!

NH: Oh, yeah. If you're still working on your own suffering and you are still trying to get a handle on why you do this, fine. Just leave other people out of it. Because for most people sex is really, really important, and it can be very hurtful to them.

BW: Yeah, sex is important. Usually "do not misuse sexuality" is interpreted in a very conservative way. I've gotten heat because I wrote for Suicide Girls, and certain Buddhist taste makers think I was misusing sexuality because I was aiding and abetting pornography.

NH: Antiporn thinking has seeped into the culture, and a lot of people believe automatically that pornography *is* harmful. That pornography *is* exploitation, that pornography *is* degradation.

BW: In the Bible it says that if you look at a woman with lust in your heart you've already committed adultery. So some people think of pornography as adultery.

NH: Absolutely they do. Technically it is; I'm having sex outside my marriage.

BW: I don't mean just those who act in porn. This extends even to those who watch it. Me looking at your video is seen as a form of adultery.

NH: Exactly. And that I have no truck with. And then there are the Christian ministers who counsel their flock not even to fantasize about anyone other than the person to whom they're married. That sets up a lot of guilt because it's just not possible. Images of all kinds of people pop through your mind when you're aroused. The idea that a thought is adultery? I ain't goin' with that!

BW: Well, a lot of religion is based on making you feel guilty about something you can't possibly help.

NH: They create the problem, then say, "Here, I'll save you!"

BW: Which is how advertising works.

NH: Creates the need, then fills it. Absolutely. So you can tell I'm not susceptible to religion that way. One of the best things about Buddhism is that it says that to feel any of your emotions you have to feel all of them. You can't feel just the good ones. You have the whole color palette, or you don't. Every family has its shame emotion and the shame emotion in my family was anger — overt anger.

BW: Overt anger? So they just simmered?

NH: Simmered, yeah. But I learned later that anger is also lifesaving. It also gets you out of bad situations. It makes you able to say things like, I don't agree with you. Are you trying to upset me? Get a fucking job! Quit your fucking bitching!

BW: [laughs] Yeah, sometimes you gotta say those kinds of thing.

NH: I don't think you need to be a conflict lover. But to be as averse to anger as I used to be, it hamstrings a person. So now I know if I'm not getting something it's on me to take responsibility that way. [Buddhist teacher] Cheri Huber talked about taking 100 percent responsibility for experience 100 percent of the time. That was a really great lesson to learn.

BW: Your mom and dad are both ordained Zen Buddhist priests, quite well-known in the American Zen community. How did the Zen background affect your career choice?

NH: Well, the Zen background didn't affect my career choice at all. When I was ten they discovered zazen and started taking instruction. When I was thirteen my mom retired from her job, and they became full-time Zen students on the bottom of the rung. They were twenty years older than everybody else there.

BW: I guess it was kind of a younger person's scene back then.

NH: So you're ten years old and you stop going places with your parents, of course. I think my initial conditioning had already taken root. I already had issues with codependence and having narcissistic parents who were very wrapped up in their own suffering. What I love about my parents was that they had no bad intentions.

BW: That's good!

NH: They were not mean people. And lots of parents are very mixed on their reactions to their children. But suffering makes you very shortsighted and inner focused. *My* suffering. So the first ten years of my life coincided with the worst ten years of their marriage. Also throughout the sixties they did other kinds of therapy. They tried everything: marriage counseling, biofeedback, body energetics, counseling. They got into mescaline, tai chi, naked tai chi... And then they discovered Zen because what they really wanted was to live a devotional life. If they'd been Catholic they each would have entered monasteries. But there's no Jewish monasteries and no Protestant monasteries 'cuz Jews and Protestants can marry and be out there in the world. So there's no place to retreat and study God. What they loved having was a spiritual, devotional life. And so they discovered Zen.

BW: So Zen was part of your upbringing.

NH: Oh, sure. In fact, I got to meet Suzuki Roshi a couple of times before he died. So I've been around it for forty years. It was really quite amazing to be a ten-year-old child in that environment. Remember, Zen was very new then. They were all trying very hard to figure out how to do the coed monastery. What are the rules?

BW: They're still working on that one! The idea of a coed monastery really doesn't exist in Asia, even today. Yet all the American ones are coed. This raises a lot of issues they've never had to face in Asia.

NH: And the organization was full of such angry people. Back then people walked like this in the hallways [does very formal Zen walk]. They tried so hard to do it right. When you're ten years old it's not a pleasant place. As for what Zen did for me, my career choice comes from the fact that I'm queer.* After twenty-five years in the business I've realized I'm a small-a artist and that sexuality is my subject matter. And I am a performer. It's what compels me the most. So what

---

* In recent years many people of nonstandard sexual orientations have begun referring to themselves as "queer" rather than using more limiting terms such as homosexual, bisexual, and so on. In fact, even some heterosexual people have begun using it to indicate their solidarity with and support of those of different orientations.

my parents offered was the idea of finding your own way to your best place in living an authentic life. I've finally disabused them of this, but for the longest time my parents thought I got into pornography because they weren't there.

BW: They thought it was all their fault?

NH: Oh, yeah! But I got into porn because I'm that way. And I think they finally have parsed out the difference. If I wasn't so exhibitionistic I'd have been a nurse and been freaky on weekends. But as things transpired, I am considered attractive enough, and I'm exhibitionistic enough to like cameras.

BW: That's lucky, I guess...

NH: I think so! But I have a message about sex. I come from the old-school seventies feminism, where it's my body, my rules. My truth is important. You wouldn't know that today to talk to a lot of the anti-sex feminists. Remember, it was Berkeley. I wasn't raised in Akron, Ohio, in the sixties and seventies like you were. I would have had to flee. Lots of queer kids end up in much worse circumstances than I have. And for them punk is exactly right. My parents moved to Tassajara, and I wanted to go to Berkeley High School. They had a really good drama department, and I wanted to do costume design.

BW: So did you reject the Zen stuff when you separated from them? A lot of kids rebel against their parents' religion.

NH: Not at all. But I'm not a religious person, so I don't have an altar and I don't sit zazen regularly or anything like that. But the Dalai Lama said there's no greater wisdom than compassion. So I realize that kindness is a choice you make.

BW: And you bring that to your work?

NH: I take compassionate awareness and acceptance as far as I can take it without being an actual temple-living, zazen-sitting observant

Buddhist. But it is the primary philosophy that I grew up with. So Zen, in terms of my daily life, in terms of compassion, infuses all of my work, especially my interaction with my fans, because a lot of people look at the people who consume pornography as losers, wankers, just completely pathetic.

BW: We are! [laughs]

NH: I don't see it that way. There are certainly many people in that world who could be considered pathetic losers. But you liking porn does not make you such a person. When I was a stripper I realized that men and women are equally fucked over about sex but in such different areas we're blind to the other's pain. So for certain kinds of guys, women are heartless bitches and cock teases and will bleed you dry before giving you a kiss. And for some women, men are asshole jerks who only want one thing. They'll love you and leave you. I don't see it that way. It's the culture keeping them equally ignorant and feeding them nonsense. And then saying, go off and get married!

BW: You learned differently when you were a stripper?

NH: Yeah. Just watching the men, just showing them my vulva . . . I realized how sad it was. No woman in their life had ever said, no, here it is, here's what I like, try it this way.

BW: We're confused! What is that thing? What are we supposed to do with it?

NH: And we women are supposed to not know what to do until he awakens us with his kiss, touch . . .

BW: Prince Charming and all that.

NH: But that's just not how sex actually works. The seventies were good that way because at the time they did encourage women to understand their own bodies, learn their own pleasure cycles, take responsibility for their orgasms, which is huge because it takes the pressure off of you men to have to know. Women are complicated, okay? From day to day. Forget woman to woman. Just one woman, month to month!

BW: I'm glad you're saying this! I never could!

NH: So the seventies were good for one thing, which was encouraging women to get a clue and start talking. My early attempts at that were quite clumsy and resulted in the guy running from the room as quickly as he could, because as I realized years later after being in porn, I must have sounded like a drill sergeant.

BW: Giving orders, you mean?

NH: [imitates reading from a book] Tell him what you want. Okay, to the left! [laughs] And in porn, you have to act a little bit: "Ooh, ooh, more to the left. Oh, yeah, right there, oh, yeah." So by talking dirty, I say what's true using the vernacular.

BW: That's clever!

NH: You don't talk dirty to make him hot. You "talk dirty" to communicate what you need. And most guys, if you go, "Yeah, yeah, just like that, a little more to the left," they'll do it.

BW: Speaking as a dude, I appreciate that kind of thing.

NH: Men want to please you. They want to be good with a woman because it's good for their ego and also because then she'll have him back! They'll get some more! So men are not selfish, heartless jerks. They're just clueless because our culture does not give us any good messages about sex. So that's what I love about porn, besides the fact it's where the naked women were!

BW: That's one place you're sure to find them!

NH: Because it's hard to get naked chicks to go home with you.

BW: Yeah. I know about that, too.

NH: I didn't know how to get with chicks either. It's hard. I want to be straight up. So I was like a gay man, "So, you wanna go home and have some fun?" And her reaction was, *Back!* But both genders are taught to just talk past each other. What they both want is connection. That's what all humans need. Just to connect.

BW: My friend Teddy has a saying. She says there are two genders, crazy and stupid.

NH: I love that. Oblivious and narcissistic! That works.

BW: I've been having a discussion with one of the models on Suicide Girls about the concept of "no-strings-attached sex." And I'll put forth my view, which I suspect you'll disagree with. I don't think there's such a thing as no-strings-attached sex. Meaning, there's always, at some level, some kind of attachment. This is my suspicion, based on personal experience. And you've had a lot more than me! But I feel that even if you are unaware of the attachments that are being created, they may still be there. The way you're not aware of your subconscious.

NH: Well, that's why Buddhism is very important. 'Cuz you sit on your cushion until you are aware of all your parts. I have an attachment to my husband. I have an attachment to anybody with whom I'm regularly sexual off camera. I like my co-workers just fine, but I don't necessarily want to go out and have a beer with them.

BW: I don't mean it's always a problematic attachment...

NH: No, but if you do sex authentically and honestly you are making an authentic connection to another human being on the feeling midbrain level. So you at least create bonds of affection. Now, that might not be bonds of obligation.

BW: No, I don't think there are necessarily bonds of obligation.

NH: But there is certainly attachment. So I have lots of lovers — potential playmates — that if I see them and the mood is right, we will do something sexual together, alone or in groups. But when we're talking about attachment or strings being attached, the way that works with most of my lovers, when we're not actively in the same room with each other, we keep in touch by texting or saying how are you. But we don't get into each other's day-to-day lives. We don't necessarily ask for or offer advice. So no strings attached means that once we're done here, you are not obligated to check in on me, I'm not obligated to check in on you. I mean, you can call me if you need someone to pull you out of a ditch or something. I wouldn't have sex with you if I didn't at least like you. But I'm not responsible for your emotional well-being and happiness when we're not together, and neither are you for me. When I'm with somebody we're having a complete, fully present interaction. When we're apart we're living our own lives. When I was less emotionally healthy I was constantly thinking about the other person and what they were doing. Now it's so much better for me mentally and emotionally to not worry about them when they aren't here. And then when they come back into my world, I'm totally there with them. When I say "no strings," that's what I'm talking about.

BW: Just to get a little bit spooky and weird here's an example of what I'm talking about. There was a moment when I was cheating on my wife. Well, that's a long story I won't get into here; we were already pretty much over at the time.* The very moment after the deed was done I got a text message from her. As if she was somehow, at some level, aware of what I was doing. And other similar things have happened. So this makes me suspect that on some level much deeper than we're usually able to access there's some kind of

---

* But if you'd like to read the whole sordid thing, get my book *Zen Wrapped in Karma Dipped in Chocolate*, available at fine bookstores everywhere!

connection. Some kind of interaction is going on. And that it might be useful to at least know that.

NH: Oh, it's always useful to know!

BW: And not pretend it's not there.

NH: Do I spend a lot of time thinking of lovers X, Y, and Z? No. But my ongoing positive experiences with them certainly inform my life, and they're working on me subconsciously all the time. It's knowing that I have a large group of friends who are supporting me and thinking good thoughts about me, who may or may not welcome a sexual encounter with me. So it's not like I don't ever think about them. And that's when I'll text, "Hey, how's it going?" Now, if the other person just had a blow job, that would seem very spooky. But it's not that I'm thinking, "What's he doing?" I'm just counting my blessings in my life.

BW: Yeah, sure. It's not that this was actually spooky to me. I accept it, and it doesn't bother or scare me. But I've noticed this sort of thing. And I think a lot of that might be connected somehow.

NH: It's your Zen practice. In my case, though, sex has been my practice.

BW: What do you mean? Like zazen is a practice? You use sex that way?

NH: It's where I always strive to be my best self. I try to be as honest as possible, as present as possible, as centered as possible, as kind as possible, as generous as possible without being a doormat. That's important there. I have thirty seconds to get someone to calm down. I meet them on the set, and it's like, Hey we're working together later.

BW: That's got to be intimidating!

NH: Sure it is. When I'm doing a shoot I have ten seconds from touching the person I'm working with for their body and their hindbrain to know it's going to be okay. I got into adult entertainment because it stripped away everything that was difficult for me. Intimacy was difficult [switches to a "dumb guy" voice]. *So, you wanna go to dinner? So you wanna come back to my place?* I just wanted to have sex! But I don't want to have sex by meeting strangers in a bar and going home with them drunk. I don't like having sex when I'm drunk. It's ridiculous. I don't like having sex with people who are drunk, or high, or whatever. Or desperately lonely. Or searching for the . . . Are you it? Are you gonna be the One?

BW: That's just miserable.

NH: But the majority of people who watch porn are unpartnered. I'd say, completely unscientifically, 35 percent of the porn market is never going to be partnered.

BW: You really think the percentage is that high?

NH: Yeah. They may occasionally buy companionship. They may go to strip clubs. But in terms of being at home and being actually able to have relationships with a person, it's not in the cards for them. Because, well, pick a reason. And porn is their sex life. It's their sexual outlet. It may seem sad. But only if you think about it in terms of the modern world, where the fantasy is held out to you that everybody is going to find a mate. Back in the day, for a man, any woman was marriageable because you had to get babies. But a man had to reach a certain level of achievement in life for anyone to consider him mate material.

BW: That's true, I suppose.

NH: If you never got out of debt, or whatever, you knew you were not going to get a partner. And it was sad, but you didn't feel angry or cheated. It was just, I didn't get to do this. Now people can be angrier at not having a partner because [adopts mock-cheery voice] *there's somebody for everybody, right?* Well, not if your skills aren't there. It takes a certain skill set to be partnered. I talk about it this way. You have the biological knowledge of the machine. What are the parts, where are they located, how do they work, what do they do? Then there is your intellectual understanding about sex, its history, what you believe about sex, what you were taught about sex. Then there's your intrapersonal skill.

BW: Intrapersonal?

NH: Your relationship with yourself.

BW: Oh, okay.

NH: Then there are interpersonal skills: "Hello, my name is Nina, what's yours?" And he says, "Yeah, great hooters!" And there's the biological awareness. There is the intellectual awareness. There's the self-awareness. There's the other awareness. And these are skills that develop at completely different times. So my intellectual and my biological awareness of sex was up here, and my emotional health was down here. I wanted to have sex, but I didn't know how to have a relationship. I was supposed to have a relationship? I was interested in the thang! So I had to wait till I was in love to have sex, then you tell yourself all kinds of stupid shit so you can go ahead and have sex. You convince yourself you're in love. Or you let him convince you that he loves you. Because you can't say, "I'm horny, you're cute, let's do it." No. I have to be in love. And so he has to lie and then later on she finds out he lied and she's all upset and hurt. But, but I tried to tell you the truth . . .

BW: That never works!*

NH: What I like about sex work, especially porn, is that it's very clear what is what. I became a kinesthetic person because I always

---

*   I was joking, okay?

overintellectualize. And feelings, for me, are a concept. Feelings? Ah, yes, I've heard of those.

BW: I think sometimes I'm like that, too. I don't seem to feel things nearly as strongly as a lot of people. It could be the Zen training. But I've always been sort of like that anyway. Kind of cool, in the sense of being unemotional.

NH: My father says there are feelings and then there are thoughts about feelings. And our family had thoughts about feelings and we had theories about feelings and we had concepts about feelings. But feelings? Huh, fascinating. Like Mr. Spock. But your body cannot lie. And I love the body because in it is everything that ever happened to you. All those feelings are there. And if you can learn to sit still and stay with them eventually all will be revealed.

BW: Well, I agree with that, of course! That's pure Zen training you're talking about.

NH: I know! For me sex works that way because I'm queer enough that I had to get settled with the sex thing or I was never gonna be settled with anything else. If I was more conventionally sexed I wouldn't have had to put so much work into it because I would have been normal. So I wouldn't have had to delve deeply into it.

BW: Sometimes I wonder if anybody's really normal, though.

NH: Okay. For lack of a better word, a heterosexually oriented monogamous person, which is as close to normal as we're going to get. But my orientation is multiple. I'm a polyamorous person. I am exhibitionistic. For me being in love and wanting you are completely different things. There's my love for my husband. I love him, and I want him all the time, and I never get enough. But you're someone different. I have people who are straight all the time ask me, "Doesn't it get confusing? Aren't you afraid that if you let him sleep with other people he's going to fall in love with them?"

BW: I think it's deeper than that. There may be a more basic reason people are generally monogamous. I think evolution has geared us toward monogamy because human babies take so much effort to raise. It takes a long-term committed effort by two parents.

NH: It takes more than a couple to raise a child. The more adults involved, the better for the parents and the child. I think evolution has geared us toward pair bonding but not necessarily monogamy. While we want the parents to be biologically related to the child, it's not necessary. As long as the caregivers are passionately caring for the child, and bonding with it, the child will be okay. Many children are best served by being removed from an unhealthy home with the biological parents or parent.

BW: So pair bonding isn't necessarily the same as monogamy. I can see that.

NH: Right. Early humans lived in small bands, and the notions of "couples" and "monogamy," as we understand them today, had yet to be invented. I think monogamy was invented after males discovered that they, too, were necessary for procreation. Since then, sexuality has been about "mate guarding" and keeping other men away from "their" women. Women became chattel property, first of their fathers, then of their husbands, then of their sons. After a while, they were declared either to be inherently "seductive," necessitating sequestering away from nonfamily members, or "pure" vessels, devoid of desire, to be used merely as brood mares.

BW: So what do you think of monogamy?

NH: I think most people are wired to be monogamous for short periods at a time. The partner who is right for me at age twenty is not the partner who is necessarily right for me at age thirty, and so on. I think, from my experiences, that about 20 percent of people are truly monogamous. By that I mean, when they're in love, they truly don't want or need anybody else. For them, monogamy is not a strain at all. Twenty percent of people are polyamorous or swinger types. They'll never be monogamous and don't want to be. The remaining 60 percent of the population are stuck somewhere in the spectrum between happy monogamy and happy nonmonogamy. Some are monogamous because they have no other option. Some are because that's the vow they took and they're basically okay with it, and they don't want to be cheaters or liars. Some are actively angry about it and pick fights. Some are unhappy with it and, while they don't cheat, they do withdraw emotionally from their partners, giving themselves the worst of both worlds. Some are actively cheating but won't leave the marriage. Some people would be happy at home if they just could get a little "strange" a few times a year and not have it be a big deal. They don't want to lose all they've built with their mates but just want a taste of something different. As I often say, "The more men I fuck, the more I love my husband." This means that, as exciting as a guy can be for one night, I understand in my bones that he'd not be good as a mate, as my long-term partner with whom I've built a good life.

BW: Somebody asked me this recently at a retreat. One of the participants was a married woman who says she has almost no sex drive. She just got married to a guy who has a fairly normal sex drive. He's not a sex maniac or anything.

NH: But his drive is higher than hers?

BW: Much higher. She loves him and cares for him, but she just doesn't want him sexually. And it isn't about him in particular. It's just that her drive is very low. Sex is just not interesting to her for whatever reason. And I asked her if she wanted to change that.

NH: Good question.

BW: She said she did. I told her I'm not a sex therapist or anything. But I thought of a couple of things I thought might help. I don't even remember what they were. So what would you say to something like that?

NH: If monogamy is the plan and the agreement — I mean real functioning monogamy, not just "I'm not sleeping with anybody else so what the fuck is your problem?" monogamy — they need to address this somehow. I would have her see her doctor and see if all her hormone levels are where they're supposed to be. I know some guys have a low sex drive and they discover that they have low testosterone. So they use a gel or patch or whatever to get them up to a more normal libido. I have a girlfriend who is in the business and she loves sex but she could not get into it. And part of it was the antidepressants she was taking.

BW: Antidepressants can do that. I hadn't even thought of that.

NH: The biggest myth about sex in our culture is that sex has to be mutually explosive, volcanic, and we have to wait till we're mutually desirous and be swept away by the passion. Wrong! That happens when you're first dating and you're drunk on brain chemicals, dopamine and serotonin and all that, and you're massively fucking like bunnies at bonding.

BW: Sure.

NH: After the initial six months or so of that your brain hormones settle down to their normal level and so the [in exaggerated French accent] *passion* seems to be missing. So within monogamy, your partner is your entire sexual outlet and you don't want anybody else. In your friend's case, there is a difference in the amount of sexual desire and they have to negotiate the difference. In my case, I don't always walk around all the time wanting sex. My crotch isn't going [adopts a monster voice], *Feed me now!*

BW: I love your imagery!

NH: But if I'm interested in sex as an idea and I'm married to you, as a female whose clitoris is not currently on fire needing to be doused,

I can let your energy come, and I'm receptive. And maybe that can kick-start my energy. It's not so much that I need to be interested in sex all the time. But I have to be willing to be gotten in the mood. Also, it works in the woman's favor to do what I call the "three-in-one." One time you make love together. One time the person with the higher libido gets to masturbate to her favorite porn with the awareness and support of the lower-libido partner. And the third time the lower-libido partner agrees to be in the room sharing the experience. I happen to like that myself. So within monogamy you agree to help each other out as much as you can. In monogamy I have to come to you with my hopes, dreams, and desires and share them with you in a nonaccusatory, nondumping manner. And I have to hear yours without getting all defensive. That's where having self-compassion and being centered comes into play. Most of us are wounded around sex, pleasure, and our bodies at a very young age. When these wounds are triggered, we revert to that age. All of a sudden you have a six-foot-four four-year-old! Can I express my feelings in a way that honors my needs without dumping, attacking, tearing down? And can I compromise? Because that's what monogamy is.

BW: You have to compromise. Sure.

NH: I know another couple. After twenty-eight years the husband developed an interest in spanking. Their youngest child was still in the house. And the wife called this "noisy sex." She wasn't down with that. So the compromise was that he wouldn't initiate noisy sex more than three times a month, and she wouldn't make a habit of saying no every time. So in monogamy desires change over time, and how are we going to make it work for us? 'Cuz I don't want you going to the spanking professional.

BW: I know a few of those...

NH: ...and I don't want you resenting me because you never get what you want. And I don't want to feel like an asshole for wanting something you hate. So how are we going to handle this? As my former therapist said, our "overarching mutual regard for each other" gets us through these times. I may not like what I'm hearing. But I can tell you're not saying it to hurt me. You're saying it because you're sharing your truth. And if I can't hear your truth, what the fuck are we doing here? Can I say my truth in a way that is not puking in your lap? That goes for all types of relationships when you're trying to operate from integrity. That's why self-care is so important, why self-compassion is so important.

BW: So, what's polyamory to you? And I should say I'm not the biggest supporter of the concept. I feel like it's very trendy right now, and it's often just a fancy word to cover the desire, usually among males, to cheat on their partners yet still have someone to come back to.

NH: Oh, definitely! Let me explain how it works for me, though. When I'm first falling in love I want the one person all the time. But I also know for me that that will eventually calm down. The endorphins will even out again and my natural polyamorous nature will assert itself. It is my Buddha nature to be omnisexual that way. Think of yourself as a harp or a piano with all these strings. If you pluck one string on a well-tuned guitar the one next to it will vibrate because that's the nature of sound waves. Well, my husband strikes a chord. He's a big guy, so two full chords. But I look at you, and if other things were equal and you were open to the concept, it's like you hit this string. You can't pluck my husband's string because he got that already, and he can't pluck yours, and on and on. There's a whole community of people like that.

BW: I don't think that would work for me. Sometimes I wish it could. But I'm just not like that.

NH: People say, "Oh, Nina, I could never be like you." And I don't even know what "like me" means to them. But everyone can be like me. Meaning, everyone can find their truth and live it. Your truth won't look like mine. Your truth is going to be monogamous and heterosexual because that's true for you. But in that way you are like me.

BW: I can see that. Each of us has a different approach to sexuality. That's for sure! But there's also what is and what is not socially acceptable. And I think you have to be aware of that and be aware of the fact that deep down you create the society that you are part of. This is true even if you find yourself at odds with that society. You are still part of it. Which doesn't mean you're obligated to be heterosexual and monogamous just because most of your society is. But in going against that flow, you're going to encounter resistance.

NH: Oh, sure! Talk about going against the flow, my husband and I have a D/s [dominant/submissive] relationship. At home he's all kink all the time. That was a new kind of sex for me. I didn't know anything about bondage or sadomasochism.

BW: You wanna do *what?*

NH: I mean, I like lots of things. But I'd never done actual, official power exchange. But it's his sexuality. He doesn't have any vanilla.* It's like being gay. His sexual orientation is kink. If it doesn't involve power exchange, he'll keep his clothes on, thank you very much. I really loved him. I wanted him. So I had to learn his language. That was a whole other chapter in itself. So anybody can be "like me." Which is getting rid of guilt and shame about sex and your desires because you can have whatever desires you want. Get okay with them. Once you stop putting your energy into repressing and being stressed over and suppressing and all the things we do when we don't want to face the truth of our desires, when that energy is gone, they are what they are.

---

* *Vanilla* is the term people into BDSM use for those who engage exclusively in so-called normal sex.

BW: We do waste a lot of energy suppressing what we are. Still, some aspects of yourself do need to be suppressed. Like the desire to kill or steal or whatever.

NH: Of course. That's morality. But I think, okay, with my other belief systems in place, are there any parts of these desires I can actually express? You have to make a choice. But it's easier to make a choice when you're not fleeing from shame, fear, and guilt. I believe that what gets you off is what gets you off. And that's biological. What stimulation my nerve endings like to help me achieve orgasm is what it is. There's no value judgment. On top of that is the cultural condemnation of what it is. You're not supposed to want someone of your own gender, you're not supposed to want someone outside your marriage, not supposed to want someone before marriage.

BW: This is funny talking about stuff you're not supposed to do. Because I'm talking to you today, and then tomorrow I'm going to go lead a Zen retreat.

NH: I love it!

BW: It's my freaky dual life.

NH: But for me it's not freaky dual. It's very compatible. I'm glad that you're here.

BW: The whole matter of sex and religion is fascinating stuff.

NH: Mel Weitsman, the head of the Berkeley Zen Center, was the first person who ever showed me compassion. I was twelve. At the time my parents were very preoccupied. Their marriage was in crisis, they had three other kids, there was a lot of stuff. I was young enough that they didn't want to leave me all alone. The Berkeley Zen Center was where Mel showed me Betty Dodson's first book back when it was still called *Liberating Masturbation*. It's now called *Sex for One*. It's a seminal book. You must get it.

BW: You said seminal!

NH: It's a fantastic book, full of beautiful drawings of vulvas. So I realized I wasn't the only one who was fascinated by them. By twelve I was interested in girls and boys. No, I was interested in vulvas and penises. The people attached really weren't that interesting to me at that point. This being Berkeley I understood there was a word for that. It was *bisexual*. The books at the time, 1971, said [adopts exaggerated scholarly voice], "Homosexual experimentation in adolescence is a normal part of growing up." So I didn't think I was sick. But at fourteen I realized this wasn't going away. I was a bisexual person. But Mel was the first person who ever looked me in the eye. He was very direct but relaxed, open, not expecting, not judging. I recognized it as something I'd never had before, something I wanted more of, but something I could barely stand. For thirty-seven years I have been circling that moment, really trying to become centered in it.

BW: That's really interesting.

NH: So for me, sex work has done that because I have to do that for other people. I can be centered because I've accepted all this about myself so I can be solid while they're freaking out. Some of them calm down, but some of them flee. Because it's just too much. When you see the truth or you see acceptance, it can either be a drink of water in the desert or a flash of fire that scalds you because of where you are in your development. Can you accept compassion or not?

BW: You describe yourself as a feminist, and yet you work in porn.

NH: Actually, the initial seventies feminism was very pro-porn. They were very pro–decriminalization of prostitution. Now a small vocal authoritarian group of thinkers have taken over the Leftist movement. These women question a woman's ability — a woman's *ability* — to do informed sex work of any kind. For them women are victims, and men are pigs. If you studied fifty child prostitutes in Bangkok, I'm sure all of them would like to go home. So from that they extrapolate that most sex workers would rather not be doing sex work. That's not scientific. Sex workers have been willing to talk to people for thirty-five years. I used to go to NOW conferences, and there'd be about a dozen of us sex workers of different kinds, and the others there regarded us as if we were unreal creatures like goblins or hobbits. We'd be saying, "As a woman, here is my experience in pornography," and they didn't want to know. If you say, "Dirty pictures skeeve me out," then we can have a conversation. I see men as equally victimized by the system. The antiporn feminists are all about "the patriarchy." But men are also victims of the patriarchy. It's like these antiporn feminists think the patriarchy gets together every Tuesday to talk about how they can use porn to keep women down.

BW: Oh, no! They know about us!

NH: [laughs] But every country has its "patriarchy." It's the same two hundred families who've run the country forever. So you're no more a member of the patriarchy than I am. They never look at men as human. Most people do jobs they don't like. Most people work too hard for not enough money. Most people are humiliated in their day-to-day work by their horrible bosses, and quite frankly men have it worse than women.

BW: How is that?

NH: Because at least women have the comfort of having girlfriends they can come to and unload their feelings and get some support and some fucking compassion. You, as a man, if you're lucky, might have a partner you can talk to about things. But the average guy can't go to his guy friends and say I'm hurt, I'm scared, I'm nervous, I'm worried, frightened. You can be angry, but that's about it.

BW: You're right. It's pretty much impossible.

NH: So men are even more isolated. If a man isn't partnered he can go days and days without being touched. When I was a dancer, I realized right away the fundamental flaw in the objectification argument. Human females are ready to mate all the time. We hide our ovulation. We're receptive to attention throughout our cycle. Most animals are receptive for about two weeks out of the year, and that's it. Humans are unusual creatures. So if I come up and talk to you because you look interesting, am I objectifying you? No. That's how I make my choice. In most animal species, the males strut and the females choose. The feminists completely denounce the concept of female sexual agency, female self-awareness, female choice. And the way they make all you men out to be robotic automatons is insulting. They refuse to acknowledge that in our hindbrains is aggression and that aggression and sexuality sit side by side. The lizard part of the brain is the first to develop. Fight, flee, fuck. And then the limbic system where emotions are. That's why animals have emotions, and emotions are contagious. Then the front brain is where thoughts are, and thoughts are not contagious. And the thinking part of the brain and the feeling part of the brain don't talk directly to each other. We have feelings, then the thinking part of the brain says we're not supposed to have those feelings. Or we're supposed to have those feelings for someone of the opposite gender or the same religion. That stress causes people great discomfort.

BW: The repression of sex is a very old thing. There may be legitimate reasons for that. You don't want children. You don't want diseases. You don't want the conflicts that jealousy ignites. So you try to regulate that area of human interaction so that society can exist. You need people to cooperate. You need agreed-on rules. As a society develops you can put aside some of the rules that really weren't working anymore. And throughout history that's been happening gradually. I think you can only push things so far. And what I see in a lot of prosex stuff is that sometimes you're trying to push it faster than society is ready to go.

NH: It's true! Of course, there have to be rules about sexual behavior and expression. You have to have consent. That's good. But what the West does is take up the Greek notion of the body being base and the spirit being pure. The monotheistic religions were built on that. Frankly, I'd like to see less sex in advertising and more freedom in private. I would like to see fewer kids being hit in public. But the idea that what you do over there harms me over here I find very disturbing. How is my happy marriage hurting your traditional marriage? How does the existence of gay marriage harm your traditional marriage? It doesn't make any sense. Of course gays should marry. They should be as unhappy as the rest of us, as one comedian put it. Actions hurt people. Thoughts don't. Whatever you're thinking about me right now doesn't harm me.

BW: No, it doesn't.

NH: Early feminists went to Arabia and said how nice the burka was because it took off the pressure of the male gaze. What are you talking about? For them male desire was also the desire to harm. You're penetrating us, conquering us! I thought we were having fun. It goes both ways. I like it. You like it. I objectify women and I look at them and I desire them without having any desire to harm. So I knew from my own experience that I could objectify and not wish to harm.

BW: You have a bit of a male perspective, I suppose you could say.

NH: I do! I'm not just bisexual. I'm very intergendered, actually. I like being a girl. I wouldn't want a dick for more than a day. But everyone wants to have a dick for a day. Or a pussy for a day. Just to see. I don't feel like I'm in the wrong gender. I am female. Yet I love women the way men love women. And I take pride in my ability to be a satisfying and good lover to women. I spent a lot of time learning how to. By the time I was eighteen I knew the idea of objectification was a flawed argument. Besides, I liked having people look at me naked. Even if they were guys. Guys are fun! And I found out that the more nudity there is the better behaved men are. Absent beer.

BW: Absent beer, yeah. I'm not a drinker myself.

NH: Men are very rule oriented. What are the rules for naked boobs being in the room? I'll follow those rules. So the boobs will stay naked in the room. I can do that! Let me know what the rules are and don't change in the middle. Women do that sometimes. That can be very annoying. I realized that part of my power over men is not just my body. I recognized my power in not hating him for wanting to look. He's a straight guy. Of course he wants to look at naked women! Duh! So instead of shaming him and taking his money, I was like [smiles], "Hey, look!" 'Cuz I like to show off. According to some feminists I'm reducing myself to a masturbatory object.

BW: I wish I could be a masturbatory object.

NH: I'm actually helping you with your next girlfriend. I'm showing you what works for me; try it on her. Men are hungry for information from an actual female who'll actually say something to them about it. So I have instant compassion for them right away as equal human beings. Equally beaten down by the patriarchy and equally lost and wandering. At least women get to hug each other. There's no place for a guy to go to get compassion unless he gets with a really good provider. There are some sex workers who provide that. But unless you find a provider who provides the so-called girlfriend experience, the GFE, men are shit out of luck if they need comfort or compassion or care. That just pisses me off. I'm always very physical with my fans. I hug them. I touch them. I squeeze their shoulders. I have to let them know that I really do mean it.

BW: I have only had one good experience going to a strip club. And that was when I knew the girl who did it.* She was a housemate who invited me to go along. Every other time I've gone it was just not interesting.

NH: But unlike a lot of guys who go there you're on a path of spiritual and emotional integration and awakening. And when you go there you see the sadness and the pain and the loneliness and alienation that create places like that.

BW: It's so depressing I don't even want to be there.

NH: It's sad. Most guys don't want to be there either, but they don't know where else to go. 'Cuz your average female is taught to keep her legs together and not put out because they still think they can't have their own desire absent your interest in them. Or if they do they have to get drunk first. Let's say I was raised in Akron, Ohio...

BW: Hey!

NH: With my biological sexuality, being bisexual, exhibitionistic, and so on, I'd have been in conflict. I want to do this, but I can't. I must be sick for wanting it. One day I'm so desperate for compassion, comfort, sex that I go and get drunk. 'Cuz I'm so nervous. Then I do things like flash my tits, fall over this guy, whatever. Then I stumble out into the parking lot. Who's gonna follow me? One of those people who misinterpreted my activity, and who knows what might happen? It would not be good. For me strip clubs were the appropriate place to go because in a strip club there are rules. I dance here. You sit there. See that bouncer? He'll break your hands. So I wasn't being considered a prick tease. I was considered a good entertainer. It has been fascinating to see that women's pain about sexuality is different from men's pain about it.

---

* See chapter 13.

BW: So do you feel the kind of work you do is what Buddhists would call "right livelihood"?

NH: For me it is. But in adult entertainment, I've often told people that they don't seem suited for this line of work. All I can say is, I have twenty-five years of experience, here are things to be aware of, here's my number if you get into trouble. I've counseled many people to get out. And most of them say thanks for the advice and do it anyway. I've only had two people take my advice. But they were ready to hear it. I want to save people. I went through a big phase of that. But these days I don't attach to whether they listen to me or not. I recognize that people have to save themselves. I keep giving out the information gladly, knowing some will take it and some will not. That's all I can do. Make myself available.

Chapter 17

What's Love Got to Do with It?

Oddly enough, in my interview with Nina Hartley we barely touched on the subject of love. That wasn't a deliberate omission. It just never came up. But I do get a lot of questions about love, which I'll try and address. Here's an email I received that covers an aspect of the topic I often get asked about. I touched on it right at the beginning of this book, in fact.

> It bugs me that Gautama Buddha left his family. The message I get from your books (and other Zen writing) is that you don't need to run away to find enlightenment, the truth, or whatever. If you happen to be a prince with a wife and child, those circumstances are not obstacles to your practice — they *are* your practice. Also, you shouldn't hurt or neglect the people and things in your life to pursue some abstract goal. It seems like this part of the historical Buddha's story is inconsistent with these principles. The way the story is usually told, I get the impression that he wouldn't have been able to find enlightenment if he hadn't left his family — in other words, having a family life really was an obstacle to his practice. I've also heard stories

of others who left their families to join his original group. So here's the question: How do you think one should interpret the fact that the historical Buddha and others in his group left their families? Also, what would you say to someone today who wanted to leave his or her spouse and children in order to devote more time to sitting?

This is a tough question to answer adequately. Let me tell you a story first. When I took the Buddhist precepts and became a monk through my teacher Nishijima Roshi, he didn't require me to shave my head. But later on I decided it might be useful and expedient to do the ceremony through the Soto-shu, which is a huge, mostly useless bureaucratic institution in Japan that certifies Zen teachers. I thought it might be nice for my name to be in the official books in their basement, or wherever they keep them. The Soto-shu requires you to shave your head for the ceremony. So I did.*

Afterward I needed to explain to friends and co-workers why I suddenly looked like a reject from the cue ball factory. I still lived in Japan at the time. So I told them I did 出家, which is spelled out in

---

* Basically, there are two tracks by which one can become an ordained teacher/monk/whatever in Zen. One is a very official by-the-books route through a large bureaucratic organization such as Soto-shu, the San Francisco Zen Center, White Plum Asangha, and so on. The other way is a very one-to-one personal style from a specific teacher to a specific student. The former has detailed requirements that must be met, such as a set number of years of training in a certain set curriculum, the completion of particular ceremonies, the purchasing of special costumes and fashion accessories, and so on. The latter is generally much looser and less defined. It depends mainly on the teacher's gut feeling that the student is qualified. Both are legitimate. There is an unfortunate trend going on these days in the States to try and standardize things and to see the more personal form of transmission as somehow less kosher than the by-the-books corporate religious version, with all the bells and whistles. Should this point of view become widely accepted, it will be the death of American Zen, freezing it into a fossilized institution populated by drones adept at aping the forms and reciting the institution's dogma from memory but without any true understanding of the practice and philosophy. But actually, the less formal way is far older and more traditional, while the more formal way is a much more recent invention.

Roman letters as *shukke* — pronounced "shoe-kay." The two Chinese characters used to spell out this word mean "leave home."
. But I hadn't left home, in the literal sense. I lived in the same house with the same wife — I was married at the time — and had the same job as before. This is not at all uncommon. Monks in Japan often live at temples but just as often do not. Since the Meiji Restoration of 1868, Buddhist Japanese monks have been legally permitted to marry, and most of them do.

Okay. So there was this Chinese-style vegetarian restaurant near my house I used to go to a lot that was run by a woman from Taiwan who was a devout follower of some sort of esoteric Buddhist sect. She asked about my shaved head, and I told her I'd done *shukke*. She turned red in the face, and steam shot out of her ears.* "You haven't done *shukke*! It's just for show! Japanese Buddhists don't know anything about real *shukke*!"

Then she brought out this scrapbook full of photos of the monks in her sect, apparently helping horribly deformed people do stuff. The photos seemed designed to emphasize the various abnormalities of the people they were helping in sharply focused, brightly lit, colorful graphic detail, almost like hardcore porn does with genitalia. "This is real *shukke*!" she shouted.

I had to admire those monks for their charitable work. I've done that kind of work in the past, and it's tough. But the woman's attitude toward that work showed me there was some kind of problem there. For her, true monkhood involved doing heroic deeds. And not just any heroic deeds, but heroic deeds that fit her view of what constituted heroism.

But I think leaving home is more of an attitude than a description of a specific act. The monks whose photos she showed me had indeed left home in a literal sense. But I wondered if they'd really

---

* Not really. But she was visibly upset.

left home at all. Of course, I didn't know them, so I can't say. Maybe they had. But the woman's attitude toward them was based on a very strong attachment to a specific and very common way of viewing the world. It's an attitude toward "home leaving" that draws a sharp division between "mundane" work and "religious" work. It's an attitude that says that "good people" do "good works" in ways that society sees as good. I wondered where she'd received that attitude. Leaving home means, among other things, leaving behind the common attitudes of your society.

So leaving home means different things to different people. Getting back to the specific question of the Buddha's life, when we read about Buddha and his earliest followers, we tend to interpret these stories in contemporary terms. But things might not have been like we imagine they were. In those days in India most people spent their whole lives in the same house with an extended family. So "leaving home" could mean moving to your own place three blocks away. In that sense, almost all of us these days "leave home." So-called home-leaving monks were probably not nearly as far away from their families as the average adult nonmonk in Western society today.

In India today some Hindus consider life to be divided into four stages, called *ashramas*. The first is Brahmacharya, the celibate student, during which one learns from a guru. The second phase is called Grihastha, the married-family-man stage. At about age fifty, a man is supposed to renounce married life and become a Vanaprastha, a wandering monk. He is supposed to leave behind his worldly ties and devote himself to religious studies and meditation. Finally, he becomes a Sanyasa, a wandering recluse, cutting all ties with family and society completely. He is declared legally deceased, and all his possessions are given away. He can't even enter into contracts because he's technically considered dead. This is serious business.

Buddha's life didn't follow this trajectory precisely, probably because it hadn't quite solidified into its current form during his lifetime. But what he did was based on an established tradition something like this. In other words, it was not the equivalent of a contemporary middle-aged guy walking away from his responsibilities to go "find himself" by moving to LA, purchasing a red convertible, and dating college girls.

But, as I've said before, what was good for Buddha in his time and his circumstances is not necessarily good for us in our time and our circumstances. It's not real Buddhism to blindly mimic what Buddha did. We need to discover the essential nature of his actions and pursue that instead.

The story has come down to us in its present form to emphasize Buddha's commitment to pursuing the truth. "Leaving home" to me means adopting the attitude that the pursuit of the truth is more vital than the pursuit of what society — your home — tells you is important. Even if your mom says the most important thing is to marry a doctor and live on a hill with a car the neighbors will envy, you need to be able to reject that and look for what's real.

But that doesn't mean running away. Running away is futile. Even if you run very far away from home to a remote mountain monastery, as long as you carry the same attitude you always had, you'll never truly get away. You'll just end up transferring all the stuff from home onto the other people in the monastery. This happens all the time.

People today who want to dump their spouses and kids to run off to the mountains ought to examine themselves and their motivations very, very carefully. Lots of people run away from responsibilities to "find themselves." But not so many of them have a real commitment to the truth. It would be better to find the truth in the life you're living, with the responsibilities you've already accepted. Responsibilities have a way of finding you, even if you run away from them.

We don't know if Buddha loved his wife in the sense that we understand the word today. But the stories that have come down to us suggest that they were very close in ways that might not have been so common in arranged marriages of his day. So what does Buddhism have to say about love?

There's a trend lately to translate the Sanskrit/Pali word *metta*, which occurs in the ancient Buddhist literature, as "loving-kindness." But to me that seems more like marketing aimed at winning ex-Christians into the fold than anything else. The word is more appropriately translated as "benevolence" or "compassion." I will get into this a little more deeply in the following mini-chapter on Buddhist philosophical terms.

Love is overrated, if you ask me. The word is usually used to denote a fluttery-butterfly syrupy-sweet emotionalism that we're probably better off without. Now I know we can talk about *agape* love, and *eros* love, and the love of a man for his fellow man* and a woman for her fellow woman.** But mainly when the word *love* starts getting thrown around, we're not talking about compassion or friendship, but about emotion.

Buddhism is about transcending your emotions, leaving them behind. That idea scares people sometimes. They worry that it means turning into a robot or a living statue. But that's not what we mean by transcending emotion. We're not aiming to turn ourselves into robots, but to become sane human beings.

Transcending emotions doesn't mean you have no feelings. You have them. But you recognize them for what they are and respond appropriately without letting them develop into what we call emotions, which are really just feelings that have been blown way out of proportion.

A typical romance begins with an overload of hormones, which excites the brain and nervous system. In this excited state it becomes difficult to act sensibly. Recent scientific studies have shown that serotonin levels actually drop during periods of high hormonal arousal, causing a person to lose his or her ability to make critical judgments.*** When you mix in alcohol and drugs, as most of us do in

---

* Very popular where I used to live in West Hollywood.
** There's some of that available on Suicide Girls.
***See chapter 7 of Hannah Holmes's book *The Well Dressed Ape* for fascinating details about this!

the early stages of romance, what you get isn't much of a recipe for sensible action. Which isn't to say that romance is bad, or relationships are bad, or marriage is bad, or love is bad, or any of that. It's just that excitement in general is something to be avoided more than pursued, though most of us are prone to chase after it.

What goes up must come down, as the cliché goes. This happens to be true. Not only does every high have an accompanying low, but in its most basic form every high *is* a low. We experience the two ends of the emotional spectrum at different times. But they are one and the same. Time is illusory. This doesn't mean we have to forgo happiness. It's just that real happiness is more stable than the emotional roller coaster ride we often mistake for happiness.

As I write this, my incredibly annoying upstairs neighbor is banging on his piano and screeching, "What's love got to do with it?" from the old Tina Turner song. Thankfully it is not 4:00 a.m., which is the time of day he usually chooses to bang on his piano. But it's still irritating. In this case, though, it's kind of appropriate because songs like that express well what society's idealized version of romantic love is all about — intense, overblown, shirt-ripping, teary-eyed fluff.

We're constantly seeking excitement and stimulation, wrenching our bodies and minds this way and that trying to find some delirious high or some delicious low. Then, after we've ripped and pulled and stretched and squeezed ourselves till we can barely stand up from the stress, we wonder why we're such a mess. Duh! The body/mind likes equilibrium. It seeks balance. Whenever you get too high, it's like stretching a rubber band. It's going to snap back or break. These are the only two options. Yet we always believe there's some high just around the corner that's going to pull us way, way, way up, where we'll stay forever and ever. If our current romance doesn't do that for us, we'll look for a new one. When the giddy high of the first date wears off, we're ready for another fix.

There's no problem with loving someone, with coupling up, with enjoying someone's company, and all the rest. But if you want to enjoy all that stuff to the fullest, the best way to do it is to stop looking for big highs, peak experiences, and sweeping flights of blissful romance. All that stuff just causes its own counterreactions. Watch your own body and mind, and you'll see this for yourself.

Chapter 18

I LOVE IT WHEN YOU DO THAT
Sex and Metta (Compassion)

Metta is a big buzzword in Western Buddhist circles these days. As I said in the last chapter, in recent times Americans have become fond of translating the Pali word *metta** as "loving-kindness." It can also mean "friendliness," "benevolence," "goodwill," "kindness," and "sympathy."

The origin of the Buddhist concept of metta comes from a story of Buddha's life known as the Metta Sutra. In this story a group of monks is trying to meditate in the forest. But the monks come to believe that demons in the trees are disturbing their meditations. They ask Buddha what to do about this, and he tells them to send thoughts of compassion toward the demons. The monks do this, and it works. According to the sutra, the Buddha told them to think something like this:

---

* Pali is the language in which the most ancient Buddhist sutras are written. Though the language itself is very old by our standards and is no longer spoken, even Pali is probably more modern than the language Buddha and his followers actually spoke.

May all beings be happy and at their ease. May they be joyous and live in safety. Let none deceive another, or despise any being in any state. Let none wish harm to another. But even as a mother loves, watches over, and protects her child, so may all with a boundless mind cherish all living beings, radiating friendliness over the entire world without limit. May we cultivate a boundless goodwill, free from ill will or enmity, and maintain the sublime abiding of this recollection.

The Metta Sutra is part of the Pali Canon, the oldest extant Buddhist texts. In the Theravada school of Buddhism these texts are considered the only authentic records of Gautama Buddha's teachings, and the folks from the Theravada school take them very seriously. So the popularity of metta in the West is mainly related to the Theravada tradition.

In the Zen tradition, however, the concept of metta is not so strongly emphasized, except occasionally in contemporary Western Zen traditions, which have adopted it from Theravada. Instead the focus is on compassion. Dogen Zenji, founder of the Japanese Soto school of Zen, said that truly compassionate action is like a hand reaching back to adjust a pillow in the night. In other words, truly compassionate action arises spontaneously without thought and is carried out in real action with no anticipation of reward and, indeed, no concept of a doer of that action. When you adjust your pillow in your sleep, you just comprehend intuitively what needs doing, and you do it. Afterward you have no idea that anything has even been done. It is still a type of compassion to be kind to yourself. When you feel better you are more able to be truly of service to others.

I'd rather talk about *compassion* than loving-kindness because it's a less loaded term. But even the concept of compassion can be twisted by the ego to serve its own ends.

There is a tremendous difference between the idea of compassion and real compassion. You know how you sometimes picture a scenario and imagine how you'd feel in that situation? Have you ever noticed that when the situation you imagined actually happens, your real feelings about it are often completely different from what you'd imagined? Some of us deal with this by trying to change our actual feelings into the feelings we imagined we'd have. But this is a big waste of time.

The same difference exists between the concept of compassion and the reality of compassion. It may not be completely useless to look at a situation and think, "What would a compassionate person do?" the way some people ask what Jesus would do. But ultimately both "Jesus" and "a compassionate person" are ideas in our heads, not reality. I think it's much more important to learn how to respond spontaneously and intuitively to a situation.

If you ask me, compassion ought to play just as much of a role in sex as passion. You may have a lot of passion for your lover or lovers, but how much compassion are you bringing to the table?* Are you open enough to see what the situation really requires over and above what your genitals are telling you to do? Would you be able to walk away from a potentially really hot and sexy encounter if you knew it wasn't right? Can you be as compassionate a lover as you are a passionate one?

Compassion can be so selfless that it almost seems selfish. There are times when both (or all) partners involved in the act of sex completely lose any sense of self and other. In those moments each one can do exactly what gives her or him the most pleasure while simultaneously and instinctively doing what pleases her or his partner(s) the most. At these times there isn't any conscious attempt to please anyone other than her- or himself because the very idea of self and other(s) has vanished. In this state it is precisely the same thing to please someone else as it is to please oneself.

_____

* Okay, maybe to the bed, since some people find it uncomfortable to do it on a table.

It would be wonderful if all of us could bring the type of compassion we sometimes find in good sex to all situations in life. Nishijima Roshi likes to say that when you establish the balanced state in Buddhism you can do what you truly want. In this state, what you truly want and what the world around you needs most become the same thing. You don't need to imagine what Jesus or Buddha or whoever would do. You just need to do exactly what you want to do.

Of course, this is not something most of us are capable of. It takes hard work and practice to get anywhere near this state. If you told most people just to do what they want, their most likely response would be to act in a completely egotistical way that just wrecks everything both for those they encounter and ultimately for themselves as well.

That may be the key right there. Truly compassionate action doesn't just benefit others, it benefits us as well. We miss that because we have such a warped and limited idea of what we, ourselves, actually are. Our happiness and the happiness of those we encounter are not really two distinct things. They are exactly the same.

Chapter 19

HUG IS THE DRUG

Sometimes people who like to describe themselves as "into spirituality" search for a different kind of love. Recently at a talk I gave, a woman told me that she felt an intense longing to be enfolded in the embrace of universal spiritual love. Lots of people have similar dreams. I spent a day with some of them a little while ago.

I went and got hugged by Amma, India's world-famous hugging saint, when she was in Los Angeles last month. She shoved my head into her fluffy right boob and whispered something that sounded like "Magilla, Magilla, Magilla, Magilla" into my ear. Or maybe it was "Medula, Medula, Medula, Medula." It was hard to tell.

Her hot breath was kind of a turn-on. I didn't expect that. But I have kind of a weakness for women whispering in my ear. Then she mashed a Hershey's Kiss into my hand, after which two of her people grabbed me from behind, kind of spun me around, and sent me off into the crowd.

It took me a while to get the whole "hug and kiss" pun.

I felt a little dizzy as they shoved me out of the way to make room for the next customer. Was that the *shaktipat* everybody was getting so excited about? *Shaktipat* is supposed to be a direct transference of spiritual energy from an enlightened being.* It felt to me more like that druggy, disorientated sensation you have when you get off a roller coaster or when you take a toke of some slightly lousy weed.

In case you don't know, Amma is a cute, short, chubby Indian lady who a lot of people believe is an Enlightened Being. She was born in 1953 in a tiny fishing village in South India. During her childhood, they say, she spent much of her time absorbed in a deep meditative state of *samadhi*. By the time she was twenty-one she'd begun to attract followers. In the early eighties she consolidated this following into an ashram and began traveling the world offering *darshan*, a Sanskrit word meaning "encounter with a saintly person," to spiritual seekers around the world.

There's a lot to like about Amma. So I'm going to start by saying some of that, because I know that no matter what I do people are gonna say this chapter trashes the poor, sweet, hugging saint. But she seems like a genuinely decent person, and I'm sure her charitable work does a lot of people a lot of good. Her charities run educational programs, distribute free food, run hospitals and hospices, build free homes for the poor, and provide lifetime stipends for mentally and physically challenged adults. It is all wonderful stuff. She's not a hate monger. She doesn't put down anyone, regardless of race, creed, or religion. She seems to be a very nice lady who wants to do some good in the world.

I do not despise Amma, and it is not my intention to trash her. But it is absolutely necessary to question what she does, and by extension what a lot of spiritual teachers are calling "love" and holding up as the ideal solution to society's problems.

---

* And if you ever had anyone pat your shakti...

Amma's setup has been scientifically designed for the maximum buildup before you get the big payoff.* When you arrive at the Radisson Hotel near LAX you take a number. Or in my case, you arrive really late after taking your friend to the airport, and you get a little pink card. After Amma gets through hugging all the people with numbers, if she's still up to hugging some more, they allow the folks with the pink cards to get a number.

The second floor of the hotel has been reimagined as a spiritual wonderland, sort of a Hindu-flavored mini-Disneyland, complete with uniformed Mouseketeers to guide you through. After you get your number you stand in a long line, slowly drawing ever nearer to the saint herself. "Have your ticket visible," I was told several times. Can't have any line jumpers! And you'd be amazed how many of these "spiritual seekers" will elbow the next guy out of the way to get their *shaktipat* first. No joke.

As you get closer, you see that Amma is surrounded by concentric circles of ever-more-devoted disciples. There are three or four guys right next to her, watching her the way a dog watches its master, as Amma speaks what I assume are beautiful spiritual messages to them, to which they dare not reply, not deigning to engage in any conversation with someone so divine. Outside that little circle of admirers are rings of worshippers swooning just to be in Amma's presence. When her handlers remove Amma's chair, many of these will run up to lay prostrate and kiss the ground on which it had sat.

As you move closer to Amma — they call her "Mother" — you gradually surrender more and more of your will. First your shoes come off. Then you're directed in a line by authoritative people who instruct you to move from chair to chair as each huggee at the front of the line gets finished. Once you get about ten feet away from the saint there are no more chairs and you are pushed into a kneeling

---

* If you think I'm gonna put a footnote here that says, "Heh, heh, buildup and payoff," you're wrong! So there!

position so that you are crawling for the last leg of the journey. Then they remove your jewelry and glasses and wipe off your face like you're a three-year-old. Finally you are pushed powerlessly into Amma's waiting embrace.

The stage is set up with Hollywood-style lighting full of vibrant orange, pink, and gold. On the wall is a fifteen-foot-high photo of Amma with a half dozen spotlights trained on her face to make it glow even more ethereally, just in case you forgot what she looks like. Backlit streamers and flags hang all around the Radisson hotel's conference room to create the image of a blissful Hindu heaven. The color scheme seems intended to generate a feeling of womblike security. The scent of incense and perfume hangs heavy in the air. People always remark that Amma smells like roses. She ought to, with all the people spraying rose-scented perfume around her!

Out beyond the inner circle surrounding the saint is the marketplace. Here you can buy Amma jewelry, Amma T-shirts, Amma bumper stickers, Amma dolls, Amma coffee mugs, Amma iPods prefilled with MP3s of Amma singing, and a whole range of other such goodies and trinkets. On the walls are advertisements for other spiritual healers personally endorsed by Amma, such as Dr. Weng's acupuncture, Effective Vedic Astrology, Banyan Botanicals, and much, much more. If that's not enough for you, you can buy all sorts of items personally used by Amma, including discarded clothing, chairs, rugs, and even Amma's Lexus. The poster for this last item helpfully includes the car's current Blue Book value ($8,000) and its starting bid ($12,000). And don't forget the food! Delicious vegetarian cuisine at reasonable prices. This I did not pass up.

Amma® is a registered trademark. None of the licensed items on offer fails to put that little circled R next to her name, lest she lose her claim. I know how this works. I used to be in charge of this kind of stuff for a Japanese company that made a superhero show, and we did exactly the same thing. She's also got a cute little logo, too, just like we did. Branding is everything! I'll bet you dollars to doughnuts she goes after bootleg Amma merch just like we went after bootleg Ultraman merch.

Later on, after my hug, I got to witness Amma teaching. She's not bad. In fact, she and her opening act, a bearded swami whose name I've forgotten, are fairly accomplished stand-up comics. That was something I didn't expect. The jokes were pretty corny but not too worn-out. There was one about a guy who walks into a bar and throws his drink at the bartender. Before the bartender can get mad, the guy starts weeping. He tells the bartender he can't help himself, it's a compulsion. The bartender recommends a shrink. The guy goes and then returns six months later, whereupon he again throws his drink at the bartender. The bartender says that the shrink doesn't seem to have helped. The guy says, "No. He helped a lot. I still have the compulsion, but now I don't feel guilty about it!" The crowd laughs, the spiritual significance of the joke is explained, and everybody sighs deeply in unison at the beauty of the great teacher's great teaching.

And just what is Amma's message to the world? Here are a few quotes from the free pamphlet (chock-full of advertisements) given out to all comers: "God-realization is nothing but the ability and expansiveness of the heart to love everything equally," "Love is what fills life constantly with newness," and "Try to cultivate a heart that never harms any being in thought, word, or deed." That sort of thing.

We are also told in the pamphlet, "To love is Mother's nature, to serve is her nature," and assured that, "As far as Mother is concerned, everyone is her child." "There is nothing preplanned about Amma's mission," the pamphlet tells us. "All her projects have been spontaneously compassionate responses to the sorrow and suffering she sees around her."

And yet, and yet, and yet . . . for all the charitable work and messages of love, kindness, and generosity, there is something deeply disturbing about the whole circus that surrounds all this admittedly admirable work.

Maybe it's because it is such a circus. Why do we need to be driven nearly to a frenzy with spiritual madness before we can be coerced into contributing to a good cause? Is excitement the same as spirituality?*

What's wrong with worshipping Amma, after all? She seems nice enough. So what the hell is my problem?

I'm going to tell you what bothered me about it. You are, of course, free to draw whatever conclusions you like.

The scariest part for me was the men standing around her transfixed just like dogs ready to obey their master. The expressions on their faces were just like the expressions you see on a Doberman waiting for its master to say "fetch" or "kill." A dog is only as good as its master. If the master tells the dog to fetch the paper, it fetches the paper. If the master tells the dog to maul the black man who just moved in next door, it mauls the black man. The dog's only criterion is pleasing its master. It has no will or moral center of its own. Blind obedience is never a good thing, even when it's directed at a supposedly "good" person.

What happens when these folks who've learned only obedience get tired of Amma? They have learned only obedience. Who will they obey next?

We need personal responsibility. This is truer now than it has ever been. As individuals we now have access to unprecedented power. This was brought home clearly by the events of September 11, 2001. A handful of people were able to cause a level of destruction and havoc that had previously taken the efforts of an entire nation. And things have only become more dangerous.

It's never a good thing to give up your personal power. You need your personal power in order to take personal responsibility.

Maybe Amma delivers pure love. That's what her press agent says, anyway. Still, I'm not sure pure love is what we need either. I

---

* Actually, I think it may be, which is why Buddhism is not spirituality.

think what's truly needed is a balance of love and hate. By "hate" I'm not talking about the kind of hate that manifests as crimes against people of other races and that kind of thing. Hate is something much deeper and more profound.

There are two sides to the universe. Spiritual people always talk about oneness, about dissolving into the embrace of universal love. But that's only one side of reality. The other side is hate, separation, aloneness. Both are real. When love and hate are balanced there is compassion and wisdom. Love alone is beautiful but powerless. Hate alone is powerful but too dangerous.

It's as bad to deny hate as it is to deny love. When we acknowledge our separation we can act in unity with each other. When we lose our sense of separation we lose our effectiveness as individuals.

The two sides of our being are not mutually exclusive. It's not that we have to give up our existence as individuals to merge into the warm embrace of all-encompassing oneness. Our essential oneness and our essential separation are manifestations of the same thing, which is neither oneness nor separation.

There are no words for this because the function of words is to divide and categorize. But reality as it is defies all categories. Even something as obvious as saying love is better than hate is an attempt to pin down and define that which is beyond definition.

We must act with compassion if we want to create a peaceful world. That's true. But compassion is also beyond love and hate. Compassion is a spontaneous response to what needs to be done right here and now.

I don't detest Amma any more than I detest Phish or Acid Mothers Temple or anyone else who offers an evening of escapist entertainment based on that heady feeling of warmth and community that can be created in an environment specifically designed to amplify those feelings while pushing all the other stuff to one side. I had fun seeing Amma, and I would go again. The food was delicious, too. I am overwhelmed by my good fortune to have friends as wonderful as Rachael and Tenaya, who accompanied me and tolerated my annoyance at much of what went on at the event. I am overjoyed to live in a world enough at peace that something like the Amma experience is allowed to happen.

What I question is when such experiences are offered up as if they provide some kind of Ultimate Answer to the world's woes. If we don't acknowledge and understand our own hate we can't effectively deal with the problems that hate creates in our world. Warm smiles and hugs don't fix everything, and they never will.

Not long after my date with Amma I got invited to yet another spiritual love fest. This time it was a concert being given at a club on Sunset Strip by an up-and-coming spiritual singer/songwriter, a blond twenty-something white boy with dreadlocks who sings songs about unity and God and the need for us all to come together and stop all our fussing and fighting. I was supposed to interview him for Suicide Girls, but the interview never happened. The club was packed with beautiful people swaying to the rhythm and feeling the love he had to share. If only we could all learn to just love one another, how wonderful the world would be!

You know how a black hole is made of matter so dense that if you took a piece out of it and put it somewhere else it would suck everything into it and create a new black hole?* That's what I felt like in that club, like I was a piece of black hole. No matter how hard I tried to feel the love, I couldn't. I tried to paste a smile on my face, but it wouldn't stay.

After the show I got taken backstage to meet the artist. As I was led through the corridors behind the stage up to the green room on the second floor, I couldn't stop thinking, "Wow, Frank Zappa's been here!" And the Sex Pistols and a whole bunch of my other heroes. There were dozens of autographed posters along the corridor from the many famous rockers who'd also been here before.

---

* Hey, kids! Don't trust Brad's physics here! Look it up yourself! He's probably wrong!

We got into the green room, which wasn't the least bit green, and the singer/songwriter held court with various members of the press who had come out to see him. He told a story of a chance meeting with a rich woman in a San Francisco restaurant. The meeting was fraught with deep significance, he told us. He knew this because, as he said, he's a "spiritual guy." He dropped this piece of information into the narrative two or three times.

I noticed the number 420 printed in lettering made of flowers on the back of his shirt. So that's how he maintained his permanent look of enchantment.*

After a few minutes the time for talking with journalists was winding down, and the woman who'd brought us backstage started herding everyone out. As we were leaving I noticed a new group was entering. A dozen or so of the most gorgeous women from the crowd were being led backstage for the next portion of the meet-and-greet. I turned to the person who brought me backstage and said, "Oh! I see how this works!" She gave me a quizzical look. Not that I begrudge the guy his groupies. But it seemed his publicist didn't really want to acknowledge this particular aspect of the "pure love" he sang about.

It's all very beautiful to stand on a stage in a Hollywood nightclub surrounded by swaying palm trees and beautiful people with plenty of money, stoned immaculate on primo weed and with all the pussy you can eat, and say that if only everybody just learned to love each other and be kind, the world would be wonderful.

But that won't solve the real problems we face. If you ignore hate you cannot find any real solutions.

There was a lot of hate in the room that evening, but nobody wanted to say that. I'm talking about hating those who oppose your dreams of a utopia of pure love, hate in the form of hating your real work-a-day life and longing to escape it in a cloud of marijuana

---

* In case you don't know, 420 is code for marijuana.

smoke, hate in the form of hating the Republicans or the businessmen or the cops. When you push forward love as a contrast to hate you're pushing forward hate as well, just as strongly. It's true that the word *love* doesn't always mean the opposite of hate. But in this context it did, as the singer kept reminding us.

Words and concepts are funny creatures. They define things by putting them against other things. We don't consciously realize it, but each time a word or a concept appears in our minds, so do all its opposites. The word is never the thing.

Compassion is completely different from love. Compassion doesn't exist in contrast to something else. I mean, sure, in terms of etymology, you could probably come up with some word that contrasts with compassion. But that's not what we're talking about here.

True compassion is a spontaneous response to circumstances. It's not situational ethics. It doesn't come from thought. It isn't a dream of some utopia that would exist if only this or that or the other condition could be met. It's real action here and now that makes things better.

Compassion doesn't need to be big. It can be very small. Shunryu Suzuki Roshi said that it's not important to try and fix the whole world. Just shine one corner. That's what God put you here to do. Not to fix everything, not to save the planet, just to make your portion of the universe a little better.

A smile is compassionate action. Yelling at some ass-wipe to knock it off can also be an expression of compassion. Both kinds of compassionate action take a lot of care. A smile at the wrong time can be as devastating as a fist in the face at the wrong time.

There is only one way to become clear about compassion. You have to be very quiet and see your own state of body/mind honestly. This is very difficult to do. But it's also not difficult at all. It's only difficult to do this because we have all devoted ourselves to developing habits that obstruct our ability to notice what's right in front of us. We obstruct our own view almost instantly. We can't see our own intuitive response because we're so used to responding only to our thoughts.

The Beatles were wrong when they said all you need is love. You need hate as well. You need to acknowledge hate. You can't ignore it or push it aside. You have to get okay with hate. When you push it into the background it doesn't go away. It's still there, roaring away. All you've done is shout it down for a while.

Some people take hate too far and try and hurt or destroy the things they hate. But that won't do you any good either. Because hate is not located in the object of your hatred. Hate is much more fundamental than that. If you succeed in destroying some object you've chosen to focus your hate on, the hate does not disappear. It will reemerge doubly strong to hate the next object.

You need that which you hate. It's part of you. It's fundamental to what you are. Even if you don't like it, or wish it weren't there, it's still you. It makes you what you are. When you can live with the things you hate, then hate transforms itself. Hate is no longer evil. It's just hate.

In some strange way, you learn to love your hate and learn to love the objects of hatred. That which you hate, that which is eternally separate from what you think of as your "self," makes you, you. By getting comfortable with your own hatred, you can come to be more comfortable with what you really are. Your response to hate then ceases to be a wish to destroy or harm those objects or people whom you believe to be its object. Nor do you seek to eliminate hate from your personality. By accepting hate and by not acting on it in harmful ways, you find that you can use that aspect of what you are in a constructive way.

Years ago I had a boss whom I hated. He was stupid and short-sighted. He had no imagination or any real understanding of the work we were doing. One day, after returning to work from a Zen retreat, it occurred to me that my boss and I were not really two different people. What I hated about him were things I could recognize in my own makeup. If those aspects were not part of me I wouldn't have been able to see them in my boss. From that moment on my relationship with him changed completely, and we were finally able to work together. It wasn't that my hate disappeared and turned into love. But by accepting hate for what it really was, I found I no longer needed to try and destroy either the hate or its object.

Saying we wouldn't have war and the other horrors we visit on ourselves if only we loved each other assumes that the reason we fight and kill each other is because of some kind of deliberate act of going against nature. But I wonder if war might actually be a survival mechanism, not for the individual, obviously, but for the species as a whole. Those who advance the idea of love as the ultimate answer seem to believe that if we returned to the natural way of love, all our problems would be solved.

But love may be one of the driving forces behind violence. This is certainly the case in so-called crimes of passion as well as when patriotism — the love for one's country and one's people — is the cause of bloodshed. An overabundance of love directed at a specific object can cause us to want to destroy that which is not the object of our love. An ability to live with what we hate might make us more peaceful, might make us less prone to war.

This is not to say that war is a good thing or that we should continue to engage in it because it's natural. War is bad. War should stop.* But I am convinced that it will take something other than warm, loving feelings to make this happen.

Make peace with your darkness. Don't try and become an unbalanced mass of pure love. Be your hate as well as your love. Act out of real compassion, not out of misguided love.

---

* Let me say that again in the footnotes just so we're very clear on how I feel about this point: WAR IS BAD. WAR SHOULD STOP.

Chapter 20

BDSM and Cult Behavior

During the past year I've developed a loose relationship with some people who practice a different kind of love — members of the BDSM community in Los Angeles and elsewhere online through the Suicide Girls website. To review, BDSM stands for bondage, domination and submission, and masochism* — in other words, kinky sex.

My initial contact came through Mistress Ivy, one of the members of the Suicide Girls, who also works as a dominatrix at a local dungeon. A dungeon is a place where you can pay for the services of professional dominatrices and submissives. A dominatrix is someone who beats you, and a submissive is someone whom you beat. Professional BDSM dungeons are legal in Los Angeles and not considered a form of prostitution. I don't know if they are permitted elsewhere. Friends of mine in the BDSM scene in Cleveland have told me that dungeons there do not operate openly or advertise in

---

* Or sometimes the *D* and *S* stand for discipline and sadism.

the papers as do those in LA, San Francisco, and other more socially liberal areas. Indeed, the dungeons in California are usually — but not always — very careful not to allow any actual sexual intercourse to take place within their walls. There's a notice on the door of the one in Los Angeles where Mistress Ivy works that warns that men who become "turgid" during a session will be asked to leave. I tend to doubt this rule is ever enforced. In fact, I know from my friends who work in the dungeons that if customers have behaved properly, they are allowed to masturbate in the presence of their dominatrix or submissive at the end of the session. This is called "release."

Mistress Ivy, my dominatrix friend, is also a practicing Buddhist in the Tibetan tradition. She's quite a scholar and is working on a master's in Sanskrit literature, which she can also read in its native Devanagari script.

Through my association with Mistress Ivy I've gotten to know a number of other women who have worked at the dungeon and was able to visit on occasion. This was quite an honor, since men who are not clients are generally forbidden to go inside. I guess they trusted me. And for this reason I'm not going to reveal too much in the way of secret information about the place.

A lot of people in the BDSM scene don't view their sexual interests as mere kinkiness or as games they play. They view it as a full-blown sexual orientation on the same level as heterosexuality, homosexuality, and bisexuality. See my interview with Nina Hartley in chapter 16, in which she talks about this. For many of them, sex is only enjoyable when it involves what they call a "power exchange." That means that one person must clearly dominate sexually, while the other acts in a submissive role. The dominant person is called a "top," while the submissive is a "bottom." Their respective activities are often referred to as "topping" or "bottoming."

This is nothing terribly unusual. In most sexual encounters some form of domination and submission occurs. Even homosexual couples tend to follow what are commonly thought of as "male" (dominant) and "female" (submissive) roles. In Japanese a dominant lesbian is called *tachi*, meaning "standing," and the submissive is called *neko*, meaning "cat."* But BDSM folks take things a step, or perhaps a few steps, further. Whips, chains, ropes, and so forth are used to enhance the experience of domination or submissiveness, and physical pain also plays a role.

I'm all for sexual freedom, and it's not my place to say what people should or should not do. I will say, though, that I have some deep misgivings about some of what little I've seen in the consensual BDSM community. I do see some therapeutic usefulness in it. But this may often be canceled out by the actual trauma involved. Acted-out scenes of rape and torture can be psychologically traumatic, even when all parties enter into the activity with full consent and even when clear boundaries are adhered to. Actors understand this phenomenon. It's tough business pretending to be angry or pretending to be traumatized. It very often tweaks the nervous system in exactly the same way as the real deal. That's some powerful mojo to be playing around with.

Which is not to say that I'm in any way against this type of sexual activity. It's just that it has to be practiced with extreme caution and care. Most folks in the BDSM community are well aware of this. And their extra awareness of the potential dangers of their preferred forms of sexual expression often leads to a degree of openness and honesty not often encountered in more standard forms of sexuality.

Since Nina Hartley mentioned her involvement in the scene when I interviewed her, I asked her about this.

BW: I wanted to ask you about power exchange. It's a key part of the BDSM experience.

---

* Let's just say I've, uh, "researched this matter through the available literature" and leave it at that, shall we?

NH: Which I do at home.

BW: I got into this discussion about how the teacher-student or guru-disciple or even Zen teacher-student relationship can easily devolve into simple power exchange. This is often the subtext of those relationships. But in the BDSM community it's very open. They say right up front, "This is power exchange. I'm tying you up, and I can do whatever I want until you say, y'know, *pomegranate* or whatever your safe word is." And I see a lot of power exchange going on in my line of work as a Buddhist teacher. But without the safe words.

NH: Oh, my God, yeah! You're gonna give them the keys to the kingdom or enlightenment or whatever!

BW: And as the teacher it's all my responsibility!

NH: Obviously power exchange is everywhere in the culture. What I like about the BDSM community is that they bring it forward, so it's no longer back in the lizard brain. And we can decide how we're gonna do this. With my husband, he's very dominant, and he doesn't switch. So in our lovemaking we think of it as something like kabuki theater or a tea ceremony. It's a form that our lovemaking takes, and in that form his true nature comes out fully. I want to dance with a partner who is fully expressing his true nature. I grew up in Berkeley, where the very notion of power exchange is seen as a terrible thing. But it is in the world. Knowing about BDSM has helped me resist the efforts of the mainstream culture to tweak that part of me. That's what Madison Avenue does. People are pushed in all different directions through the use of soft power by advertisers. They don't know this is going on. It's very hard for BDSM people to be swayed by advertising because they see it coming a mile away. And the more integrated kink folk I know cannot be made to feel guilty about their sexuality. So in any teacher-student situation in or out of the dharma there is power exchange. And power exchange is the number one thing people play with in sex. It's out there all the time.

BDSM apes it and burlesques it. Because we understand that power imbalance is an essential aspect of nature. Bunnies are made to be eaten.

BW: Sounds like a good title for a children's book!

NH: But ungulate animals, their role in the world is to turn sunlight into protein for other animals to ingest. They eat grass and turn it into meat. I can choose not to eat them. But that's their role. Bunnies turn grass into fox food because foxes can't eat grass. This is what I love about zazen. It forces you to deal with that. Being able to sit with uncomfortable feelings without running away or stuffing them down is a huge gift. You realize that moods change. If we stuff the feeling here, before it reaches its crescendo, we don't realize it'll stop if we give it time. It'll pass if you don't feed it or stuff it away, thereby giving it more power. Part of what makes us happy or unhappy is what we pay attention to. And it takes a lot of energy and effort to sustain an emotion, like anger, for example. It's exhausting to be angry. Half the time we feel we can't help what emotions we're experiencing. But if you sit on the cushion long enough and watch them, you realize, "Oh, this is a choice I'm making." And after a while eventually you can calm down enough to see that moment where you have the choice to act like an asshole or to choose differently. The Dalai Lama said, "There is no greater wisdom than compassion." The wisdom in choosing the compassionate response is real. It's not even an altruistic thing. It feels better to act compassionately.

BW: I knew a person who worked for a BDSM club. She witnessed some stuff there that was all perfectly consensual, but it really seemed to be exacerbating the traumatic stuff that the client brought to the scene. So I wanted to ask your opinion. Just because something is consensual, is it okay?

NH: Since the person is an adult, of sound mind and body, if I'm a dominatrix I don't get to say to him, "Wow, man, that's a sick trip."

I get to say to him, "That's not my trip. I choose not to take your money for this. I cannot be the other side of this equation." Just because a person is reinforcing or recapitulating negative or harmful behavior doesn't mean he doesn't get to do it. I can agree not to participate.

BW: That's an area of responsibility. It's like being a bartender and refusing to serve drinks to someone who's clearly had too many. And if you're running a business that may be a difficult call to make.

NH: In the professional BDSM business if one specific provider wasn't gonna go for it, very likely there'd be another one who would. Because that other provider doesn't see what the client wanted as dangerous, or doesn't care. Unfortunately that happens, same as it does in lots of other businesses, like bars or gambling houses.

I want to take this a little further and clearly state my conviction that just because everyone involved consents to an activity, that doesn't automatically make it okay. There are still consequences, even if the scenario is handled as responsibly as possible.

Plenty of other books explore these issues in greater detail and from a far more informed standpoint than I can bring to the discussion. But I'll take a crack at it. One of the people I know who worked in the professional BDSM world said she often witnessed situations in which things plainly went too far. Everyone in the room was a willing participant. But they were very obviously pushing themselves and each other into unhealthy areas. Kind of the same way lots of people do with recreational drugs.

They were being outwardly responsible in the sense of adhering to the protocol of the scene, observing safe words, and so on. But what was happening was traumatic, and they were not really dealing with that aspect. I'm not talking about a little bit of light spanking or gentle rope play here. Some of what went down was pretty heavy stuff, especially in the psychological aspects, which got very deep, even when the physical abuse was tempered. Again, it's vital to keep your balance in such situations, and most of us have no idea how to do that.

One of the interesting phenomena I've observed in this world of kinkiness was the "lifestyle player." BDSM folks often refer to the stuff they do in the context of their sex lives as "playing." "Playing" might include tying each other up, flogging, playing cop and speeder or teacher and student, cross-dressing, and so on. A lifestyle player does not stop performing his or her role when the sex is done. They keep it up 24/7, or as close to 24/7 as is practical. For example, a woman may remain collared and naked at all times when in the house. My former girlfriend, the one I talked about earlier who worked at the dungeon, once visited the home of a pair of lifestyle players where the woman remained sitting naked on a chair with her legs spread wide open while people walked by, chatted with each other but not with her, and generally went about their business. My friend said it was kind of weird and disconcerting. I'm sure it was. But to each his or her own. It's none of my business to judge.

The reason I'm bringing all this up in the context of a book about Buddhism is that, as I mentioned to Nina in the interview above, there are a lot of parallels between the way BDSM people — especially the lifestyle players — behave and the way some people act in the context of religious organizations. In many ways these people are lifestyle players at their religions.

I received an email that addresses some of these issues.

> Brad, here is my hunch. Folks are paying megabucks to various gurus and spiritual masters not just to receive the verbal teachings but because covertly they are thrilling to power and to power imbalance.
>
> I do not practice BDSM, but I am more and more convinced these days that the adult kink community does a far better job than the spiritual-seekers scene, because the

kink practitioners are thinking consciously about power and have learned to communicate beforehand what they all want, what the boundaries are.

Yet in the spiritual kink scene, people are obsessed with power but unconscious of it, and determined to stay unconscious of it. There is no way to talk consciously about power, and there are no safe words a bottom can use to signal that he or she is being traumatized instead of challenged and wants to scene to stop.

The result is, in the world of BDSM kink, people examine and name their desires and set it up so that both top and bottom can exit the scene feeling satisfied — which is more than can be said for many sectors of the so-called spiritual scene. I suspect that many don't feel they are spiritual unless they are thrilling to a power imbalance.

You once wrote about how your teacher looked at one of the superhero books made by the Japanese company you worked for. He said that superhero shows taught children to worship power — that some benevolent being could come to the rescue, every time. Some worship Ultraman, or the Science Patrol. Others worship roshis and gurus and never examine the deep structure of all this.

And if you pay a lot of money to some spiritual master for his teachings, as many do, or if you give over your entire life to him, you have an incentive not to want to examine this. It's too painful to face that you paid thousands of dollars to fulfill a child's fantasy of rescue.

I agree. In most cases, in the spiritual scene, everyone involved is almost completely blind to the power exchange issues involved in their relationships.

I once asked Nishijima Roshi about koan practice. I talked about this earlier, but let's review. This is a tradition followed in certain schools of Zen wherein the teacher assigns an abstract question to the student, and the student is supposed to answer it. The most famous of these is "Two hands when clapping make a sound. What is the sound of one hand?" Traditionally, pretty much no matter what answer you bring to one of these sessions, the master tells you it's wrong and sends you away.

Nishijima Roshi said, "In koan practice the student usually just enjoys being defeated by the master." In short what he's saying is that it's a classic D/s* relationship.

Now, I know that koan practice is not forever and always a corrupt thing. But Nishijima's answer expressed a lot about the way the teacher-student dynamic can malfunction, even in cases when koans are not used. Students enjoy giving up power to their teachers, and being defeated by them is a great way to do this. The power exchange is maintained, and the student feels relieved of responsibility. A whole lot of other things that go on in the spiritual teacher-disciple relationship derive from this same desire of the student to give up power to the master.

The religious lifestyle player gives up all his or her power to the autocratic structure of the religion, thus becoming the ultimate submissive. After all, who could be a bigger dominatrix than God or Buddha? The words used by various religions, especially in Eastern traditions, could almost come out of the submissive's playbook. *Surrender*, *devotion*, and *piety* are just as highly valued by a lifestyle BDSM submissive as they are by any religious acolyte. It's all about relinquishing power and thereby relinquishing responsibility.

I will say it over and over until we're all sick of hearing me say it: responsibility is the key. Responsibility is crucial. We can no longer afford to give away our responsibility. There is too much at stake.

There should be no lifestyle playing in Zen. Generally, people who enter Zen monasteries are encouraged to spend a bit of time there and then get out. Zen monasteries are not a place to stay your entire life the way it is in some religions. Some people need to be there longer than others. And, unfortunately, there are numerous

---

* Dominant/submissive.

cases where folks stay and stay and stay much longer than they ought to.

I have some doubts about teachers who spend all their time in monastic communities. I'm not saying every last one of them is terrible.* But when someone has spent decades living in isolated monastic communities and having his needs met by his followers, of course he's going to come off all serene and enlightened. He's never had to deal with what the rest of us put up with all the time!

Which is not to say there's no value to periods of isolation. And there are certainly people who simply cannot handle so-called ordinary life because the lifestyle too many of us accept as normal is so fucked up. There may even be a lot we can learn from people who are too sensitive to live in mainstream society. But I think we also need to be aware that while some of these folks have nice things to offer in terms of a heightened sensitivity, they also often lack important social skills.

I believe it's ultimately better to integrate practice into your ordinary life as much as possible. It's better to keep a real job in the real world and to routinely associate with people who don't have the first clue about Zen. People who live full-time in Zen places tend to get a little inbred. For example, they often start using words and phrases that nobody in the outside world can understand without even realizing they're doing so, kind of the way people who are into anything deeply nerdy do. It's better to learn to communicate with the wider community in its own language.

It is absolutely necessary for any human community — including a Zen monastery — to have some kind of power structure. No community can exist without some kind of power structure, and such structures, by their very nature, must be imbalanced in terms of who has power and who does not. But I think it's better to get out of any religious community before you start to buy into the power

---

* And even if I did, why would you give up your power and take my word for it?

structure there. You can accept it and allow it to operate as it must. You can obey its rules for the good of everyone involved. But trouble begins the minute you actually begin to believe in it.

People are always trying to give up their power to Zen masters. They even try giving it up to me. Mel Weitsman said that the way to tell if a Zen teacher is good or not is if he or she wants you as a student. If the Zen teacher *doesn't* want you as a student, that's when you know you're on the right track. Ultimately it's a very personal practice, and if a teacher needs students maybe her practice isn't really very pure. If she needs to take personal power from others, that's a very bad sign.

Power exchange may be a necessary evil in establishing and maintaining a community. But when it comes to your direct relationship with a teacher there should be no power exchange at all. It's very difficult to negotiate this because we are so used to operating in terms of power exchange, especially in teacher-student relationships. But when power exchange exists in a Zen relationship, real communication is impossible.

I spent years working on this, from the time I encountered my first teacher until the moment Nishijima Roshi said he wanted to ordain me, which accounts for close to twenty years. So I am by no means trying to make this sound easy or effortless. It's perfectly normal and okay for a Zen student to keep trying over and over and over again to give up power to a teacher. Things only go awry when the teacher starts accepting that power.

The power to see what you truly are is yours and yours alone. No one can awaken you any more than they can look at the world with your eyeballs. Zen isn't for spiritual lifestyle players.

As to the question of whether you can be kinky and still be Zen, though, the answer to this, as it is with every other answer, rests with you alone. I would only caution that you should be careful of anything that seems too exciting. There will always be some kind of a rebound as the body/mind returns to its preferred state of stability.

Chapter 21

I Fuck, Therefore I Am What I Fuck?

I'd like to go a bit further into what I started to discuss at the end of the last chapter. I've noticed that people involved in BDSM, as well as others of variously "queer" sexual orientations,* who are interested in Buddhist practice are often especially troubled by the Buddhist precept against misusing sexuality.

Given what we usually hear from teachers of Western religious traditions, it's easy to imagine that anything outside strictly vanilla monogamous one-on-one heterosexual relations in the standard missionary position for the express purpose of procreation might constitute a misuse of sexuality in the eyes of religious authority. Let's talk about homosexuality specifically, since there is a longer history of Buddhist views on the subject than there is on some of the other sexual variations.

---

* Again, *queer* is a word many in the nonstandard sexual orientation community have adopted for themselves. I felt very uncomfortable using it at first. Then I realized I'm as queer as anyone else. And so are you, regardless of your sexual orientation. None of us really fits society's standards perfectly, even if some of us come dangerously close to doing so.

In India it was already accepted long before Buddha's time that groups of men living together in monasteries occasionally got it on with each other. In early Buddhism there were rules against male homosexuality. When the order of nuns was established they added rules against hot girl-on-girl action to the list. Sometimes these ancient regulations are trotted out by people who don't like Buddhism and presented so as to make Buddhism seem as antihomosexual as any other religion. But these rules were intended to establish strict celibacy rather than to specifically condemn homosexual sex. They were a way of saying, "Hey, you monks, you know that rule we have against having sex? That also applies to you guys having sex with each other, okay?" The rules against having homosexual relations, like the rules against having sexual relations in general, applied only to monastics, not to the general population.

It's also hard to speak about these ancient regulations in contemporary terms. The very concept of homosexuality was unknown in Asia until the nineteenth century. This is not to say that men never fucked men and women never fucked women until then. It's just that the category of human interaction we now call "homosexuality" had not yet been introduced.

In fact, the word *homosexual* is of very recent origin, having been coined in 1887 by neurologist Charles Gilbert Chaddock in his translation of Richard von Krafft-Ebing's *Psychopathia Sexualis*. That word was subsequently translated into the Japanese word *douseiai*, literally "same-sex love." Before that the closest Japanese term was *nanshoku*, "man love," which usually referred to relationships between Buddhist monks. There was no word for lesbianism. In ancient India the Sanskrit word *kliba*, which often gets translated these days as "homosexual," could mean a man who was sterile, impotent, castrated, or a transvestite; a man who had oral sex with other men, or had anal sex as a recipient; a man with mutilated or deficient sexual organs; a man who produced only female children; or a hermaphrodite.[*]

---

[*]   Sudhir Kakar, "Homosexuality and the Indian," *Little India* (August 2007).

All this makes it impossible to say exactly what the ancient Buddhists really thought of homosexuality because for them homosexuality really didn't exist the way it does for us. Regardless of what people did with each other in the bedroom there was no homosexuality because the category itself had not yet been invented. The word is not the thing.

So while something we can retroactively call homosexuality and people we can retroactively call homosexuals have existed ever since human beings first appeared on the planet, it may not be realistic to think of ancient societies according to our current ways of defining things. Bernard Faure's book *The Red Thread*, which I've already referred to a bunch of times, goes into this in great detail as it relates to the history of the Buddhist response to homosexuality. So I don't think it's necessary to discuss this history at length in this book.

Still, one historical fact does warrant mentioning. While Christians were burning homosexuals at the stake for their sins, the Buddhists never had any particular problem with people of nonstandard sexual orientation, except when their activities disrupted monastic living. And in such instances they had pretty much the same problems with homosexual relationships as they had with heterosexual ones — that they messed up life in the monasteries, nothing more. Like sex in general, homosexuality, bisexuality, and all the rest of it were never considered sins in Buddhism.

As far as Zen Buddhism is concerned it's all pretty much up to each individual to determine for him- or herself whether or not nonstandard sexual relationships constitute "misuse of sexuality." I heard my own teacher, Nishijima Roshi, comment about this only once. He never expressed his views on the subject until one day someone asked him if he thought homosexuality was "misuse of sexuality." He didn't answer as to whether it was misuse. But he did say that he believed that if more people established the balanced state one can find in Zen practice, homosexuality would vanish. When asked why, he said that homosexuality was obviously not the natural way since it doesn't lead to procreation. He was careful to say this was just his own opinion on the matter and not some kind of "Buddhist truth" on the subject.

Now, before you go calling him a reactionary, intolerant homophobe, remember that he was specifically *asked* for his views on the subject. He would not have talked about them otherwise. It wasn't an important topic to him. He did not say that homosexuality was evil or against Buddha's Way or that homosexuals should be persecuted. He just gave his opinion. I think most Zen teachers are like that. The issue of a person's sexual orientation is so trivial as to be irrelevant to their practice. So any opinion a Zen teacher might have would just be a result of whatever environment they've grown up in.

As for my opinions on Nishijima Roshi's views, personally I don't know what would happen to nonstandard sexual orientations if everybody did zazen. I don't really share Nishijima's belief that everybody would become hetero. Although he didn't actually say that. Maybe he meant that everybody would become celibate. I don't really know. In any case, I think it's a moot point since we've clearly not arrived at a time when everyone is in a balanced state, so anything we say about it is just speculation.

Other teachers have other views. A lot of people got pretty bent out of shape when it was reported that the Dalai Lama said, "From a Buddhist point of view, [gay sex] is generally considered sexual misconduct." In saying this he was no doubt referencing the ancient regulations I talked about at the beginning of this chapter. But even Mr. Lama did not express strong condemnation. In fact, he expressed the view that homosexual relationships could potentially benefit society, be mutually enjoyable, and were, on the whole, pretty harmless in and of themselves.

The point is, a person's sexual orientation has never been considered a key issue in Buddhism. Even if your teacher has definite ideas about what people should or shouldn't do in the bedroom, you're not likely to hear those views unless you specifically ask. This is as it should be. Morality is a personal matter. Nishijima Roshi always says that the precepts are a list of the common habits of Buddhists, not rules Buddhists must follow.

My own history with regards to homosexuality probably colors my views on the matter somewhat and may have in part led to my acceptance of all types of sexuality. All through high school I was subject to harassment and threats because it was widely known throughout the school — not suspected, mind you, but *known* as an absolute fact — that I was a flaming faggot. The only trouble with that was that I was completely straight — probably straighter than some of the people who'd labeled me gay. I have no problems with gay sex. It's just not something I'm interested in trying for myself. Like skydiving, it looks like it could be fun, but I just don't want to do it.

I think the way it became so widely known that I was a homo was that there were these two greasy horrible guys who didn't like the punk rock–inspired clothes I used to wear. These guys would sit at the entrance to the school and make rude remarks to me pretty much every morning because I didn't dress the way they thought I should or have the same ugly haircut their moms gave them. One day one of them shouted at me, "I heard you was a homosexual!"

So I turned around and said, "Yeah, that's right!" then kept on walking. These guys apparently didn't have the capacity to understand sarcasm. I had a girlfriend, for God's sake! A hot redhead named Charmaine who had the cutest butt you ever saw.* Neither of those guys had girlfriends. Maybe that's why they sat around harassing people. In any case, once I had openly admitted my gayness, that was all anybody needed.

So I saw firsthand how incredibly cowardly homophobes are. I remember this football player named Tom. He was a big guy and a major star at the school. The social life of the town I grew up in revolved entirely around high school football, not just among the

---

* Hi, Charmaine, wherever you are!

kids but among the adults, too. It was incredibly pathetic. So this guy was like a celebrity in Wadsworth, Ohio. Probably got good seats in Cleckner's restaurant down on the town square and everything else. Where is he now, I wonder? I kind of feel bad for people like Tom because you never really live down being a star in high school after you grow up.

Anyway, Tom was especially upset by my supposed homosexuality. Whenever he was with his buddies he'd yell at and threaten me. But during our senior year it just so happened that his locker was right outside my first-period class. I was always late to this class because I'm a generally lazy person and always have been. Tom, being a big star, was pretty much able to wander in to his classes whenever he felt like it, so he was late most days, too. Thus it transpired that nearly every morning we would pass each other in the nearly vacant hallway in front of Mr. Gorman's English class.

At first I was scared of him. But then I noticed that not only did he not hassle me when he was alone, he would not even look at me. And this guy was way bigger than me. He could've beaten the crap out of me even without his buddies around to help. So I got into the habit of staring at him whenever we passed in that hallway. He never once met my gaze, the wimp.

In any case, I may have a bit more understanding of what it feels like to be persecuted for being of a nonstandard sexual orientation than most straight guys because I actually dealt with it a tiny bit. I know that what I went through was far different from living with this kind of harassment your entire life. And since I wasn't actually gay it was more a matter of those guys being stupid rather than one of feeling that my true lifestyle was somehow "wrong." But I had a small taste of what it's like to be picked on in that way, which is more than most straight people can claim.

But I digress.

These days a lot of people are trying to make Buddhism more

accessible to "queer" people. San Francisco was the place where Soto-style Zen practice first took hold in America. And given that city's special history regarding homosexuality, it's also the place where some of the most visible work of integrating people of non-standard sexual orientations into Buddhist practice has occurred.

The San Francisco Zen Center has a Queer Dharma Group that meets regularly. The San Francisco Zen Center also hosts various queer-themed seminars and suchlike at the Tassajara Zen Mountain Center. The Hartford Street Mission in San Francisco is a group dedicated to spreading the dharma among the city's gay, lesbian, bisexual, and transgendered community. And this isn't just going on in San Francisco either. There are dozens of similar things happening throughout Buddhist communities in the West, as well as online.

My friend Daigan Gaither, the monk at the San Francisco Zen Center I mentioned earlier, often leads these groups. He's gay, which I guess ought to go without saying, but I'll say it anyhow. He told me, "What it means to be a fag today is a totally different social construct from what it was in Buddha's time. Or in Dogen's time or in Bodhidharma's time. There wasn't a word for it. What Buddhism says to me is don't let sexuality create an 'other.' That's how you avoid abusing sexuality."

He also said that in Buddhist communities "your gaydar gets totally fucked up. All the guys in Zen are a little gay in that classical secular perspective. They act a little gay. I can't tell you how many people I was convinced were gay who turned out not to be. Part of it is that straight men in Zen communities are more affectionate and open to intimacy. That's not our experience of straight guys."

On the subject of special gay and lesbian sitting groups, he told me, "What it means to be 'open' to someone from a white male hetero perspective is totally different from what it means to be open to someone else who comes from a disenfranchised group."

He continued, "It's important for gay and lesbian people to see not only that we are accepted here but that we're not asked to get rid of anything. Our relationship to spirituality has been really abusive. You're told you're welcome here, but only if you cut off this part of your life or hide it. You have to include gay and lesbian people and say that specifically. For years churches have said that everyone is welcome and it's like, we welcome everybody — *except you*. My experience with religious organizations has always been like that, so I infer that of all religions. I don't allow other religions to be what they are. So it's good to state it explicitly."

My view on this is that it's fine but possibly unnecessary. I hope that at some point we'll be able to make it known that when we as Buddhists say everyone is welcome, we truly mean *everyone*. I'd be reluctant to start a queer dharma group of my own because I wouldn't want to exclude anyone who didn't feel that the word *queer* applied to them. But perhaps my view is a little too idealistic. And being too idealistic is not a good thing, to my way of thinking.

Regardless of one's sexual orientation, the main thing Buddhism stresses is the need for balance. So whatever your sexual orientation it's important to be as balanced with it as possible. It's just as easy to be unbalanced and straight as it is to be unbalanced and queer.

I was at a precepts ceremony at Green Gulch Zen Center in Northern California a few years ago. Green Gulch is a remote, isolated community that functions much like a traditional Asian Zen monastery. After the ceremony there was a little reception. I didn't know too many people there and ended up walking around just listening to everyone talk. A couple of women were talking very loudly and seemed intent on letting anyone who happened to wander within earshot of them know that they were committed lesbians. Who loved each other. And had sex together. Last night. And it was good. How nice for you, I thought. You're gay and you live in the San Francisco Bay Area. How incredibly unique and worthy of special attention.

Feh. I personally don't give two shits what your sexual orientation is, but I do get very annoyed by pretentiousness.

A strong tendency to identify oneself as a member of some particular group tends to become a hurdle to overcome once your practice deepens. This is even true for those who identify too strongly with being Buddhists. In fact, identifying too strongly with Buddhism may be the biggest hurdle of all!

Just as every straight person has a few queer sexual desires that will tend to show themselves during practice — they sure asserted themselves in mine — so, too, does every queer person have some straight sexual desires that will manifest as well. All of us are a big stew of stuff. The aspects of ourselves that manifest as our particular orientation are not all there is. When you identify rigidly with certain aspects of yourself you're actively suppressing those aspects that don't fit that identity. If you continue your Zen practice long enough you'll start becoming acutely aware of this.

I'm not saying that lesbian practitioners are going to be suddenly jolted by visions of hard cocks, or gay men by visions of dripping vaginas. I'm sure most people who consider themselves queer are open enough about their sexuality that the discovery of hidden inclinations toward the so-called proper sexual orientation won't come as a huge shock.

But what will break down is the heavy identification of the self with *any* of its aspects. And this is often a painful transition, no matter what your sexual orientation is. Zazen can be tough stuff.

Daigan told me, "People in some forms of Buddhism say you have to get rid of your identity. But for me, I spent a lot of time getting molested over my identity. What do you mean get rid of it? This is what we got. But later on I saw that it's not the identity we get rid of. We change our relationship to it. We try not reify it or lock it into some place. It's seeing identity as empty. It's just there. It doesn't have any intrinsic value. It's not good, and it's not bad."

The upshot of all this, though, is that a person's sexual orientation is not terribly relevant to his or her Buddhist practice. Defining oneself as straight, gay, bisexual, kinky, or whatever designation you prefer is one way for the ego to try and delineate itself. Such a definition may be provisionally true and may have some use. But ultimately it's not who you truly are. Buddhist practice is about trying to uncover something far more fundamental.

Chapter 22

[SEXUAL ANGLES ON BUDDHISM]

I PREFER BEING JUKED WITH A BABY OCTOPUS*
Sex and Preferences

There's a famous Chinese poem called "Faith Mind Inscription."
In spite of its lousy title, it's one of the most profound pieces
of literature in all of Zen. The first verse sets forth the premise of the
poem right away: "The Great Way is not difficult, just avoid preferences. When love and hate are absent, everything becomes clear
and undisguised."

Of course, when talking about sex and preferences, the first
thing people think of is sexual preferences and all the nonsense our
culture has piled on top of the matter of who a person prefers to
fuck. I've already talked about that stuff enough. So let's look at some
other issues involved with the Zen idea of avoiding preferences.

I suspect most people, when they first hear this notion of avoiding preferences, think of it the way I did when I first heard it. You
think, "Oh, my God! I like vanilla better than chocolate! I like the
Ramones better than Air Supply! I like lying on the beach better
than getting hit in the face with a two-by-four! I have so many preferences! What am I going to do?"

---

* Apologies to Frank Zappa.

In other words, you think, as I did, that preferences are a solid thing that must be gotten rid of. You imagine that some kind of bizarre mental gymnastics must be involved in forever ridding yourself of all like and dislike so that someday when you go to Ben & Jerry's and they ask you what flavor you want, you'll just smile beatifically and say, "Give me whatever you like, for lo, I am free from preferences."

I mean, my God, it gets even worse as the poem goes on. The next line is, "Make the smallest distinction and heaven and earth are set infinitely apart. If you wish to see the truth, then hold no opinions for or against anything." How could anyone do that? Ever?

But it's not as awful as it sounds. We're actually talking about something very immediate and direct. It's related to the question every Zen teacher is asked more often than just about any other, the one that goes, "My brain is all clogged up and scattered when I do zazen. Am I doing it wrong?"

But here's the deal. Your brain is all cloudy, but you'd *prefer* that it not be. The difference between what you are and what you think you ought to be causes your imagination to leap wildly. You want to go from where you actually are to some idealized state your confused mind has created. But it's a losing battle, because the attempt to change from what you are to what you think you should be is the very problem.

The solution is to simply forgo preferences. Don't make any effort to be what you're not. Just allow what you are to fully manifest. Keep your posture and stay still. Sit with it. Don't go against it. Don't go for it. Only sit and let it be.

In terms of sex, we all have lots of preferences. This goes for people of all "sexual preferences," by the way. It's not just a matter of which gender you prefer to shag. Sex brings out all of our loves and hates in a very big way.

For example, we're not in love, and we hate that. Or we're in love, but things are going wrong and we hate that. Or we're in love with this girl/guy/stuffed animal, but we want to sleep with that other one, too, and girl/guy/stuffed animal #1 isn't into the whole polyamory thing. Or we can't get enough sex. Or we're getting too much sex. And on and on and on it goes.

Sex is such a hot-button area in terms of getting us into our various likes and dislikes that this is certainly one of the reasons Buddha recommended that his monks be celibate. But this is a book mainly for people who are interested in Buddhism but not in celibacy. So what are we gonna do about preferences if we want to keep on getting laid?

One bit of good news is that the more we can get beyond our preferences, the better our sex lives will be. Instead of wallowing in how things aren't the way we want them to be, we can dive right in to what we have at this moment and enjoy it thoroughly.

Part of avoiding preferences is learning to like the very fact that you dislike something. In an episode of *Star Trek: The Next Generation* there's a scene in which Data, the android character, is given a special computer chip that, for the first time in his robotic life, allows him to have preferences. He orders a drink, gulps it down, and goes, "I hate this! Give me another!" He's never disliked anything before, and this itself is a source of great joy and fascination.*

The idea of avoiding preferences doesn't mean that we need to be complacent and leave even the worst situations in life just as they are. The first step in effectively changing something that clearly needs to be changed is accepting the way it actually is. Then we can do what needs doing to make things different without wasting a lot of energy wishing things already were different. For example, you may find yourself in a relationship that's bad and you gotta either make it better or end it. If you sit around wishing things were different and wallowing in your malaise, you'll never do anything to fix it.

But bringing the matter of avoiding preferences into even tighter focus than that, being without preference means that when

---

* I know I already gave this example in *Hardcore Zen*, but some of the people reading this haven't read that book. So deal with it!

you have preferences — and you always will — you let go of any notion that you should not have them. You let go of your preference for being free of preferences. Even having preferences is not a problem. The real root of our problems as human beings is the way we fly off into imagining how things could, or should, be.

Chapter 23

Is Zazen Dangerous?

I was at the Bodhi Tree Bookstore in West Hollywood the other day. It's one of the world's largest Buddhist bookshops, though these days they do more business with dodgy new age tomes like *The Secret* than by selling the occasional copy of the *Dhammapada*.

Anyhow, when I was browsing through the used-books section I overheard an interesting conversation. The guy at the shelf next to me had apparently been Joshu Sasaki Roshi's translator for several years. Sasaki Roshi is a fiery Rinzai Zen teacher who arrived from Japan in the early sixties and now, at age 103, lives on Mount Baldy, just a few miles south of Los Angeles. My first teacher was briefly a student of Sasaki's. Singer Leonard Cohen is probably Sasaki's most famous student. This guy was talking to a woman who was very impressed by his association with Cohen.

She said to him, "I read a line in one of Leonard Cohen's books of poetry about sitting zazen in a monastery seething with hatred toward the person next to him. Do you think he really meant that?" She seemed upset by this.

The guy said, "You've never done a Zen retreat, have you?" I could've told him she hadn't ever attended a Zen retreat just by the question. And I'm sure he knew the answer as well. Because if she had ever sat a Zen retreat she'd have known exactly what Leonard Cohen was talking about. At some point in any retreat you pretty much always end up seething with hatred at the person next to you!

Hating the person next to you at a Zen retreat isn't really a problem unless you start acting on those feelings. Lots of crap comes up, and sometimes you end up misdirecting your anger at the most available target.

One time I was making some special effects for a homemade sci-fi film that I never completed. I built some fake buildings out of cardboard boxes and borrowed a friend's pet iguana. I put some Matchbox cars among the buildings and had the iguana terrorize my little city. But the iguana didn't really do much except walk lethargically through the set. And that was when he wasn't just falling asleep. So the iguana's owner asked if I wanted him to bite the cars. "That'd be cool," I said. The iguana's owner started pulling the lizard's tail, which was out of camera range. And sure enough, whenever his tail was pulled, the iguana bit whatever was in front of him. Seeing what that lizard did, I thought, "wow that's exactly what people do. When we're bothered we don't always deal with what's really bugging us. We lash out at what's closest."

One of the things that often surprise people when they first enter a Buddhist organization, or sangha, is that a lot of the people there often have some really deep and troubling issues. I guess they've seen too many bad TV shows and expect everyone who follows the path of Buddhism to be wise, well-adjusted, and happy. But if you think about it for a few seconds, it makes perfect sense. Who would want to do all the hard work required by Zen practice if they weren't profoundly dissatisfied with their life in some way?

Survivors of various kinds of sexual abuse often find their way to Zen centers in their search for ways to cope with the trauma and its lasting effects on their lives. I myself am not an abuse survivor, nor am I any kind of expert in the subject. But I haven't seen any other writings about the role of Zen practice in the lives of abuse survivors. So until some survivor or expert writes an account of her or his Zen experiences, my inadequate musings on the subject will have to suffice.

One of the members of the first sangha I was part of was a sex abuse survivor, and this experience affected her in some pretty serious ways. But I was too young and full of myself to be of any real help to her. Now in my work as a Buddhist teacher I've often spoken with people who have survived sexual abuse about their practice.

One of the interesting issues from my own standpoint as a Zen teacher is how incredibly hard it is for someone with these kinds of issues to talk to a meditation teacher. Even when a specific meditation teacher is not a straightlaced, sexually repressed person, the aura of holiness that surrounds him or her can be very off-putting for people who need to talk about unusual aspects of their sex lives. Many sex abuse survivors also have rather nonstandard sex lives, not just because they've suffered abuse, but because the abuse they've suffered has made it difficult to interact sexually the way so-called normal people do. As a result a lot of people who could use a bit of what meditation has to offer will never approach it because of the mistaken impression that they are somehow too "dirty" to be involved in such lofty things. This is sad.

Of course, this doesn't apply just to sex abuse survivors. I myself would have found Zen utterly unapproachable if I hadn't come across someone like my own first Zen teacher, who was not afraid to curse and fart and offend nice people. Had I not met him I, too, would have assumed I was far too weird or perverted or corrupt for the kind of purity required to partake in what I saw as pious activities like meditation. I will be forever grateful to Tim McCarthy and all his vile jokes.

Some very specific issues apply to sex abuse survivors who want to practice zazen. So let's get into them, shall we? I'll start with an email I received from a friend of mine:

> Is meditation dangerous? Is zazen safe for trauma sur-
> vivors? I know a lot of people in difficult situations (like
> people in jail) get a lot of benefit from meditation, but is
> sitting a retreat dangerous if you have all kinds of fucked-
> up shit sitting under the surface?

It's a fact that zazen brings stuff up. No matter what kind of stuff you have locked away in your mind/body, it's going to come out during a sitting. It's also true that zazen is different from other forms of meditation — if zazen is even a form of meditation — in that it is not directed at any ideal condition. In zazen you allow whatever comes up to just come up as it will, rather than attempting to move the mind toward a specific desired state, as most forms of meditation do. This means that trauma survivors may be more likely to face repressed memories and suchlike while doing zazen than while doing other forms of meditation.

I don't think it's truly dangerous for trauma survivors to do zazen. But they have to be careful. Of course, anyone should exercise caution while doing the practice. But survivors of trauma possibly need to be even more careful. Some misguided Zen teachers as well as meditation teachers of other varieties see the goal of practice as having some sort of "enlightenment experience," or "moment of awakening," or "opening," or *kensho*, or *satori* — there are a whole slew of euphemisms. It may be best for trauma survivors to avoid that kind of thing since a practice that's focused on having an enlightenment experience tends to force you to move more quickly than you actually need to. So it's more likely to bring this stuff to the surface before you're ready to deal with it.

But here's what a sexual abuse or other trauma survivor might expect to encounter in traditional Zen practice. Most of this is also applicable to anyone who practices zazen, trauma survivor or not.

There's not a person in the world who doesn't have some unacknowledged stuff buried below the surface.

On the most superficial level zazen will bring up memories. At first these will be familiar ones, meaning they won't be particularly surprising, just stuff you haven't thought of in a long time. For a trauma survivor, this can mean starting to recall events from your past that are painful and that you have avoided thinking about but that you are basically aware of. The reaction to this runs along the lines of the response you'd have even if you weren't sitting zazen. But sitting tends to intensify emotions. You might start crying or having other similar responses. This can be a bit embarrassing in a crowded zendo. But you should know that you are not alone in having feelings like this.

On the next level zazen can bring up things you have deliberately repressed. At this level the memories can be surprising since you might start recalling things you were not consciously aware had happened. You may even be unsure if they're true memories. Indeed, some may not be true at all. That's important. Just because you seem to remember something doesn't necessarily mean it actually happened. The mind can get very tricky. These memories might make you confused, angry, and so on. Again, the fact of sitting zazen can intensify this experience.

As you continue to practice you get to stuff that is hard even to recognize as memory. You may get strange impressions of vague things or just bare emotions devoid of any particular context. These are harder to deal with because they're impossible to figure out. You're better off not even trying to figure this stuff out because doing that just piles more thought and emotion on top of what you already have to deal with. Acknowledge it and, as much as possible, try and just let it be. It will pass. Again, you're not alone. Remember those people I talked about who started hating the people on the cushion next to them?

Sometimes — even when they try not to — practitioners will

assign these emotions to events and people inappropriately, just like that iguana did with those Matchbox cars. People who experience this kind of thing and don't understand the source of it — and no one could possibly understand the source of it — may blame it on their teachers or on other people practicing. Like Leonard Cohen did, and like I have done myself on occasion. It is often the difficult duty of a Zen teacher to bear the brunt of some of this misdirected stuff. So be kind to us, please! Or practitioners may blame themselves or have a whole lot of different responses. Don't worry about your responses either. Let them go. It's easier said than done, I know. But try.

I should point out here that it generally takes months or years to get to this level. It's not the kind of thing you're going to encounter in your first zazen class. What you generally encounter in your first few times doing zazen is utter boredom!

So what do you do if the heavier stuff starts to happen? By the time you get down to the more difficult strata of buried stuff you will probably have developed a relationship with a teacher. If you have a teacher, discuss it with him. That's what he is there for. As longtime practitioners, they have experienced this themselves. Remember that most of us in the Zen teaching game came into it because we had our own very serious stuff to deal with. Since your teacher has watched his own stuff come up in a similar matter, he should be able, at the very least, to tell you how he dealt with it. He can also assure you you're not going crazy.

Whether or not any of this comes up in this way depends largely on the practitioner. If you're very gung ho and in a big hurry to reach some rarified state of consciousness or — God forbid! — enlightenment, you're more likely to encounter this kind of thing faster, when you're not ready for it. If your practice is more gentle and unhurried, you're less likely to get this stuff too quickly. If it does come up, you'll already have some grounding that will allow you to handle it. So I suggest taking it slow and easy. Just enjoy sitting zazen for its own sake, and don't try to get anywhere with it. If you do it that way, the stuff that comes up will come up in smaller portions over time and won't confront you before you're ready to deal with it.

In spite of all the foregoing cautionary material, I still believe zazen can be a very good thing for survivors of traumatic experiences. Maybe even the best thing. It can put you directly in contact with the source of the trauma itself. By slowly and carefully removing the psychological barriers you've erected to protect yourself from these memories you can finally become aware that the memories themselves are just thoughts in your head. No matter what the content of your thoughts are, they are all just thoughts. This is easy to say but very difficult to truly understand because we've been taught since birth to believe in our own thoughts.

This is why we practice. Anyone can tell you this stuff, and anyone can understand it intellectually. But applying it takes practice. It takes repetition. Sitting there on your cushion, you allow stuff to come up over and over and over again, and you just sit there with it, not running away, not reacting, just sitting. This is how you learn *your own way* to deal with it. Not someone else's way, even if that someone else is the Greatest Master Ever Known, because no one else's way will work for you as well as your own. By taking it slowly, you first learn to deal with the little things, and eventually, when the big stuff hits, you've already had loads of experience.

Merely reading about zazen will not help you put its lessons into effect any more than reading about baseball will turn you into major league material.

Once you've seen what these thoughts and memories truly are, you will come to see that they have far less power than you imagined they did. And once you've seen how powerless all thoughts really are, you can then transcend these memories and the detrimental effects they've had on you. The key is to see what's going on right now, rather than trying to see into the past through memory or into the future through thought.

Here is what one sexual abuse survivor told me about his practice:

> I tend to go into these four-day funks of self-destruction. My therapist showed me a diagram with baseline emotions for people who have not suffered trauma, and superimposed over it a diagram of baseline emotions for people who have. Apparently people who have suffered severe trauma build neuropathways that lead them to predict traumatic events and then react to them, even if they aren't happening, and this fucks people up their entire lives. She believes it's my yoga practice and daily zazen that keep my funks to four, maybe five days, instead of lasting for months, or even years. She went on to explain a bit about neurogenesis and studies being done right now about building new neuropathways. I think zazen is beneficial for trauma survivors because it instills in them enough calm and insight to not react in ways that have long-term self-destructive effects. On top of which it builds new neuropathways, rewiring conditioned reactions to trauma, both real and imaginary.

I believe this is true. In fact, I'm sure zazen functions pretty much the same way for everyone. I've often felt during practice that I could almost feel my own neural pathways rearranging themselves.

We human beings generally subject our brains to a lot of abuse. We create neural pathways where they are not needed by constantly rehashing pleasurable or painful experiences in order to more fully develop our sense of self. This is sometimes our own damned fault, and sometimes it's brought on by outside pressures.

This is how my friend Linda described her experiences as a child sexual abuse survivor and Zen practitioner:

> When a child is abused, there is pleasure followed by agitation. This teaches the child that any kind of pleasure is dangerous. For instance, in my case, I couldn't even enjoy something as simple as a good film because I was always waiting for it to end

so I could go home. Going to parties was hell because, just as with the movies, I was checking my watch and waiting to leave. Then there were bigger kinds of pleasure such as amusement parks, driving, and Rollerblading.

Going down a hill on blades creates a sensation in the stomach of excitement. The excitement would set off my panic button, and I would lose my balance, thus falling and getting hurt.

It took me a long time to realize that I was frightened by the sensation of excitement. This is part of my panic disorder brought on by the sexual abuse. Doing zazen, I was able to unlearn the response, in that I started to experience the moment of excitement as something new in every situation. It's like that line that you can never cross the same stream twice. But I also learned that the excitement was a physical response to stimuli. I can now enjoy films and parties because I try to be present in the moment rather than waiting for it to be over so I can escape the pleasure. The last few times I went Rollerblading, I was able to take hills with a sort of *Wheee!* attitude rather than panic.

I talked about some of this stuff with Nina Hartley. Like me, Nina is not a sexual abuse survivor. But in the adult business a lot of people are, so I figured she might have some insight. Here's what she had to say:

BW: A lot of people who have been sexually abused seem to come to me for advice. And I often don't know quite what to say because I don't have that background.

NH: But you don't have any judgment. And that's what they're suffering from.

BW: Yeah, maybe.

NH: Because with abuse you feel so guilty. The abusers say, "I'll hurt somebody who's close to you," or, "Nobody's gonna believe you." It totally fucks up a young person's sense of safety and security. So it's great just to be around someone who doesn't get salaciously interested in details or judge you for having somehow been responsible.

BW: I have a friend who has been practicing Zen for a long time, and she was talking about how we build up these neuropathways in the brain. Whether or not we've experienced sex abuse, we all do this. And so whatever energy is in there, your brain just wants to route it somewhere, and when an experience comes up it routes it into the one it knows. In her case any experience of pleasure gets routed into this horror area.

NH: When I talk to Future Therapists of America I tell them that what often drives people into treatment is the constant tension between what the organism naturally wants for pleasure and what they've been taught to think about those desires. We're not even talking about behavior here. They just feel guilty about what they think. And this is why I'm so careful about not misusing sexuality. Because I know how to manipulate a body and have infinite patience until it has a good time. No matter what the forebrain says. If I were an evil person I would find vulnerable people who are desperate for that kind of experience and give it to them. That would form an intense attachment. I would come across like a savior. And then I could mess with them. What's really horrible is just because a person doesn't want to be in a situation does not mean that their body cannot be coaxed into having an authentic pleasure response to the stimulation because the forebrain doesn't have to be involved. It's a physiological process. So for the midbrain, if I stimulate the body in a certain way it will eventually have rhythmic contractions. So I don't doubt for a moment that her abuser was able to get her body to respond, even though she didn't want to be there.

BW: That's what happens in a lot of child sexual abuse.

NH: Absolutely. So it prematurely and inappropriately sexualizes children. And it also produces shame and horror of it all. And I do believe Zen is very good for this because it helps a person learn to sit still with all their demons.

BW: That's what she told me. She's been practicing for ten years or so, and she found that zazen practice really helped because you just watch this stuff happen.

NH: Yes. And you see how your forebrain does its tricks. My mother used to talk about this. She'd go into zazen in a completely fine mood and she'd come out really enraged or completely engulfed in grief or whatever. This is because the front part of the brain has to tell a story. And what story it tells about the desires you're feeling depends entirely on the experience, history, age, gender, culture, birth order, family history. All these things have fed whatever story your forebrain tells. They are not real. They're conditioned mind, or small mind.

Small mind and *big mind* are terms that often come up in Buddhism these days. Though the concepts are very old, it seems that Shunryu Suzuki deserves the credit for coining these now-standard English translations. Some jackass has stolen the term *big mind* and registered it as his own trademark. But real big mind doesn't belong to him or to anyone else, for that matter.

Small mind is our conditioned mind. We have a personality. This is natural and necessary. But we make mistakes about it. We fear that if we don't continually reinforce our sense of self, we will disappear, or we'll be hurt, and so on. This is not true. Nor could you lose your unique personality even if you tried as hard as you could to destroy it.

Survivors of sexual and other forms of abuse often try even harder than the rest of us to build up their sense of ego-self. I'm not using the word *ego* here in the way it's often used in popular culture as a synonym of positive self-esteem. Ego-self can be built up and maintained even better through negatives than it can through positives. If you keep telling yourself you're weak, you're useless, you're unlovable, and so on, this acts as a tremendous boost to the sense of ego-self. If I'm horrible, I must exist!

Big mind, on the other hand, is much harder to define. In fact, one way it can be defined is by its very inability to be defined. It is emphatically *not* something you can pay $150 to have some two-bit Zen master provide you an experience of, which is what that doofus who registered the name will tell you it is. Big mind is also not God in the way we usually understand God. It's not far away. It's elation and bliss, but it's not *exclusively* elation and bliss. It underlies absolutely *all* your experiences, including the experience of reading this book right now as well as everything mundane, boring, or painful in your life.

Big mind and small mind are the same thing. Some old Zen master said, "When the room is ten feet wide, the entire universe is ten feet wide." Your limited experience and perspective as an individual and the unlimited experience and unlimited perspective of the universe are the same thing. I know this makes no sense. It's not supposed to make sense. But you don't need to take it on faith. Do zazen practice for long enough, and this will become your real experience.

And it still won't make any sense!

Be that as it may, I think survivors of sexual abuse may have a slight advantage over the rest of us. It takes most of us a very long time to learn the true nature of suffering. We're like Bullwinkle when he tries to pull a rabbit out of his hat — "This time for sure!"* People

---

* For those of you who didn't grow up watching these cartoons, Bullwinkle the moose dresses up like a magician and tries over and over again to pull a rabbit out of his hat. Every single time something other than a rabbit comes out. Sometimes it's a bunch of flowers, sometimes it's a lion, and so forth. It's a great metaphor for life. I'm sure there must be clips on YouTube.

who've suffered abuse in childhood are often already past that phase when they begin their practice. Not to trivialize what they've gone through, but in some ways their experience can act as an aid to practice. We all have to work with what we have and what we are.

Chapter 24

GOD KNEW MY SOUL
BEFORE I WAS BORN

Speaking of trauma, let's talk about a subject that causes a lot of people, especially religious people, a lot of trauma — abortion. Someone who obviously does not favor the practice of abortion put up a big billboard in El Paso, Texas, with a picture of an adorable baby, along with the slogan "God knew my soul before I was born."

I saw the billboard when I was invited by the poet Bobby Byrd to give a talk in El Paso in May 2009. Separated by just a few feet of the Rio Grande from Juárez, Mexico, El Paso is almost like a Mexican city that just happens to be on US soil. If you don't speak at least a little Spanish you'll have a hard time getting around in some parts of town. There's a gigundous Mexican flag, about the size of a football field, waving just across the border.

Given the city's heritage, it's not surprising that the major religion in El Paso is Catholicism. I assume the Catholic Church had something to do with the billboards, though I can't say for certain. There was a whole series, all with similarly delightful little babies on them. One said, "Fragile and innocent." One said, "My heart began beating when I was eighteen days old." Another said, "Embryos are tiny babies."

When I went looking for this on the Internet I saw that one blogger had parodied the billboard that said "God knew my soul before I was born" by replacing the photo of the cute little baby with one of Adolf Hitler. If you believe in the kind of a God who knows babies' souls before they're born, you have a lot to account for.

But the slogan "God knew my soul before I was born" also says a lot about why abortion is such a hot-button issue in Christian countries and basically a nonissue in Buddhist countries. I never heard, or even heard *about*, a single prolife/prochoice debate in the eleven years I lived in Japan. They just don't happen except maybe among the country's tiny Christian minority. I know of none in any other Asian countries either.

Yet for Christians, abortion must seem like the most abominable crime anyone could commit because it usurps the power of God. As I understand Christian cosmology, the idea is that every human being has a unique soul. This soul is created by God sometime before the person is born. The soul then takes human form so that it can act according to its own free will. It is completely innocent at birth but gradually becomes less innocent the longer it lives. Then the person dies, and the soul is judged by God according to the actions it took during its human life. If the person has dedicated his or her life to Christ, the soul goes to heaven. If not, the flames and torments of hell await.

If you abort a baby you are robbing that soul of its one and only opportunity to live a mortal life. Moreover, you prevent that soul from doing anything either good or evil, thereby foiling God in his one and only chance to judge that soul. He then has no idea if the soul he created was good or evil, so he has no idea where to send it. That's a huge crime against God. It makes the person who does the abortion more powerful than God, since God can't prevent him or her from doing it. This is some nasty stuff!

But what is the Buddhist take on abortion? In the Dharani Sutra, Buddha is reported to have specifically called abortion a violation of the precept against killing. In this sutra he says, "There are five kinds of Evil Karma that are difficult to extinguish, even if one were to repent of them. What are the five kinds of offenses? The first one is killing the father, the second one is killing the mother, the third one is abortion, the fourth one is to injure the Buddha, the fifth one is to create disharmony among the Sangha assemblies." Besides this, the *vinaya* rules add that a monk can be excommunicated for convincing a woman to have an abortion.

The fifth-century Theravada Buddhist scholar Buddhaghosa was more equivocal. He condemned abortions when they were performed for the purpose of "concealing extramarital affairs, preventing inheritances, and domestic rivalry between co-wives."* But his objections seem to be based more on the reasons for the abortion rather than on the abortion itself. I think it's also very important to bear in mind that an abortion in Buddha's time, or even in Buddhaghosa's time, was a very different thing from what it is today. The procedure was certainly far more brutal and dangerous and I would have to guess was usually carried out much later in the term than is the norm these days. In more recent times (1993), the Dalai Lama said, "Of course, abortion, from a Buddhist viewpoint, is an act of killing and is negative, generally speaking. But it depends on the circumstances. If the unborn child will be retarded or if the birth will create serious problems for the parent, these are cases where there can be an exception. I think abortion should be approved or disapproved according to each circumstance."**

One thing I find personally relevant in all this in terms of what Buddhists believe about abortion is that in spite of twenty-five years

---

* From Michael G. Barnhart, *Buddhism and the Morality of Abortion*, from the website Urban Dharma.
** From "Buddhism and Abortion," from bbc.co.uk.

of study and practice I myself was unaware of any of these statements until I started researching Buddhist attitudes on abortion for this book. I think that alone says a lot about the Buddhist attitude on the matter. These views on abortion are not considered key teachings. A female friend stated that I would have been more aware of this stuff if I were a woman, especially one contemplating abortion. And that's true. But it's hard to imagine anyone, male or female, practicing Catholicism for more than twenty-five years without being aware of the Church's stance on abortion. The same would be true, I think, for those practicing just about any other type of Christianity.

So why don't Buddhists make a big issue of abortion, while we in the West seem to see it as so important? Well, for one thing, in Buddhism there's no belief in a creator God. You can't rob God of his opportunity to judge a soul's worth since there is no God to rob of that opportunity. And certainly widespread overpopulation in many of these countries is also a factor. But a more important philosophical reason that abortion is not a big issue in Buddhist countries may be the widespread belief in reincarnation among Buddhists. Because of this belief, in the minds of most Buddhists, you cannot rob a unique soul of its one and only chance for life by aborting a fetus.

If you accept the idea of reincarnation, then you also accept that the aborted fetus will have another chance at life — in fact, probably a better life than he or she would have had if he or she had been born to someone who didn't want a child. In Buddhist terms it is strictly and unambiguously a decision the potential mother and possibly the potential father have to make without recourse to trying to guess what an unknowable being like God might think about it.

It seems to me that according to the received wisdom of Western pop culture all Buddhists are supposed to believe in reincarnation. And statistically it's probably true that more Buddhists believe in reincarnation than don't. But I'm not a great believer in reincarnation myself. Dogen categorically denies that reincarnation is in any way a Buddhist belief. According to him it's a mistaken belief that comes from the Indian religions that predated Buddhism. I'd like to talk just a bit about that before we move on. Dogen says, "According to the non-Buddhist view, there is one spiritual intelligence existing within our body. When this intelligence meets conditions, it can discriminate between pleasant and unpleasant and discriminate between right and wrong, and it can know pain and irritation and know suffering and pleasure — all [these] are abilities of the spiritual intelligence. When this body dies, however, the spirit casts off the skin and is reborn on the other side; so even though it seems to die here it lives on there. Therefore we call it immortal and eternal."*

The view he's denouncing here is the basic Brahmanistic or Hindu idea of reincarnation. As I've said, these days what passes for Buddhism in the West is a mash-up of a lot of Eastern philosophies that are often vastly different from one another. Unfortunately this mixing of philosophies isn't confined to the West, which is why so many Asian Buddhists believe in reincarnation. All I can say is that I'm more convinced by Dogen's view of things. It just makes better sense to me.

In contrast to the non-Buddhist idea of reincarnation, Dogen says, "Firewood becomes ash; it can never go back to being firewood. Nevertheless, we should not take the view that ash is its future and firewood is its past. Remember, firewood abides in the place of firewood in the Dharma. It has a past and it has a future. Although it has a past and a future, the past and the future are cut off. Ash exists in the place of ash in the Dharma. It has a past and it has a future. The firewood, after becoming ash, does not again become firewood. Similarly, human beings, after death, do not live again."**

This is a pretty strong denial of the concept of life after death. But he goes on to say, "At the same time, it is an established custom

---

* From *Shobogenzo*, vol. 1, "Bendowa," translated by Gudo Nishijima and Chodo Cross.
** From *Shobogenzo*, vol. 1, "Genjo Koan," translated by Gudo Nishijima and Chodo Cross.

in the Buddha-Dharma not to say that life turns into death. This is why we speak of *no appearance*. And it is the Buddha's preaching established in [the turning of] the Dharma-wheel that death does not turn into life. This is why we speak of *no disappearance*. Life is an instantaneous situation, and death is also an instantaneous situation. It is the same, for example, with winter and spring. We do not think that winter becomes spring, and we do not say that spring becomes summer."

For Dogen, then, discussions of reincarnation were pointless. Life is what we have at this moment, and that's what we should pay attention to. Death will be whatever it is. What we are at this moment is utterly different from what we were a moment ago. Yet we can't deny there is some connection between the two.

It's also important to note that in Buddhist terms life is not something we *have* so much as something we *partake* of. Life is much bigger than your life or mine. Life will continue after we're gone. What we are right now is vast and infinite. Shunryu Suzuki Roshi, a great follower of Dogen, once said, "You will always exist in some form or another." Yet this idea is vastly different from the belief in reincarnation.

On the other hand, those who try and guess what God might think about abortion, as well as what God thinks about other issues, have it very tough. According to Brandon Keim, "Some scientists think [the belief in God is] just an accidental byproduct of social cognition. They say humans evolved to imagine what other people are feeling, even people who aren't present — and from there it was a short step to positing supernatural beings."* This is similar to the belief R. Elisabeth Cornwell espoused in the article for Suicide Girls I talked about earlier. Since we depend on other people for survival, it is vital for us human beings to be able to guess what other human

---

* From "Religion: Biological Adaptation, Accident — or Both," *Wired* (March 9, 2009).

beings are thinking about what we do. It's just a short step to imagine the Ultimate Human Being, God, and try to guess what he might think of our actions.

But unlike our spouse or our dad, we can't just walk up to God and ask what he thinks of us. So we need to rely on books we believe God has authored or on people who we believe have the ability to speak on God's behalf. This is very tricky because even our best sources of information are secondhand.

In the case of an issue like abortion we are on incredibly shaky ground. If we injure or murder an adult or even a child or animal, we get immediate feedback about how that feels. The victim screams or hits us or struggles to save its life. But in the case of a fetus we have no means by which to judge whether we have actually caused pain or suffering. None of us can remember what it was like to be in the womb. So we're left with trying to guess what two beings think of our action — the fetus and God. In other words, we are completely reliant on the thoughts in our own heads to guide us.

But Buddhist practice has to do with seeing beyond your thoughts, or seeing *through* your thoughts, to find a reality that underlies thinking and feeling but is neither thinking nor feeling. We're left, then, in the realm of intuition. Most of us are very uncomfortable with intuition because it is, by its very nature, vague and difficult to pin down. Yet in Buddhist terms, intuition is far more valuable as a guide to right action than thought could ever be.

Clearly then, if we go by that we are, as always, on our own when it comes to abortion.

If I were to give my own opinions about the subject of abortion, I'd have to start out by saying that it's a choice I never had to face personally. It's impossible, therefore, to give my "true feelings" on abortion. I would only be able to do that if I'd actually gone through it. Otherwise it's all speculation.

So rather than doing that, I'd like to let you hear from a friend of mine who is a Buddhist and who went through the process herself.

She prefers to remain anonymous, but she has graciously allowed me to include her story in this book. I have left it exactly as she wrote it.

I volunteer for an arts organization. I was selling tickets, ushering in guests for their annual film festival. I remember getting ready for the event. I put on makeup and borrowed a bright purple sweater from my more fashionable roommate. I met a guy during one of the films. The two of us sat by the window in the lobby and talked. He asked me for my phone number.

I borrowed a different sweater for our date the next weekend. He decided we should go to a restaurant he knew in Minneapolis. It was still early when we finished eating. He said, "I live right around the corner, why don't we go back to my place?"

He said, "Here, why don't I mix you a drink?"

He said, "Why don't I bring out the arguilah?"

He said, "Why don't you sit a little closer?"

He said, "You're so beautiful, why won't you let me touch you?"

My initial protests of, "I really need to go. The buses will stop running soon." "No, please, I'm fine." "No, I want to go," gradually became less and less audible. I was a candle nearing its base. My flame flickered and weakened until I was submerged in the final pool of hot wax. I was extinguished. All that was left of me was this hazy trail of smoke.

I remember the struggle as he pushed me from the couch. I remember the way his strong arms felt holding me down. I remember my tights torn, my skirt pushed up around my waist. He wouldn't look me in the eyes as I whimpered in protest. I could only see his moving chest, the side of his face, his arms pinning me down. He was spilling his sweat onto me, drenching me and my remaining clothes in his odor. His stench seeped into me, violating my every pore, polluting my core. My body tensed against him. None of it made a difference. I waited, frozen, for the end. I was engulfed in hardened wax.

He slept.

I managed to find my borrowed sweater crumpled on the floor. It was a daisy-yellow cardigan, the kind of thing you wear to visit your grandparents or a museum. It mocked me as I pulled it around my body in a vain attempt to withstand the cold, and made my way out of this house alone in the dark.

My hot tears silently turned to ice on my face. It was snowing lightly. I saw the Witches Tower. Everyone knows the Witches Tower, but no one knows its purpose. It's situated at the highest point in the Twin Cities. It towers above its neighborhood — watching over all the trees and front porches. The top is lit throughout the night, like a beacon, but for God knows what. It can be seen for miles. It looked ominous, lighting individual flakes of snow on their descent. I dialed information for the number of a cab, with the tower as my only reference point.

I woke up the next morning and saw the crumpled sweater lying on my floor. My roommate would know what had happened just by looking at it. She would know how disgusting, how foul, my body was now. I showered again and again. I scrubbed until I was pink and raw. I didn't talk to anyone. I cleaned and cleaned and cleaned. My body, my clothes, my room. I wanted them all spotless.

I had a spot that could not be removed. A growing cancer. It was a knot at the pit of my stomach. I knew. Cold fall turned into a raging Minnesota winter. I bundled up in layers of wool to brave the barrage of snow on my way to the pharmacy. Once there I bought a tube of toothpaste, Band-Aids, cotton balls, a pregnancy test. My red face and downcast eyes told too much of my story.

Two lines. Locked into the tiny stall, I wept for or, I suppose, with my child.

I saw my baby being delivered in a flood of its own tears. We would be covered together in a thin layer of salt. I would kiss its forehead and taste only tears. The child would become a pillar of salt. But it was not Lot's wife. It did not turn back and see fire and brimstone as an act of its own will. This pestilence was forced upon it. It was innocent. Where was justice now?

I recognized a pair of shoes, and I slid the test across the floor to my friend. I reluctantly opened the stall door. "I'm so sorry," she murmured. She took me to her bed, pulled the covers over us, and held me until I could cry no more. She held me firmly as day turned into night. She held me until I remembered a mother's embrace, until I gained the strength to hold the concept of my growing child on my own, until I slept.

The questions and doubts consumed my waking life. Then I stepped back; I sat still for a long time and saw them simply as what they were. I watched the sun as it rose and fell. The steady rhythm of the light, streaming through the window, hitting the wall in front of me. I remained there, watching the days pass, now voluntarily. It's a little like searching for your glasses, only to remember you're already looking through them. I had what I needed. There was value in suffering, in being lost.

This body I had come to know as my own was not mine. It never was. It was intertwined, tangled up with the rest of the world, with my growing child. When I went to breakfast, I felt like vomiting. That nausea was also my child's; its needs were spilling out through my emotions and actions. They were a part of my emotions and actions. They were the entirety of the decision. I loved that baby more than I can say.

There was a crowd of protesters outside the clinic that morning. They yelled, as an elderly woman volunteer escorted me to the door. She had understanding eyes and short white hair. I sat in the waiting room. When it was my time, I declined the pain medication. It was only right for me to really feel this death. I didn't want to disconnect from it or numb it; I wanted to be there and bear all the consequences. It was my child the doctor was removing from me.

I lay there with my legs spread apart, feet placed in stirrups, as the doctor and nurse hollowed me out. They put larger and larger metal objects into my vaginal canal until I was stretched enough to place what is effectively a fancy vacuum into my uterus. There was a noise from the machine for about a minute, and then they pulled all of their instruments out of me. That was it. No incision. No anesthesia. There was about five minutes of discomfort and pain, where I clasped the hand of the woman there to talk with me, ask me questions, keep me relaxed. A cluster of cells the size of your fingernail removed. I was emptied. The woman sat at the side of the sturdy clinical bed, blotted my tears with a tissue, and told me that I had done all right. She hugged me with such tenderness that I finally felt that way. She walked with me out of the clinic, sheltering me once again from the shouts of the protesters. I didn't even hear them.

Spring came and went. In the summer, I traveled to a monastery to meditate in silence. I needed time. The monastery acted as a container for all that had happened to me. I was held in by the fields and wooded hills. There was refuge in the bells at dawn; the sounds of the birds all day; the faint creaking of the wooden porch as I walked step by step across it. Sometimes I walked up the path to Katagiri Roshi's grave and did bows among the insects and leaves. I helped one of the monks during the afternoons with work. We installed a plumbing system in the outdoor showers. I hauled firewood. I weeded, watered, and harvested the garden. I cooked with the fresh vegetables that I had helped grow. The flavors of the food were so imbued with life. I gained physical strength then, too. That was when I started doing push-ups. It was empowering to develop the ability to support myself, to not feel broken or violated. Physical strength did not have to be used to oppress, to hold others down. This strength was for sustenance, for nourishment, for support.

I did a Jizo ceremony with women from the area. We sewed little red bibs and hats for our lost children. The ceremony is rooted in Buddhism and Shintoism, but this form arose in Japan in the 1960s after World War II. During that time there were many prostitutes servicing soldiers without birth control and getting pregnant. Many of these women had multiple abortions. These women were undergoing an immense amount of silent suffering. The Buddhist community recognized a need and began to hold Jizo ceremonies to help them cope with their grief. Jizo is the bodhisattva of compassion and is regarded as the caretaker who guides women, travelers, and children who have died. Maybe he will help guide my lost child home.

I really can't add anything to that. But there is one side issue I'd like to address. I have a slightly different take than most people on the issue of aborting a fetus because it might be deformed or diseased.

My mother's side of my family carries a genetic disorder called Huntington's disease. My grandmother on my mom's side died from this just after I was born. At the time my mom was pregnant with me, her mother was exhibiting advanced symptoms of the sickness. In the films of my parents' wedding my grandma is grimacing and gesticulating like Joe Cocker singing "A Little Help from My Friends" at Woodstock.* My parents both understood when they got married that any children they produced might develop the disease. My mother died from Huntington's in 2007.

Yet when my mom got pregnant with me, they still decided to follow through. I've gone back and forth as to whether or not I'm grateful for that. When I was a bitter teenager this was yet another

* Look it up on YouTube, kids!

in a long series of reasons I resented even having been born. I was a depressed kid, and knowing I might live a short life terminated by a horrible disease did nothing to make my disposition sunnier.

These days, though, I'm glad they made the decision they did. The shadow of that disease is, in a large part, what drew me to Buddhism. I wrote extensively about this in my book *Zen Wrapped in Karma Dipped in Chocolate*, so I won't go into it in great detail here. Suffice it to say that early knowledge of my own mortality spurred me to be far more serious about Buddhist practice at a far earlier age than most.

In any case, you never know what's going to happen once a baby is born. Even if it's not born with some kind of handicap, a lot can occur. I don't condemn anyone who thinks the presence of a handicap is a legitimate reason to have an abortion. When I worked for the Board of Mental Retardation I saw a lot of people who lived for decades essentially as infants, even though their bodies continued to grow. I can't imagine the agony their parents had to face. I do not know what choice I would make if I were really faced with that decision. This is just speculation.

I don't think I could abort my own child. But I have no desire at all to legislate what others can and cannot do in that area. Abortion should be safe, legal, and available to anyone who feels they need to do it.

I disagree with the idea that abortion is murder. A fetus is not a person. A fetus has the potential to become a person. I don't want to try and speculate about at what point it does become a person. I think the laws currently in place in the United States already do a pretty good job of that — of speculating, I mean. Still, their speculations are about the same as mine. I think the whole "personhood begins at conception" view is nonsense.

And although I just conceded that in some sense I think life, as opposed to personhood, begins at conception, as a Buddhist I would take it much further even than that. In Buddhism we believe that everything in the universe has some level of self-awareness, some level of life. Even rocks and blocks of wood and glasses of diet soda. So a fetus has some kind of self-awareness, too. But I don't think a newly conceived fetus has any more awareness of itself than, say, a kidney or a spleen, and we have no moral compunctions about removing those.

And yet a fetus is not a rock or a block of wood or a glass of diet soda or even a bodily organ in the usual sense. Though abortion is not the same as murder, it is a case of taking life. One should never take life carelessly, even if it is the life of a cow or a pig or even a carrot or potato. As a potential person a fetus has a right to dignity and a right to respect. Buddhists don't believe in souls. But we do believe in dignity and respect for all living things, sentient and nonsentient alike. If I ever had to allow a fetus I had played a role in conceiving to be aborted, I would also insist on the performance of proper funeral rites. I think a certain period of mourning should be observed as well.

There is also karma involved in the decision to have an abortion. I'll get into the notion of karma in the next chapter. But suffice it to say here that Buddhism has what Dogen calls "deep belief in cause and effect." This means that we accept that any action we take has some effect, some result, some kind of consequences. Whatever word we use to describe it, there is some kind of reaction for every action.

In the case of an action like abortion, one might be concerned about the possibility of accruing what they call "negative karma." There might be some worry that by having an abortion or enabling someone else to have one, you might be setting yourself up for some kind of backlash from the universe for doing an evil deed.

When I used to hang out with the Hare Krishnas I was amazed that some of them believed they knew what the karmic outcome of any given event would be. One guy assured me that John Lennon had been reborn as a tree. Apparently one time the head of the Krishnas visited Lennon, and he answered the door naked. This proved he was an exhibitionist, and exhibitionists get reborn as trees because trees have to stand naked and be looked at all the time.

In spite of their certainty about these matters, I personally believe it's impossible to ever say what the karmic outcome of any specific action might be. If a person acts consciously without any violent or murderous intent, the karmic outcome, I believe, will be of the same nature. As long as you're aware that there will be some kind of karmic effect and you don't take the decision lightly, there is no reason to worry unduly about what will happen as the effect.

My friend mentioned the tradition of the Jizo, and I'd like to leave you with a few more details about that. Originally a bodhisattva named Ksitigarbha, Jizo is seen in Japan as the guardian of children, particularly of children who died before their parents. In more recent times Jizo has come to be regarded as the guardian of what they call *mizuko*, or literally "water children," meaning children who were stillborn or aborted. I used to see statues of little bald Jizos all over the place in Japan, usually beside narrow roads or walking paths. Often they're decorated with little red bibs and surrounded by offerings of toys and flowers. When someone has an abortion, it's traditional to leave such an offering or put a new bib on the neighborhood Jizo. Statues of Jizo were always bald like a baby even in ancient times, but these days their features are often exaggerated and babylike. This seems like an appropriate way of honoring the deceased, and it has the effect of making the parents feel they have atoned for any wrongdoing they may feel they have caused.

Chapter 25

[SEXUAL ANGLES ON BUDDHISM]
If You Do That, You'll Go Blind
Sex and Karma

Karma is yet another one of those Buddhist concepts that's talked about a whole lot these days. But, as is typical of such words, pop culture mostly mangles its meaning.

The word *karma* means "action." But it also contains the idea that every action comes with some kind of effect. We've all grown up with the scientific method. When you boil it down, science is really just the study of cause-and-effect relationships. We're accustomed to accepting the idea that all events in the material world are governed by the law of cause and effect. Dogen told his students that they should have deep belief in cause and effect, that they should never believe that there are any exceptions to this law.

The Buddhist belief in cause and effect extends the material law of cause and effect that we all understand to the nonmaterial realm. Dogen quotes an ancient Buddhist master who said, "Not to commit wrongs, To practice the many kinds of right, Naturally purifies the mind; This is the teaching of the buddhas." He comments on this by saying, "We cause right-and-wrong, cause-and-effect, to

practice; but this does not mean disturbing, or intentionally pro-
ducing, cause-and-effect. Cause-and-effect itself, at times, makes us
practice. The state in which the original features of this cause-and-
effect have already become conspicuous is 'not committing,' it is
'[the state] without appearance,' it is '[the state] without constancy,'
it is 'not being unclear,' and it is 'not falling down'—because it is the
state in which [body and mind] have fallen away."*

We Buddhists believe that cause and effect works just as clearly
in the realm of moral action as it does in the realm of physical
processes. Sometimes it seems like people who do good get shit
on, while people who act like jerks reap all the rewards. There's an
old Buddhist story about this.

> Gayata, a student of the nineteenth patriarch, Kumaralab-
> dha, said to his master, "In my family, father and mother .
> have always believed in the Three Treasures yet they have
> been beset by ill health and, in general, are disappointed
> in all their undertakings. My neighbor's family has long
> done the work of butchers yet their bodies are always in
> sound health and their doings harmoniously combine.
> What is their good fortune? And what is our guilt?"**
>
> The master replied, "Why do you doubt the rule of
> cause and effect? The lengths of time between cause and
> effect are of three kinds. The first one is immediate, the
> second one is a little while between the cause and the
> effect, and the third is when there is a much longer time
> between the cause and the effect. Because of such differ-
> ences in time between cause and effect, it seems that a

---

* From *Shobogenzo*, vol. 1, "Not Doing Wrong," translated by Gudo Nishijima and Chodo
  Cross.
** As mentioned earlier, in ancient Buddhist scriptures butchers usually are considered evildoers because their business violates the first Buddhist precept, which
  says not to take life.

kind person dies early, or a violent person lives longer, or a wrong person seems to be happy, or a right person seems to be unhappy. Therefore people sometimes think that there is no rule of cause and effect, or there is no relation between sin and happiness. They do not know that the relation between cause and effect is just the same as the relation between a thing and its shadow, or between sound and vibration."

Often this relationship between cause and effect is phrased in terms of a person's current lifetime and his or her future lives. But there is no need to believe in reincarnation or rebirth to see this happening. Once you start to see how it works in your own life it becomes impossible to doubt. A regular zazen practice is a good way to develop the intuition to become aware of the workings of cause and effect.

Sometimes we call the effects of our actions "results." But the Buddhist philosopher Nagarjuna questioned the notion of a result. While he agreed completely that every action had an effect, Nagarjuna was pretty adamant that there was no such thing as a result.

There are two main reasons that even though all actions have effects, there is no such thing as a result. First, all actions have effects that spread throughout space and time in ways we cannot possibly perceive. Any time you say that "this is the result of that," you are limiting the actual effects of whatever action you're looking at and ignoring most of what's really going on. Second, Nagarjuna looks at time in the Buddhist sense, in which there is no real past or future, only the eternal present moment. In the present moment there can be no such thing as a result because what is is just what is. The cause that produced the effect is in the past and therefore removed from reality here and now.

That's all very heady philosophical stuff. If you're really interested you can read the translation of Nagarjuna's masterwork, *Fundamental Wisdom of the Middle Way* by Gudo Nishijima Roshi and me, which was published by Monkfish Books just before this book you're reading now.*

But in terms of sex, karma obviously plays a major role. All action has effects. The effects of certain kinds of action are less significant than others. But sex is a very significant kind of action and always has very significant effects.

People talk about "no-strings-attached" sex. But I don't believe that really exists. You can have sex without commitment, sure. You can even have sex in which there are no obligations for the parties involved ever to interact with each other again. But sex is so significant of an action that it always creates some kind of bond between or among the people involved. You can ignore those bonds if you want. But that doesn't make them go away.

This is why you need to be really careful with sex. The obvious and superficial among the possible negative complications stemming from sex — like STDs, unwanted pregnancy, jealousy, and so forth — are just the tip of the iceberg. Of course there are lots of good effects of sex — like intimacy, pleasure, fun, *wanted* pregnancy, and all that nice stuff. But I want to focus for a couple of seconds here on the complications that can arise because when we're hot for some bumpin' of the uglies we tend to dwell only on the positives and not on the complications.

These complications are not all necessarily negative. And even the ones we usually think of as negative don't always have to be negative. It's just that when people intertwine their bodies they're also intertwining a lot of other stuff. Remember that Buddhists don't believe in the distinct separation of body and mind. So, to the Buddhist way of thinking, it's impossible to have sex that is strictly bodily. Things of the mind come together and slosh into each other even if we're only focused on the physical aspects of the interaction.

So be aware that every time you have sex with someone you are sharing something more than mere bodily fluids, even if you

---

* You gotta take your plugs where you can get 'em!

choose never to see or speak to that person (or those people) again. You ought to take that seriously, even if the sex itself is just for fun. Sex can be a beautiful thing. But it has to be handled properly. When it's handled correctly, that's when it's most beautiful.

The karma you accrue when having sex with other people always has some kind of effect on your life. If I were more into phrasing things in the typical "Eastern spiritual master" way I might talk about how sexual activity leaves impressions on your astral body or whatever. But I don't really go in for that kind of talk. I just know from personal experience that every sexual encounter I've had, no matter how brief or seemingly "meaningless," has left some kind of mark on my consciousness. I don't think I'm different from anybody else in this respect.

You're also affecting the people you have sex with. So you should never be reckless. You're becoming part of their karma as well, part of their personal story. You wouldn't want someone to carelessly mess up your life just so they could have a bit of fun, so don't do that to somebody else. Even so-called casual sex should not be handled casually, or at least not thoughtlessly.

The karma of sex also comes from your past. A lot of people stress out big-time over how to find true romance or at least how to find some quick nookie. They do all kinds of things to try and make it happen. But your past actions determine to a large degree whether or not that will be possible. You can't force the universe to cough up that special someone you so desire just because your ego is telling you that you just gotta, gotta, gotta meet that person *right now*. The universe has its own timetable, and it's a timetable that, in a very major way, your own actions have created.

Also, who you meet is largely a function of past karma. I always think of any supposedly "chance encounter" as having some kind of significance. I don't get too deeply into speculating about what that significance is or how it came about. There's no possible way I can know that. But I don't view any encounter as random or meaningless.

In terms of relationships, this means I try to be open to the actual relationships that occur in my life rather than imagining better relationships and wishing I could have them instead. Which is not to say I never have such thoughts. I certainly do. But I know that thoughts along those lines aren't very important.

All this relates to how sometimes misguided people ask me how to make their love lives better. Let's talk about that next.

Chapter 26

ZEN DATING AND MARRIAGE ADVICE

Well, that abortion stuff was kind of heavy. Let's lighten up a bit, shall we?

Weirdly enough, even though I wrote a book about the breakup of my marriage and the fact that I dated a woman who came to my Zen classes,* thus proving I have no idea how to successfully be married or meet women, I sometimes get requests for dating and marriage advice. Here's one:

> I am a very dedicated Zen practitioner, and I go to the local Zen center in my city several times a week to sit, and I am currently single and on the marriage market, looking for a wife who is into meditation or at least appreciates it. I am getting extremely old (forty-nine, last time I checked) and the marriage "market" is pretty grim in the US for people in my age category. Since I am into Zen and also very interested in Japan, and since there are still some Japanese

---

* *Zen Wrapped in Karma Dipped in Chocolate*, in fine bookstores everywhere!

women interested in white guys (though apparently not nearly so many as there were forty years ago), and since single Japanese women over thirty apparently find it difficult to get married, it occurred to me to ask you what you thought about the idea of looking for a Japanese wife (based in Japan) who is into Zen and aged about thirty-five to forty-five.

Now, that's an unusual one! But I get questions about the topic of dating fairly frequently, often referring to some supposed knowledge of Japanese women I might have. I told the guy that I really have no idea if he could find a Japanese wife who is into Zen. I found one, but she dumped me a few years later. I'll get to that in a minute.

Anyway, it is true that even today Japanese women still tend to be fascinated with Western men. I was amazed when I first got to Japan and I'd see these nerdy white guys over there with these smoking-hot women they would never have had a chance with back home. Of course I became one of those guys myself, so who am I to criticize? It's not quite as easy as it once was, since there are so many more of us over there these days. But non-Asian men are still comparatively rare and tend to be viewed as exotic and therefore desirable. Even so, you still have to be a decent human being. Don't think that the color of your skin is going to open every door and unbuckle every pair of jeans for you just by itself.*

But as far as Zen goes, be warned. Japanese people in general, male and female alike, generally know far less about Zen than any Westerner who practices it or even reads about it a lot. It's not an exaggeration to say that nearly everyone reading this book has more knowledge about Zen than any random person you might meet in Japan. Zen is nearly as exotic a thing to them as it is to the average truck driver in Peoria.

---

* By the way, I hear that black guys are more popular in Japan than white guys these days. So white guys, hit those tanning booths!

Sure, they've seen it around the neighborhood, so they're not scared of it like the truck driver might be. They don't think it's devil worship or a cult. But they usually don't have a clue what goes on inside the temple behind the convenience store just around the corner from their house or what the philosophy is or any of that. When I was living in Japan I'd always see TV programs supposedly showing what life was like in a Zen monastery. The standard scenario was to enroll some comedian in a training program and watch him get whacked with sticks every time he did something wrong. I have even been asked by Japanese people if Zen is a form of Buddhism. No joke.

So I told the guy that any average Japanese woman he might encounter would be likely to find his Zen practice eccentric at best or even downright weird. Most folks at the Japanese company I worked for thought it was kind of strange that I had a Zen practice. They seemed to sort of admire it, but at the same time they regarded it as odd. There wasn't a single other Zen practitioner among the company's hundred or so employees.

Now, as far as unmarried Japanese women over thirty being more desperate to get married than Western women that age, it's hard to say. In Japan they used to call unmarried women over the age of twenty-five "Christmas cake" because nobody wanted them after the twenty-fifth. But that's not necessarily true anymore. Just like Westerners, Japanese people are getting married later these days. I asked the guy if he really wanted to marry someone who is desperate. He said that was the whole point and didn't seem to find it at all ironic. Okay.

Like I said, though, I've already been married to a Japanese woman who was into Zen. So I'm not personally so anxious to find another. And I've already written a whole book about the breakup of my marriage,* so I'm not going to rehash that stuff too much in this one. But I'll try to say a few things that I haven't already said.

---

* See previous footnote.

Yuka, my ex-wife, was not a Zen practitioner when I met her. Her family was nominally Zen. This meant that on the rare occasions anybody in the family went to a Buddhist temple it was a Zen temple rather than a Pure Land Buddhist temple or a Nichiren Buddhist temple, which are the two other most popular sects. They were not in any way devout practitioners or believers. They probably went to a temple once or twice a year for ceremonies that were more community functions than religious rites. They might have recognized the name Dogen as being that of a revered ancient Zen master, but they certainly didn't know anything about what he taught. No one in her family had ever sat a single period of zazen. Like the folks where I worked, they thought my practice was admirable but weird. They were impressed when I became a monk, but also a little baffled by my decision to do so.*

I'd already had my practice for more than a decade by the time Yuka and I started living together.** For most of the time we were together, every morning and every evening I sat zazen alone. Yuka was usually asleep during the morning ones, and for the evening sittings I just found a spot in the apartment where I couldn't hear the TV. Every weekend I went by myself to lectures and group practices led by Nishijima Roshi. Once or twice a year I attended Nishijima's three-day Zen retreats, also on my own.

After a while Yuka became curious about this stuff and started to tag along. She started sitting occasionally at home. After a few years of sending me off on those three-day retreats by myself, she started attending them with me. She enjoyed them a lot and quickly became a regular, eventually assuming a lot of the administrative duties that went along with running the retreats.

All this time I never asked her to start doing zazen or come to the lectures and retreats. She always knew where I was going, and she

---

* As I was and still am!
** In sin!

knew she could come along if she liked. It was her decision to start attending.

I think this is probably the best way to approach the matter for anyone who practices and has a significant other who doesn't. There's no sense in trying to force the issue. Someone who is forced to do practice will almost never stick with it anyway. This would also be my advice for Zen practitioners with children. They'll take to the practice if and/or when they feel the need to. It's fine to make the practice available. But it's best not to do any more than that.

Yuka and I were married by Nishijima Roshi in a Zen ceremony. Zen wedding ceremonies are rare, even in Japan. In fact, Buddhism never even got into the business of sanctifying marriage until fairly recently. The early Buddhists had no reason to develop wedding ceremonies and the like, since theirs was not a religion in the Western sense. The notion of a Buddhist wedding would have been something like the notion of a Marxist wedding or a Three Stooges Fan wedding. It just wasn't part of what Buddhists did. Nowadays, there are Buddhist weddings. But in Japan, at least, they are comparatively rare.

Most Japanese weddings are Christian — sort of. There are very few actual Christians in Japan. But Christian-style weddings are seen as the cool way to get married. Often the ceremonies are performed by foreigners who are part-time actors and usually make their living as English teachers.

These guys are not ministers or priests. But that doesn't matter. There are no legal stipulations that they have to be, and nobody really cares. Marriage is not considered a religious function in Japan anyway. It's cooler to have a white guy do the ceremony in heavily accented Japanese than to have a real Japanese Christian minister or priest do it.

I attended one of Yuka's friend's weddings once, and sure enough, they'd hired one of these guys to perform the ceremony. I saw him flinch a little when he spotted me in the audience. But he gave a good performance. He was nowhere to be found after it was over, though.

A Zen wedding is basically a modified precepts ceremony. The couple agrees together to uphold the Buddhist precepts, and then they exchange rings. The Zen master dips a pine branch in water and sprinkles it on them, and you're done.

In the West, Zen weddings tend to be further modified to conform to our customs and expectations. There's really no set form. I've only performed one wedding, for my friends Emily and Doug. Since their families were both Catholic I made up a ceremony that was more like a standard Catholic wedding and eliminated the taking of the Buddhist precepts altogether so as not to freak out the folks even more than they were already freaked out by my showing up in my Zen robes.

As you know, my marriage did not last. I was once asked in an interview, if we both had this Zen practice why couldn't we make the marriage work?

It would be lovely if everyone who practiced Zen came out of their practice with all their problems solved and with the ability to make any relationship work. But, alas, it doesn't work like that. The break-up didn't have anything to do with Zen. It wasn't like we disagreed on Dogen's view of Being/Time or something. It had to do with all the usual things that break marriages up.

I will say that when it happened it was far freer of drama than most other divorces I've been around. I think the Zen stuff had a lot to do with that. When it became apparent that the marriage could not be saved, we did what we needed to do without a lot of anger and pettiness.

When my break-up with Yuka was happening, I spoke to Nishijima Roshi about it. First he told me that if I was breaking up with Yuka because I was interested in another woman he thought I was extremely stupid. But that wasn't the case, and I said so. He encouraged me to try and work it out, but try as I might that proved impossible. Then he told me he thought a Buddhist monk should either be married or celibate.

I wasn't ready for celibacy, although I can see the logic in that choice. We've already been through this in an earlier chapter. But I do feel that it's the choice that's more likely to lead to a more balanced life.

Following my divorce I plunged into the nightmare world of dating. For a time I was involved with a woman who was a very dedicated Zen practitioner — so dedicated, in fact, that she decided she'd be better off living in a monastery than living with me. So much for the shared-interest-in-Zen thing!

I'm not a good source for dating dos and don'ts. I only know what not to do. In fact, I can't even say I know what not to do. I make every mistake a person can possibly make in these matters. But that didn't stop Maura Kelly, who writes a dating blog called "A Year of Living Flirtatiously" for the Marie Claire website from calling and asking me for my dating tips. She turned the interview into an article called "Zen and the Art of Dating: Insights from a Zen Monk." Nice title. But I think any actual insights from a monk — me — were sort of lacking. Still, I'll try my best anyway.

She asked me how to deal with rejection, like when you meet someone and he's clearly not interested in you. I told her a story about how I was at a party in Hollywood and I was talking to a woman there. I wasn't even trying to pick her up or anything. I just happened to be talking to people at the party, and she was one of those people.

Like a lot of people who go to parties in the greater Los Angeles area, this person was mainly looking for opportunities to further her career ambitions. When she found out I wrote books about Zen for a living, she immediately tuned me out. She started actively looking around the room for someone better to talk to *as I was speaking to her*. It was so unbelievably rude and obvious it was actually funny.

I didn't get mad. I just wrapped up what I was saying. She wasn't listening anymore anyway, so I ended whatever sentence I was in the middle of as gracefully as I could. Then I walked away. I'm not sure she even noticed I left. There's no sense talking to someone who doesn't want to talk to you.

The woman who wrote the article also asked how to deal with feeling crappy about having been treated badly by someone you have the hots for. In the version she posted she had me saying, "Let your emotions come up and recognize them and move on. Don't fixate on them too much." I think she got that from a Thich Nhat Hanh book!

What I actually said was something like what I've already said in this book before. You can't really help feeling whatever you feel at any given moment. But you do have a choice whether or not to pursue those feelings and roll around in them like a dog who has just found a dead skunk in the woods.

She said, "So it seems that what you're saying is: Let people who don't seem interested go. And keep looking for a good person to come along: someone you can connect with. Stay open to all the possibilities. Don't let disappointments distract you from the fact that there are tons of other opportunities and possibilities out there."

In the published interview she has me agreeing with that, and maybe I did. I don't recall. But about the matter of finding someone to connect with, a lot of people carry around the idea that if they only found the perfect mate then they'd be happy. It's a common fantasy that's promoted heavily by moviemakers and novelists because it sells so well. It is indeed nice to meet people you have some kind of connection with. Sometimes you might even get to have sex with them. Hooray for you!

But I don't think you can have an idea — even a vague idea — of the ideal person, make strenuous efforts to meet that special someone, and then have it happen. It doesn't really work that way. These things have to happen by themselves.

Some people try very hard to find that someone, though. And for them there are Internet dating services. I joined one of the Buddhist dating services on the Internet recently. I'd seen the ads these guys placed in the Buddhist rags with an appealing young couple meditating back-to-back and thought those ads were hilarious. I figured it was worth checking out just for this book, if for nothing else. I didn't get too far, though. The "free" site asked me to pay a monthly fee of $15 if I wanted to send messages to any of its members. I didn't really want to anyhow. What I found in my brief excursion was pretty grim.

For starters, it looks like most of the Southern California–based women on this nominally Buddhist dating site identify their religion not as Buddhism but as Scientology. I found that a little surprising. And Scientologists or not, most of the folks there are looking for the elusive "soul mate." It was just such a sad place to visit — so many people wanting something so desperately that even if that something should cross their path they wouldn't recognize it since they're so blinded by wanting it. They get so deeply into the mind-set of looking for their ideal that the real world becomes a mere shadow.

It was also weird to see the term *soul mate* used so often there. It's difficult to fit the idea of being someone's soul mate into Buddhism since Buddha denied the existence of the soul. The idea of a soul is just a feeble and inadequate way of conceptualizing what human beings are. Still, sometimes there are unexplainable attractions between people — romantic and otherwise. But there's still no great need to try and understand why such things occur. When they do, you just do what needs doing. Easy.

As Mr. Spock said, "Sometimes having is not so pleasing a thing as wanting. It is not logical, but it is often true."

Searching for a soul mate is a losing game anyway. There are some things you just can't force to happen. In fact, I'd say most things in life fall into that category, especially great interpersonal relationships. This same thing goes for searching for a Buddhist teacher. There's at least one "Zen master" out there who'll sell you a personal meeting with him for $50,000. But you can't buy a

Buddhist teacher who can really teach you any more than you can buy a lover who can really love you. You can put yourself in the most statistically likely spot to find your soul mate or your perfect Buddhist teacher. But that doesn't always work either. Statistics are an iffy thing to base your life decisions on. In any case, the relationship has to develop organically. And I'm naive enough to believe it will develop even if you fail to put yourself in the most seemingly likely spot for it to happen.

Relationships often do not look at all the way we expect them to. We've been lied to by television and movies and books written by people wishing to fulfill in fiction dreams they can't realize in this world. What they've told us about romance is mostly bullshit, and so is what they've told us about ideal teachers.

As for making the ideal romantic relationship the goal of your life, I don't think it's really a good idea. It's funny to me that I should be so down on the idea of true and lasting romantic relationships since my own parents had one of those. As I said earlier, they stayed together literally "till death did them part." They made their vows on November 23, 1962, exactly a year before JFK got shot, and parted on January 12, 2007, when my mom died. Both sets of my grandparents also stayed together until one of them died. So I grew up with a strong belief in the idea of mating for life.

This may seem an ideal situation to grow up with. So many people who don't have parents who stick together through thick and thin wish they'd had a set like mine. And yet I think this actually led me to make some unfortunate choices. I found myself often unable to break up with someone who I clearly should have broken up with because I had no basis for that. It's not that I regret anything I've done. Even if I did there's no point in regret. And certainly this is hardly the worst thing that can happen to a person. I'm not really complaining about it. It's just that I think this demonstrates the way that no matter how closely our upbringing might match what the prevailing culture thinks of as ideal, there are still problems to be faced.

When the ideal relationship is your goal, that means your goal is an ideal — remove the "l" at the end and it means your goal is an idea. It's an image.

Marriage is a funny thing, too. I agree with Nina Hartley that most humans have a strong pair-bonding instinct but that this may not be the same as what we call monogamy. I know this may seem to contradict what I've said in earlier books. And I'll get to that. In any case, marriage as an institution is an invention of human thought. Buddha neither approved of nor condemned marriage. He himself was married. And, although he left his wife to pursue his path, he did not get divorced in the sense that we understand the term.

Marriage is a social contract. Once entered into it should either be honored or legally dissolved. In Japan Buddhist monks were allowed by law to marry after the Meiji Restoration of circa 1868. Celibacy wasn't really being honored anyway, and that was becoming obvious. Also, the government realized that married monks wielded less political power than celibate ones. They were too busy with their families to get very involved in affairs of state. These days a lot, perhaps even most, Japanese Buddhist monks are married. And a lot of Buddhist teachers are divorced, too, by the way, though they rarely make this widely known. Why should they make it known? It's not really relevant to the job.

There is no set Buddhist view on marriage. But I'll give you my own take on it in brief.

Marriage turns the natural inclination of humans to pair-bond into a legal institution. This is fine. We humans do a lot of this sort of thing. We've reined in our natural inclination to eat whenever we're hungry and turned it into an institution of eating at three specified times of day. We've turned our natural inclination to care for the members of our community into a bizarre system of taxation and government. The list goes on and on. Why should pair bonding be spared?

Marriage is neither good nor bad in and of itself. There are a lot of reasons to recommend it. And this is why I came out so strongly in favor of monogamy in my other books. I'm still very much in favor of it when it can be accomplished, and I still highly recommend it. It solves a lot of problems by making clear boundaries on sexual behavior. I found this extraordinarily useful when I was married. Until our marriage became clearly unworkable, the idea of actually cheating on my wife never occurred to me. Oh, sure, there were plenty of times I *wanted* to. Are you kidding? I lived in Japan, where every third woman you see is so beautiful you want to die, and a great many of them just love foreign guys. But I was married, so I would never actually carry those ideas through. The restrictions made my life a lot more orderly and easy to deal with.

But marriage also creates difficulties, such as making it very problematic to end a pair-bond situation that is no longer viable. Having said that, though, I think in most cases a married couple should try as much as possible to find ways of preserving their marriage if they believe there's a chance it can be preserved. But when it can't be preserved, they should be free to end it.

The world of marriage and dating is a new one for Buddhism. As the philosophy and practice continue to grow and develop, so will its relationship to marriage and dating. We Western Buddhists bring a lot of baggage concerning religion and its relationship to marriage to the table when we approach the matter of marriage within Buddhism. It's going to take some time before we really come to terms with what Buddhist marriage can be.

As for Buddhist dating, I'm afraid you're pretty much on your own.

Chapter 27

WHEN GOOD SPIRITUAL MASTERS GO BAD

I saw some of you readers out there flinching in the last chapter when I casually mentioned that I had been dating. I have Zen master powers that way — I can see you right through the pages of this book. Even if those of you who flinched might be okay, at least in the abstract, with the fact that a Zen teacher can have sex, you're probably thinking of all the issues involved with a Zen teacher kind of person dating. Like what if a teacher dates a student? That's the one that drives everyone batty. So let's go into that a bit.

Those of you who have read my previous book, *Zen Wrapped in Karma Dipped in Chocolate*, already know I have some personal experience in this area. But I promise those of you who haven't read that book you won't have to have read it in order to follow what I'm going to say here.*

Anyway, Scott Edelstein, a guy I knew ages ago who was a friend of my first Zen teacher, contacted me recently. He was working on a

---

* Not that I couldn't use the money...

249

book about sex and spiritual teachers. He said it was about why so many spiritual teachers go astray and how to keep them from straying. He wanted to interview me for it because in my previous book I talked about my affair with one of my "students." We'll get into why I put the word *students* in quotation marks in a bit. But let's start by talking about the issue of "spiritual teachers going astray," especially as it regards sex with students.

First off, I have to say that I genuinely appreciate the way he likens spiritual teachers to dogs that have to be kept from straying by the members of their communities. There is a good reason that members of such communities feel that way.

Members of spiritual communities tend to believe that their teachers ought to be required to behave in ways that they approve of because they generally see their teachers as authority figures. Even the most fascistic authority figures are ultimately seen as servants of the people they rule. In the case of spiritual authority figures, the lines are blurred. They're not elected rulers of their community, and the boundaries of their authority are not usually spelled out too clearly.

Spiritual teachers are expected to be the embodiment of the collective ideals of their communities. If a spiritual leader presents himself* as the living incarnation of all that is holy, pure, and chaste and if he demands such chastity from his followers, but his followers discover that he has been dipping his holy scepter into the baptismal fonts of his parishioners, there's gonna be some reckoning.

There are a number of legitimate reasons spiritual teacher–student relationships are generally seen as problematic. The biggest is the issue of power abuse. Spiritual authority figures are in positions of power. And power can be used as a means of forcing or coercing others to do what the person in power wishes. There is a long history of spiritual authority figures using their power as a way to get their students to have sex with them.

---

* Or herself.

The other side of this is that power is attractive, whether the person in power intends it to be or not. A lot of the folks who end up becoming spiritual leaders spent most of their lives being kind of nerdy and, frankly, fairly unattractive. Who wants to get boned by some guy who spends most of his time studying ancient texts and meditating?

Quite often these people find themselves late in life surrounded by admirers. Somehow, without any real effort to do so, they have suddenly become attractive. They often have no idea how to handle this because it has never happened before. Add to this the fact that almost no one becomes a spiritual leader until at least the time they're just about ready for their standard midlife crisis. And add to *that* the fact that the difficulty many of these people had in relating to the opposite sex may have contributed in a large way to their choosing a path that required a lot of alone time. It's a volatile mix.

Buddhism has been rocked by numerous sex scandals since it has come westward. As far as Zen in America is concerned, probably the most famous of these is Richard Baker Roshi's various dalliances at the San Francisco Zen Center in the early 1980s, chronicled in Michael Downing's book *Shoes Outside the Door*. The story goes that Baker was having numerous affairs with his students, some of whom were married, while serving as the spiritual leader of the Zen Center.

Several other Zen Buddhist masters in the West have similarly shocked their communities with their sexual behavior. Maezumi Roshi in Los Angeles was rumored to have had some affairs with students. Eido Shimano Roshi in New York was said to have done a few of his disciples. Katagiri Roshi in Minneapolis allegedly had a few discreet liaisons with willing young ladies who came to his Zen sittings, though nobody knew about it until after he'd been dead a few years.

It's somewhat ironic that these turned into scandals because Zen Buddhism has never presented itself or its teachers as being the embodiment of sexual purity, at least in the standard Western

Judeo-Christian sense and especially not in the heavily Puritan-influenced American sense. Of course in the cases mentioned above there was more to it than simply sex. There were issues of hypocrisy, cheating, and so on. Even so, when I looked into these scandals I often got the feeling these teachers were sometimes being judged according to standards they themselves never claimed to embody or uphold. It often *did* seem as if their communities were aghast that they were having sex *at all*. Their followers often seem to have taken them to be otherworldly creatures who should not have any interest in sex. This doesn't excuse everything that happened in the cases I've cited, as well as in others. But it's important to bear in mind that Zen does not claim that its teachers are the embodiment of sexual purity.

Much of the problem may be the very notion of Zen teachers as spiritual authority figures. In my view Zen teachers are not spiritual authority figures at all. I know not everyone in this business sees it that way. There certainly are Zen teachers who do play the role of spiritual authority figure. No doubt about it! But if you want my opinion, and you must because you're reading this book, Zen teachers should never act as authority figures.

My personal approach to being a Zen teacher is that I see myself not as any kind of authority but more like an artist who uses his own approach to life as a way of demonstrating how he has solved certain problems. Whether these solutions are right or wrong, they are the ones I have used. Life is an ongoing experiment. But whoever your teacher is, his or her way of solving these problems is not necessarily yours. What is being conveyed is an attitude and an approach rather than a set of specific behaviors to be emulated.

I admit that considering Zen teaching as art is an uneasy fit. But so is considering it as religious instruction.

The general public doesn't really have a clue as to what a Zen teacher is. So they usually base their assumptions about what a Zen teacher ought to be on the model of religious instructor.

And it isn't just the uninformed masses who do this. A great many Zen teachers conceive of themselves this way as well. This is especially true in Japan. The modern Japanese Soto School is essentially an imitation of the Roman Catholic Church. In the Meiji era, the Japanese looked to the West to provide a framework for understanding the world. They adopted the Western classifications of various forms of knowledge and the divisions thereof, such as science, philosophy, and religion.

It's important to recall that even in our own culture there was a very long time during which there were no such divisions of human knowledge and understanding. There wasn't really a category of philosophy that was separate from religion. And even aspects of what we now recognize as the scientific view were mixed into a generalized stew of knowledge that included religion and philosophy. Other aspects of human understanding, such as mathematics, law, art, and a whole lot of other forms of understanding that we now consider fundamentally incompatible with one another, were also mixed into this stew.

But by the time the Japanese were ready to adopt the Western outlook and way of life, these classifications had already been well established in our culture. These classifications were not, however, nearly so well established in Japan or in the rest of Asia.

So when the Meiji-era Japanese needed a place in which to classify Zen Buddhism, it seemed like the best fit was in the category the Westerners called "religion."

Once it was decided that Zen was a religion, Japanese scholars and clergypeople alike began to look for the commonalities between Zen and Western religions and to largely downplay those aspects that did not fit the established Western mold.

And so the idea has come down to us a hundred and some years later that Zen is a religion. I'm aware that there has been considerable debate about this. But mostly the debate has been framed in terms of the question, "Is Zen a religion or a philosophy?" I used to side with the faction that said it was a philosophy. But I'm not so sure this is even the right question anymore.

One aspect of religious instruction is that as a representative of some specific religion you usually have an institution behind you. They decide what their reps can and cannot say and how their reps should dress and behave. The institution takes responsibility for the individuals they choose as their representatives. Thus, if a parish priest in Des Moines is caught fondling choirboys, the main office in Rome is held responsible.

The Zen model doesn't really function that way except perhaps when it comes to large institutions such as the Soto-shu of Japan and maybe a few others in the West that follow their model — which, in turn, is based on the Catholic Church, ironically.

Art instruction works differently. I am a competent enough guitarist that I could teach someone the basics of the instrument. I can show you the chords, the blues scale, how to hold your pick real tight and make that squeaky sound like the guy from ZZ Top, and so forth. Once I have instructed you, how you use that knowledge isn't really my business. You may choose to use it for good, or you can use what I've taught you for evil purposes, like playing guitar in a Julio Iglesias cover band, for example.

It's really up to you. Furthermore, beyond the basics I teach you, it's up to you to come up with your own style of playing. Your style will be influenced by what I've taught you. But if you're any good at all you'll be able to incorporate those influences into something uniquely your own.

I think that's how good Zen teaching should function as well. Good Zen teachers shouldn't try to unify what they teach any more than poets should try to make their poems all sound the same or novelists should try to write the same book. That would be counter to their art.

As for the matter of authority, any decent Zen teacher will toss back any authority you try to hand her like a hot potato. A hot potato with spikes on it. That explodes. In other words, a decent Zen teacher does not to take your authority away from you. Her job is to help you learn to manifest your own authority.

Still, whether or not the teacher is an authority figure, we do have this idea of not misusing sexuality. And it is problematic when the members of a Buddhist community come to the conclusion that their leaders have been misusing sexuality, at least in the way that the members of the community have come to define what is and is not a misuse of sexuality.

Not every instance of a teacher's sleeping with a student constitutes a misuse of sexuality. Sometimes even when it's clearly not sexual misconduct, people still get upset. When people get upset, it needs to be dealt with.

One of the odd things I've noticed is that there seem to be cases when a teacher-student sexual relationship is clearly consensual, does not involve the teacher using power to coerce the student into sex, does not involve cheating, does not involve any spouse, does not involve the breaking of public vows of chastity or hypocrisy on the part of the spiritual teacher by demanding standards for the community that he does not live up to, and so on and on, and yet the community still finds the very existence of the relationship upsetting. I have a theory about that, which I'd like to share. I don't think my theory addresses the only reason this kind of thing happens, or even necessarily the main reason. But I've never heard anyone talk about this when they discuss all the things that these kinds of relationships touch off in people's minds. So here goes.

Members of spiritual communities often tend to think of themselves as a kind of family. The head of the community, usually male, is often seen as a father figure. In some traditions, such as Catholicism, this relationship is even made explicit by calling the head of the church "father" and the monks and nuns "brothers" and "sisters." There are Hindu orders in which similar terms are used for people in similar positions. But even when the various positions aren't named in this way, there is often an underlying sense that the spiritual organization is a group of kinfolk.

So let's say your "father" starts spending a lot more time with your "sister" than he spends with you. That's gonna raise some issues. And if you find out that "Dad" is having sex with your "sister," oh, my God! Furthermore, ideally there are very few boundaries between real family members. They generally know each other's business and feel no hesitation to comment on it. So members of spiritual communities often feel a right, perhaps even a duty, to know their leader's business and to get into it in as much as they might get into whatever it is their actual dad might be doing.

Even when people know perfectly well that the spiritual leader isn't *really* their dad and that their spiritual sister isn't *really* their sister, let alone "Dad's" actual daughter, it's nearly impossible to avoid these subconscious reactions. These reactions can be much more powerful than the reactions we are able to consciously acknowledge.

I watched this happen in my own case when I began dating the woman who was considered by some to be "my student." Just to be clear, though, I do not consider anyone to be "my student." My bottom line with the groups I nominally "lead" — again, I use *lead* like *student*, for want of a better word — is that I sit zazen every day, and at a specific time and place each week I open my doors and let other people join me.

In any case, the very existence of this relationship made a couple of people in my group extremely upset. But it was never apparent to me exactly why they were upset. I've made it quite clear that I am not celibate. I was single, so there was no issue of cheating involved. There was never any concern that I had used my power as a teacher to seduce this person. I had several long discussions in which I tried my best to get the folks who were concerned about who I was dating to articulate just what the problem was. The closest I got was when one of them described it as "shitting where you live." This was not at all how I thought of the relationship.

So should I not have entered into a romantic relationship with someone who sat zazen with me? Is this a boundary that no one should ever cross?

It's hard to say. Lots of organizations have specific rules about this. My friend Nina is a yoga teacher, and the studio she teaches at has a rule that if one of the instructors becomes romantically involved with someone who attends her classes, that person is no longer allowed to attend classes led by that instructor. At the San Francisco Zen Center, where students and teachers must formally and publicly accept each other as such, they have a standing rule that should a romance begin between teacher and student, they must sever their formal teacher-student bond. The student is free to take another teacher from the Zen Center and the romance itself may continue, but not as one between teacher and student.

This all makes perfect sense to me. I think these are good policies. But they are also the product of institutions in which the student has the option to take another teacher. What about smaller organizations in which there is only one teacher? And what about in situations, like mine, in which there is no formal teacher-student relationship?

This is a tough call. And there is no possible way anyone can establish a blanket rule that will cover every situation. Each such relationship is different. It all depends on the context.

There are a lot of reasons teachers in spiritual traditions end up in romantic relationships with their students. Most of these reasons have nothing at all to do with issues of abuse of power or other misuses of sexuality.

Think about it. Here you have a person — let's assume a heterosexual male, for the sake of not having to say "he or she" for the rest of these paragraphs, although it could be any gender or orientation — whose practice is extremely important to him, probably the single most important thing. But, like anyone else, he longs for companionship. Where is the most likely place this person is going to encounter someone who shares his passion about the thing that is number one in his life? You guessed it! Among his students or fellow practitioners.

A relationship formed under such circumstances can be every bit as real and true as any other romance entered into by people with a mutual attraction and common interests. It would be a tragedy to categorically deny people the ability to come together in this way just because it might make the other members of their group uncomfortable. And I'm not sure it's such a terrible thing to make the community uncomfortable. Sometimes a little discomfort can be healthy.

In my own case, the relationship formed under these circumstances was as honest and deep as any other I have been involved in. And let me be clear about this, I very much resented the community's unwarranted interference with my personal life. I still do. I'm not just saying this to bitch about it. It's a significant matter. If you're a member of a spiritual community and there's something like this going on with your teacher, you need to examine your own reactions very carefully before you decide it's your business to intervene. Your teacher is a human being with real feelings just like yours.

But I'm also aware that I brought this upon myself to a large degree. It has made me rethink my whole approach to Zen teaching. It was in part because of this that I decided my bottom line was simply "I sit, and you can join me." I don't regret the romance. It was necessary. It was right. The relationship that occurred was far more important to me than any duty I might have had not to upset the members of my sitting group.

I can't speak for every Zen student and every Zen teacher. And I certainly can't speak for all teachers and students in all spiritual traditions. But I can say that teacher-student romantic relationships will always be a part of the landscape of Zen and other spiritual traditions. It's important to understand that these relationships do happen and to understand that when they do, the reasons are always various and complex. Sometimes the relationship is clearly abusive and wrong, but not always. In fact, I'll be so bold as to say that most of the time there is nothing any more sleazy or abusive going on than goes on in any other romantic relationship. It's also vital that members of the community examine the real reasons behind whatever feelings they have about the matter. This is, after all, what the practice is for — self-examination rather than the examination of others.

Chapter 28

WHEN GOOD SPIRITUAL MASTERS GO REALLY, REALLY BAD

AIDS and Other STDs and Buddhist Practice

The facts are pretty well established. Chögyam Trungpa Rinpoche was a Tibetan Buddhist master who came to the West in the sixties, eventually ending up in Boulder, Colorado, where he established Naropa University, the first accredited Buddhist university in the United States. William Burroughs and Allen Ginsberg taught there. And, for a very brief time, so did my first Zen teacher.

Trungpa wrote a book called *Cutting Through Spiritual Materialism*, which deserves its status as a classic in the field. But Trungpa was a problematic teacher, to say the least. By the time he got to America he had already given up his monk's vows and openly drank, smoke, and slept with his students. There are rumors of him holding orgies in which unwilling Naropa students were forced to participate. Trungpa died in 1987 at the age of forty-eight from cirrhosis of the liver.

But he left a successor, a man he gave the spiritual name Ösel Tendzin. His real name was Thomas Frederick Rich Jr. My first teacher used to refer to him as "Asshole Tension," even when Tendzin was still alive. Tendzin died in 1990 at age forty-seven of

AIDS, but not before spreading the disease to an unknown number of men and women with whom he had unprotected sex. One of his conquests alleges that he was held down by Tendzin's guards and raped. Tendzin apparently believed that his Buddhist practice would prevent the disease from spreading to others.

There must be a million issues about Buddhism and sexuality in even this highly truncated version of the story. While not every rumor about Trungpa or Tendzin has been verified or admitted to by their estates and successors, if even a few of them are even partly true, they stand as evidence that the Buddhist ideal of not misusing sexuality was interpreted very liberally by these teachers.

But even if we can forgive their promiscuousness, it's impossible to reconcile Tendzin's alleged belief that his spiritual development would protect the men and women he fucked from contracting AIDS. This is pure nonsense and not at all in keeping with the Buddhist belief in the natural law of cause and effect.

AIDS was unknown in Buddha's time, and while there were certainly some forms of sexually transmitted disease active in his day, the medical understanding of such things at the time was very limited. So he never addressed this topic at all.

I've said that keeping a vow of celibacy doesn't solve all the problems related with sex. But I have to admit it *does* solve the problem of sexually transmitted diseases.

Still, most of us aren't interested in that option, so what do we do? Just being sexually responsible people requires that we take all the standard precautions. Use condoms, get tested, don't engage in unsafe sexual practices, you know the drill. Even if we aren't Buddhists, common decency requires that we do at least this much.

I started this chapter off with the story of Ösel Tendzin because I don't want to whitewash things for you. I don't want to make the case that everyone who calls him- or herself a Buddhist is necessarily a shining example of how to behave sexually in the age of increased awareness of STDs and AIDS.

But, in fact, there are a lot more examples of Buddhists who have dealt with the issue of STDs in general, and specifically with AIDS, in highly humanistic and honorable ways than there are of Buddhists who have behaved like assholes when dealing with it. This is what makes Ösel Tendzin's case so remarkable. His case is not at all typical of a how a Buddhist deals with sexually transmitted diseases.

A much better and more representative example of a Buddhist practitioner with AIDS is that of Issan Dorsey. I'll call him Issan because that's his Buddhist name. It means "one mountain." His given name was Tommy. Issan was a gay man who came of age in the forties when it definitely was not okay to be open about alternative sexuality. After a stint in the US Navy, where he first encountered other gay men, Issan ended up in San Francisco just as flower power and consciousness-raisings were becoming all the rage. And, it just so happened, right as Shunryu Suzuki was organizing what was to become the San Francisco Zen Center.

After having his fill of drugs and living on the street, Issan gravitated toward Zen practice and became one of Suzuki's most devoted early students. He was ordained as a monk and played a very key role in the development of the Zen Center, as well as the Tassajara monastery.

Issan's presence drew a number of gay men to the San Francisco Zen Center. Eventually a satellite temple called the Hartford Street Center was established in the Castro district, the gayest section of San Francisco, and Issan went there to be its spiritual leader.

When the AIDS epidemic began claiming the lives of many in the Castro, Issan decided that the Hartford Street Center should do whatever it could to help make things better. Many of those affected by the disease had no resources to call on. A great number of them had been disowned by their families and friends, were shunned by government-sponsored social services, and had even been outcast by fellow members of the gay community who didn't fully understand their condition and were understandably afraid. So Issan turned the

Hartford Street Center into a hospice for those dying from AIDS who had nowhere else to go.

This was not a popular decision. Issan faced a lot of resistance, not the least of which came from Zen students, both straight and gay, who felt that this was not the proper use of their facilities. But Issan persevered, and the Hartford Street Center helped a lot of people through some very difficult times and provided them a place to die with honor, dignity, and friendship.

As we've already discussed, Zen monks are not bound by an oath of celibacy. So Issan continued to have long-term affairs and short-term sexual liaisons throughout his career as a monk. Unfortunately Issan himself did not take proper precautions in all his sexual encounters, and he ended up getting AIDS. But even till the end of his life he remained a devoted practitioner and Zen teacher, delivering dharma talks even when the disease was at its worst. He is well remembered as a beautiful example of how one can live a dignified and useful life even under the most trying of circumstances. David Schneider wrote a moving autobiography of Issan called *Street Zen* that is well worth checking out.

Another good example of a Buddhist practitioner living with AIDS is someone we've already met in these pages, Daigan Gathier of the San Francisco Zen Center. In fact, it was AIDS that brought Daigan to the practice. He told me:

> When I came to this practice, I was miserable. I had already been HIV positive for five years and had just been told I now had AIDS, the love of my life had just died, and I had run out of options to run away or to get over my grief. I was sure my life was completely broken.
>
> AIDS is my karma and my teaching. When I got infected in 1990 I was told, "Most folks are living about two years." Not really what someone who is twenty-four wants to hear.
>
> I grew up in a fundamentalist Christian family. Their response was to look outside of yourself, to God. To their way

of thinking the whole reason you have AIDS is 'cuz you're a big fag anyhow.

So I decided to check out different spiritual paths. For me it was all of this grief and loss since so many of my friends had already died of this thing. A friend of mine found a little sitting space. The teacher there was named Howie Cohen. He said, "Nothing is broken, so what are you trying to fix?" and my response was, "What the fuck are you talking about?" If there's nothing broken and nothing to fix why am I so messed up? That's not my experience.

By the time I was twenty-five I had been to more than three hundred funerals. Add to this the stigma of being gay, and a government that couldn't care less. What do you mean nothing's broken? And Howie said, "Look, all you have to do is find a way to make that useful. This is the life you got. What are you gonna do about it?" And he showed me how to not make a big deal about it. He said, "Your road is difficult, but this is your road." He wasn't callously saying just get over it. He was saying, "This is what you got, what are you gonna do?"

I never don't have AIDS. I never get a break from it. There are no days off. A few weeks ago someone was asking me about what my memories were from before being infected. I don't remember. Even before the virus was in my body, it was in my life. When I was younger there was a short time before the bomb hit and all my friends started getting it, but not long. And then life changed. My first AIDS death was when I was seventeen, and it was a guy I had fucked around with in a park. Afterward my friends and I all sat in that same park drinking beer and wondering what the hell happened. I feel like I am doing that still a lot of the time. Only without the beer.

What practice gives me to get through it is permission to not get through it. Just that this is it. Or better is Suzuki Roshi's quote, "Our way is to accept what is, as it is, and to help it be its best." In the case of this disease, it is what it is, and so how can I help it be its best? What is "its best" when it comes to AIDS? Interesting koan, no?

Daigan's story is about what is perhaps the most extreme of the various negative consequences that can occur from sex. We live in an era where one of the possible unintended outcomes of a pleasant roll in the hay is that you can die a slow and fairly nasty death. This is yet another reason that sex is serious business and needs to be approached that way.

No matter what you believe about the whys of how it happened, it seems clear that Western society got way too fucking cocky after we managed to come up with effective birth control and conquered the major sexually transmitted diseases like syphilis and gonorrhea. We went through a couple of decades when it seemed like we could do pretty much whatever felt good and rest assured that nothing really awful would happen. Nothing that couldn't be cured by a simple shot in the arm. This assumption turned out to be very wrong, and lots of people have paid a heavy price for it.

I'm a little concerned these days by what seems like a swing back to something like the same cocky attitude toward sex that was in vogue in the sixties and seventies. Now that we know the basic methods of preventing the spread of AIDS, many of us seem to be getting a little too relaxed about things. It's good to see that the term *safe sex* has morphed into the more realistic *safer sex* — an admission that even cautious sexual practices are not necessarily risk free — and that lots of people are taking much greater precautions these days. But it's also good to be aware that a lot of the earliest victims of the AIDS epidemic were practicing what was believed at the time to be safe sex. We don't know what's coming up next, and so it's important to be very careful.

In the age of AIDS and other STDs, the Buddhist ideal of not misusing sexuality can be seen even more clearly as not just some old-fashioned fuddy-duddy restrictive religious approach to something fun but as very good advice on how to avoid literally ruining your life.

Chapter 29

[SEXUAL ANGLES ON BUDDHISM]
Sex with All the Lights On
Sex and Enlightenment

O ne of the longest-running debates in all forms of Buddhism starts with the question, "Can a householder become enlightened?" And just a little aside here; I hate the way pretentious wannabe contemporary Buddhists throw around the word *householder*. It's a bad translation of a very old euphemism for someone who can have sex. So why not just frame the question more directly: "Can you still get enlightened if you fuck?"

Okay. I'll concede that there's more to the definition of *householder* than just someone who gets to have sex. It basically means anyone who is not a monk,* someone who participates in society like a so-called normal person, who has a job, maybe has a spouse and kids, maybe even has — or "holds" — a house.

The earliest forms of Buddhism that we know of seem pretty unequivocal on the matter. According to them, householders have

---

* Again, in case you forgot, I include both male and female Buddhist clergy under the heading "monk."

266

no chance of attaining enlightenment. The best they can hope for is to be reborn as monks.

People who study the writings of Dogen* often accuse him of flip-flopping on this issue like an Old South politician. In *Bendowa*, one of his earliest writings, Dogen says that everyone, regardless of whether they're householders or home-leavers (monks), can and should practice zazen. Since Dogen regarded zazen as equivalent to enlightenment, the implication is that you can still get enlightened even if you're getting laid.

Yet in one of the final chapters of *Shobogenzo*, "Thirty-Seven Elements of Bodhi," he says, "For the last two or three hundred years in the great kingdom of Song [aka China], people calling themselves priests of the Zen sect have habitually said, 'Pursuit of the truth by a layman and pursuit of the truth by one who has left family life are just the same.' They are a tribe of people who have become dogs, for the sole purpose of making the filth and urine of laypeople into their food and drink." In other words, monks only talk about laypeople becoming enlightened so they can take their filthy layperson money. And this is just the beginning of a rant that goes on for about three pages.

The matter of whether or not laypeople could become enlightened has played a very key role in the development and spread of Buddhism, and Dogen's rant points to the reason for this. Since there are a lot more laypeople than there are monks, and since laypeople often provide financial support for monks, it is practical and expedient for Buddhist teachers to state or at least imply that laypeople can get enlightened. And we can see from the historical record that, in spite of the rant cited above, Dogen seems to have been at least sometimes prone to do the same thing himself. What

---

* To review, the thirteenth-century founder of the sect of Zen in which I was ordained.

he actually believed, we can only guess. And scholars have been guessing for ages. But I'm not gonna bother.*

In any case, this debate also raises the question of what the heck this "enlightenment" business is to begin with. Here's one common definition. Lots of folks think that enlightenment is something only certain very special people possess. These enlightened people also have the power to confirm the enlightenment of other people. Who but they would know what it looks like? Lots of people would like to have this kind of confirmation because it gives them political and social power. It might even get them a book deal from New World Library! This is as true today as it was in the past. This belief is the basis for pretty much all the corruption that exists in Buddhism and has ever existed. Enlightenment confirmations in Buddhism have often been sold or bartered as cynically as the medieval Catholic Church sold and bartered indulgences, or forgiveness of sins. This is not to say that all such confirmations were given for lousy reasons, but it is a fact that many of them were.

Me, I don't believe in that kind of enlightenment. Any enlightenment that needs to be confirmed by an outside authority isn't really enlightenment.

Having said that, though, I am also very dubious of people who claim to have been enlightened without any sort of training or teacher and without being part of any tradition at all. There are people, like Jiddu and U. G. Krishnamurti (no relation to each other) to cite just two examples, who seem to have achieved a very deep understanding and to have led exemplary lives without being part

---

* Okay. If you must know, my suspicion is that Dogen said different things to different audiences to encourage them in their own way. It's a fucking hard life being a monk even now, and it was way harder in Dogen's day. Unless you feel like there is a very special reason to live the monk's life, it's easy to give up. So Dogen delivered fiery sermons of encouragement to his monks about how important and special their job was. Yet when he spoke to laypeople he assured them that they, too, could do the same kind of zazen the monks did. I'm sure he meant every word he said to every audience he spoke to, even when his words directly contradicted each other.

of any tradition. But they're exceptions. And those guys never really claimed to have had enlightenment as such. The ones who do make such claims almost always seem like dipshits to me.

As to whether having sex prevents a person from attaining a deep sense of the truth, I don't really see why it would. However, if you want to see very, very deeply into yourself — which is to see very, very deeply into the nature of the universe — you're going to have to do a lot of work. To put in this kind of work you need to forgo a lot of other things. It's the same as a guy who wants to be a really shredding guitarist. He has to devote years of his life to staying in his basement practicing scales till his fingers bleed. He can't be spending all his time going to parties and getting laid. And seeing deeply into the nature of the universe is way harder than learning all of Yngwie Malmsteen's hottest licks.

These days people call a whole lot of things "enlightenment experiences." These range from "eureka" moments, to psychotic breaks, to supposedly mystical states, to drug-induced euphoria. Most "enlightenment experiences" are pure horseshit. On the other hand, though, people who pursue zazen for a long time often have glimpses into the deeper layers of reality. You do not need these glimpses confirmed by any outside authority any more than you need an outside authority to confirm that you just caught a glimpse of the girl next door in her undies.* If you actually saw it, you know for certain. If you need someone to tell you whether or not you saw it, you didn't see anything.

At the same time, there is value to having a teacher you can communicate with about the various things that come up during your practice. For the most part, if your teacher's any good, he'll listen politely to your stories of wonderful insights and then tell you to go back and sit some more till you get over it.

But then there may come a day when you and your teacher see eyeball to eyeball, when your view and hers line up exactly. When

---

* Or the dude next door in his boxers.

that happens she may ask you if you'd like to do the traditional ceremony confirming it. You are then free to choose whether or not to do so.

At any rate, some of the people who've had glimpses into the deeper nature of reality had sex lives at the time, and some did not. It's more a matter of the depth of that glimpse, and the understanding that it brings. If you're not distracted by other things — like sex, for one — your understanding is likely to be more thorough.

But there's a downside. I once asked a Zen teacher friend about a highly respected master with whom he'd briefly studied. He said the guy was all right. But he also said he was kind of an "empty person." I asked what this meant, and he explained by likening him to a highly trained classical pianist. Those kinds of people are often brilliant musicians who have no understanding of the rest of life. They've dedicated themselves to the piano so much that they have no ability to interact socially because they've almost never had the experience. They emerge from their training incredibly good at whatever they've been trained in but otherwise empty as people.

How much enlightenment does a person really need? This is a very hard question to answer. It's not like you can't live a happy and fulfilling life without having some kind of mystical insight into it. Though I believe, without any doubt, that regular zazen practice will make any kind of life you choose happier and more fulfilling.

But as far as the experience of enlightenment goes, it's all up to how much that sort of thing matters to you. If it matters a whole lot and you want to go right down to the very deepest of depths, then you'd better drop everything else and get to work. Don't fool yourself into believing there's any easier way than that. If, on the other hand, you just want a bit more stability and a bit more understanding, a daily practice of thirty minutes to an hour will probably do just fine. And you can still "do it" as much as you feel like.

Chapter 30

HAPPY ENDING, BUDDHIST STYLE

Whether or not you're a Buddhist, sexuality is a vital part of everyone's life. You were born because two people fucked. As far as your biology is concerned you're still around so that you can fuck and make more copies of your genes. No matter where you live, your society has been profoundly shaped by its attitude toward sex. Biologists are now beginning to theorize that the nature of our bodies and minds themselves have been shaped by sexuality. Certain structures in the brain, they say, are there because they were beneficial to our ancestors' reproductive success. No matter how far you run, you're not going to get away from sex. Sex is a big deal.

I've talked about Buddhism as a kind of art. But I think even more fundamentally than that, Buddhism is an attitude. It's a way of approaching what life presents you with. I believe the Buddhist attitude, when applied to sexuality, can provide a means to make sex more rational, safer, less harmful, and perhaps most important, a whole lot more enjoyable than any other attitude we humans have tried so far. Life is a whole lot more fun when you can put aside your delusions about who you are and what you want and actually simply be who you are and do the things you truly want to do.

I remember being shocked when I first heard Nishijima Roshi say that Buddhism was all about doing exactly what you want. I'd been practicing for ten years by then, and it never seemed at all to be about doing what I wanted. Who *wants* to sit and stare at a wall for hours and hours? Who *wants* to try and abide by a bunch of restrictive ancient rules? Who *wants* to go on stupid retreats where you get alternately bored out of your skull or freaked out by all the weird shit your subconscious coughs up?

But through this practice I've come to see that what I really wanted all along was just to be authentically who I actually am. Most of what I thought I needed, I didn't really need. Most of what I thought I wanted, I didn't even really want. The false sense of self I thought I had to build up, defend, and sustain 24/7 turned out to be a phantom, to be nothing at all. Yet like Suzuki Roshi said, "Just to be you is enough, you know."

The Buddhist attitude toward sex isn't about being one specific way. It's not about being straight and monogamous. It's not about leading your life according to a specific formula. It's about being authentically what you are.

Buddha taught the Middle Way, the way that avoids the extremes of hedonistic excess and the extremes of self-mortification and denial. He didn't say what he said because he wanted us to be more repressed and inhibited. I am fully convinced that what Buddha was really after was a life that did not suck. That is, after all, the basis of the philosophy. The common interpretation of Buddha's famous First Noble Truth amounts basically to "life sucks." His main interest was in finding out what we could do to make life not suck so much.

Sex can make us very happy. But it can make us intensely miserable, too.

Remember what I was telling you in the beginning about the retreat I went to where I was so heartbroken? Love sometimes passes away. Heartbreak always does. Even when love continues, it changes. Nothing lasts eternally except this eternal now, where we always seem to find ourselves when we get out of our heads. I got over that heartbreak, and things got better. The sun still shone. The birds still sang. The trash still needed to be taken out and the cats fed.

The best thing to do when you're heartbroken is to live your life. It's because of heartbreak way back in the early 1990s that I can still play Robyn Hitchcock's song "Chinese Water Python"* on guitar. It's the kind of complex finger-picked piece I am not usually capable of. But I'd been dumped, and I needed to find some way to deal with all that energy. People often do great things when they get dumped. So maybe all that misery is good for something, when you can let it be good for something.

Most of us, when we think about how we'd like to live, want to find some magic formula that gets us all the happiness and none of the misery — not just in terms of sex, but in terms of everything. And if that's what you're convinced you need, there are a million and one hucksters out there ready to tell you that's what they're selling. The shelves of the store you shoplifted this book from are loaded down with promises of a life of all ups and no downs.

I won't lie to you. If I believed I could find that kind of life for real I'd be the first one to sign up. But I've seen enough to know it ain't ever gonna happen that way.

Buddhism isn't about how to find a life that fits our deluded ideas of perfection. But it is about how to find the real perfection in the life you're leading right now, no matter how ridiculously far it is from your ideas about what your life ought to be like.

Sex is held out by some as the key to ultimate happiness. There are others who'll tell you that the only way to end your suffering is to give up sex entirely. Although certain Buddhists advocate the latter approach, the whole of Buddhism offers a much broader range of

---

* From the album *Eye*.

possible solutions to the problems and complications sex so often creates.

In these pages we've looked at how some contemporary Western Buddhists have dealt with a wide range of issues regarding sexuality. And I've given you some of my own opinions on the matter, informed by a life of observing and experimenting with different Buddhist-informed approaches to sex. Ultimately, though, the path you choose will be yours. No one else's way will ever work for you.

One of Buddha's most important pieces of advice on how to have a life that doesn't suck was to avoid misusing sexuality. He didn't leave us with a concise list of dos and don'ts to let us know how that could be accomplished. He knew that such a list would be worse than useless. It's really up to us to find out what is and is not the misuse of sexuality in our own lives.

When I was talking to people about this book as I was writing it I often ended up saying that its entire message could be summed up in three words: Just be careful. Although I've said a whole lot, it really boils down to that. Don't be reckless with sex. You can really hurt someone if you are, and you can really hurt yourself. Buddhists believe that the repercussions of all our actions spread out across the world and even into the rest of the universe. We have a great responsibility. We shouldn't take that lightly.

I've misused sexuality in my own life, and I've seen the consequences. But I've also been blessed by sexuality. My experience with sex is that if you treat everyone involved with complete honesty and absolute respect, almost anything is possible.

So have fun and don't hurt anybody, including yourself.

Appendix

How to Do Zazen

I couldn't just leave it like that. Like in a broken romance, I say my final piece and then I turn around and say something I'll regret later...

But this is different! I want to leave you with a little something from Dogen, the thirteenth-century Japanese monk who brought zazen back to Buddhism, and vice versa. I've already written extensively about Dogen in my book *Sit Down and Shut Up!* and about zazen in *Hardcore Zen*. But I don't want you to have to go out and buy two more books just to figure out what this one's all about.* So I thought I'd provide a brief primer on zazen practice in case you're interested in where all the foregoing stuff comes from.

Dogen explains all you really need to know about the practice in a short piece called *Fukan Zazen-gi*, which means "Universal Guide to the Standard Method for Zazen Practice." There are probably a dozen translations out there. I'm quoting from the one in volume

---

* Well, three, actually, since there are some references to *Zen Wrapped in Karma Dipped in Chocolate* here, too.

275

one of *Shobogenzo*, as translated by my teacher Gudo Nishijima and his student Chodo Cross.

It starts off, "Now, when we research it, the truth originally is all around: why should we rely upon practice and experience? The real vehicle exists naturally: why should we put forth great effort?" This is a reference to Dogen's own question when he first began his practice. If, as the sutras tell us, everything is as it should be right now, why bother doing zazen?

He answers his own question saying, "However, if there is a thousandth or a hundredth of a gap, the separation is as great as that between heaven and earth; and if a trace of disagreement arises, we lose the mind in confusion. Proud of our understanding and richly endowed with realization, we obtain special states of insight; we attain the truth; we clarify the mind; we acquire the zeal that pierces the sky; we ramble through remote intellectual spheres, going in with the head: and yet, we have almost completely lost the vigorous road of getting the body out."

I love that passage. First he describes everybody's meditative dream date, complete with special states of insight, the attainment of truth, and a zeal that pierces the sky. Then he says that ain't it. Ouch!

Next he cites examples of the great masters of the past who made zazen their practice both before and after they had whatever insights made them famous. "The ancient saints were like that," he says. "How could people today fail to make effort?"

He tells us, "We should learn the backward step of turning light and reflecting. Body and mind will naturally fall away, and the original features will manifest themselves before us. If we want to attain the matter of the ineffable, we should practice the matter of the ineffable at once."

So how do we do that, Mr. Dogen?

Next he gives us the details. "In general, a quiet room is good for practicing [Za]zen, and food and drink are taken in moderation. Cast aside all involvements. Give the myriad things a rest. Do not think of good and bad. Do not consider right and wrong. Stop the driving movement of mind, will, consciousness. Cease intellectual consideration through images, thoughts, and reflections. Do not aim to become a buddha."

That's the intellectual side of practice. Now for the physical.

"We usually spread a thick mat on the place where we sit, and use a round cushion on top of that. Either sit in the full lotus posture or sit in the half lotus posture. To sit in the full lotus posture, first put the right foot on the left thigh, then put the left foot on the right thigh. To sit in the half lotus posture, just press the left foot onto the right thigh."

You can also put your legs the opposite way around in the Burmese posture, which is like a half lotus but without the legs crossed. The main thing is to get both knees down on the ground, or as close to the ground as possible. If this proves too difficult you can place some extra cushions under your knees.

If you absolutely cannot manage to sit on a cushion on the floor, then sitting on a chair is better than not doing zazen at all. But as soon as you say that, every able-bodied person in the room runs for the chairs! Chairs are not very conducive to the practice. They force *their* idea of balance on the body and make it nearly impossible to find your own. If you really, truly must use a chair I'd recommend one of those backless ergonomic kneeling chairs that computer geeks sometimes use. If you let some object balance you, you'll never find your own balance.

People sometimes think I'm too dogmatic about posture. But if a yoga teacher saw you doing downward-facing dog in a bizarre way and then corrected you, would you feel she was being dogmatic? Zazen is a physical practice, not an arbitrary pose you take to work on something mental.

I'm well aware that there are people in this world who absolutely cannot get into anything close to even the Burmese posture. But there are far fewer of those people than there are people sitting in chairs at Zen places in the United States and Europe. Don't be lazy. Make some effort. Take a yoga class and loosen up those legs. It's worth the effort. Still, it's more about balancing the spine than about how well you can twist up your legs.

Then Dogen tells us to "Spread the clothing loosely and make it neat. Then put the right hand above the left foot, and place the left hand on the right palm. The thumbs meet and support each other. Just make the body right and sit up straight. Do not lean to the left, incline to the right, slouch forward, or lean backward. The ears must be aligned with the shoulders, and the nose aligned with the navel. Hold the tongue against the palate, keep the lips and teeth closed, and keep the eyes open. Breathe softly through the nose." Clear enough.

He continues, "When the physical posture is already settled, make one complete exhalation and sway left and right. Sitting immovably in the mountain-still state, *Think about this concrete state beyond thinking. How can the state beyond thinking be thought about? It is different from thinking.* This is just the pivot of Zazen."

This is a reference to a story about a conversation between Master Yakusan Igen and a monk. The monk asks his master, "What are you thinking in the mountain-still state [zazen]?"

The master says, "Thinking the thought of non-thinking." The monk asks how to do that and the master says, "It's different from thinking." He leaves it at that. If he said any more it would just be more descriptions of thought, which would be counterproductive. Each of us must find our own way to think the concrete state beyond thinking.

Dogen tells us, "This sitting in Zazen is not learning Zen concentration." It's not about getting some great mystical state. "It is simply the peaceful and joyful gate of Dharma. It is the practice-and-experience which perfectly realizes the state of bodhi." It sounds like nothing. But Dogen assures us it isn't. "The Universe is conspicuously realized, and restrictions and hindrances never reach it. To grasp this meaning is to be like a dragon that has found water, or like a tiger in its mountain stronghold. Remember, the right Dharma is naturally manifesting itself before us, and darkness and distraction have dropped away already."

He next alludes to the so-called enlightenment experiences of the great masters of the past. He asks, "How could they be known through mystical powers or practice and experience? They may be dignified behavior beyond sound and form. How could they be anything other than criteria that precede knowing and seeing?"

This is important. He's saying that our real state in zazen is the truth itself. It doesn't matter if it feels like what you imagine mystical insights ought to feel like. The state of zazen itself is beyond anything as tawdry as what you imagine mystical insights ought to feel like.

I love the next bit. "Therefore, we do not discuss intelligence as superior and stupidity as inferior. Do not choose between clever people and dull ones. If we single-mindedly make effort [in zazen] that truly is pursuit of the truth. Practice-and-experience is naturally untainted. Actions are more balanced and constant." In other words, it don't matter if you're a dunce like me. You can still do zazen!

"Although there are myriad distinctions and thousands of differences," Dogen says, "we should just practice [Za]zen and pursue the truth. Why should we abandon our own seat on the floor, to come and go without purpose through the dusty borders of foreign lands?" You don't have to travel the world to find the truth. It's always right where you are. He says, "If we misplace one step we pass over the moment of the present. We have already received the essential pivot which is the human body: we must never pass time in vain." In other words, don't waste time because "the body is like a dew-drop on a blade of grass. Life passes like a flash of lightning. Suddenly it is gone. In an instant it is lost."

Dogen concludes by saying, "If you practice the state like this for a long time, you will surely become the state like this itself. The treasure-house will open naturally, and you will be free to receive and to use [its contents] as you like."

You couldn't wish for a happier ending than that one!

Elsewhere in his writings Dogen recommends that his monks do four forty-minute periods of zazen every day. That's a bit much for most of us. Personally I put in about an hour each day — generally forty minutes right after I get up and another twenty before bed. If you can't manage that much, just do however much you can. As long as you do it every day, even five lousy minutes is better than nothing at all.

If you are wondering where to practice, you can start out right now, today, in your own home. You don't need to go to a Zen center or a temple up in the mountains. But if you do choose to go to those places, there are hundreds around, with more opening up every day.

If you go to your local Zen place and it doesn't suit you, then stop going there. If there's no Zen place nearby, just do your practice by yourself. Communal Zen is nice and can be helpful. But it's not essential.

People always ask me how to tell if a Zen teacher is good or not or if a Zen center is decent or awful. The answer is that there are only a tiny number of bad Zen teachers working the spiritual scumsucker circuit. The worst you're likely to run into is someone who is well-meaning but kind of clueless. There are also some very good teachers out there who don't advertise or promote themselves. They don't write books. They just do good work. These people are much better than me. Go look for them!

In any case, why should you trust me? I'm just a guy you don't know who wrote a book. Trust your instincts. Ultimately you are going to have to make the call yourself. So there's no sense asking me about it anyway.

You're the one who matters most in this. It's about finding true independence and true interdependence, which are ultimately the same thing. If you are sincerely interested in the practice, every insight that was available to Buddha and Dogen and Bodhidharma and those big Buddhist masters on the covers of the magazines at the checkout stand of your local natural foods market will be yours too. So go get started!

I'll see ya at the zendo!

ACKNOWLEDGMENTS

A whole lot of people helped me write this book. Some of them are mentioned in the text specifically, but others aren't. So here goes.

Thanks to Tim McCarthy and Gudo Nishijima for more than words can ever convey. Thanks to Tonen O'Connor, Zuiko Redding, and Dokai Georgeson for being wonderful inspirations. Thanks to Dan Warner for being my dad, to Sandy Warner for being my mom, to Stacy Shelton for being my sister, and to Ben and Skylar Goldman for being my nephew and niece.

Thanks to Daigan Gaither and Nina Hartley for their major contributions to areas I would not have known about without their help. Thanks to Helen Jupiter, Erin Broadley, Nicole Powers, and Missy, my editors at Suicide Girls, for making much of this book possible. Thanks to Catie Braly and Lori Glenn for giving me a place to stay while I finished the book off. To Bee Jellyfish for also providing space for this book to be written in. Thanks to Harmony for lessons in some of the rougher stuff. Thanks to Eli Block for valuable introductions. I hope I wasn't too harsh. Thanks to Rachael McCrary for putting up with my crankiness at the Amma thing. Thanks to the folks who wrote to me at my blog (hardcorezen.blogspot.com) and at Suicide Girls who gave me stuff to write back about.

Thanks to my editors at New World Library, Jason Gardner and Mimi Kusch, for wading through this stuff and making it better. Thanks to Kim Corbin for getting people interested in my books.

Thanks to Yuka for being there in spite of everything. It has really meant a lot to me. Thanks to Leilani for a lot of life lessons that went into the construction of this book. Thanks to Nina for being my friend. Thanks to Svetlana for being my Eastern European friend. Thanks to Katy and Jamie for teaching me things I never knew I didn't know.

About the Author

Brad Warner was born in Ohio in 1964. In 1983 he met Zen teacher Tim McCarthy and began his study of Zen while he was still the bass player of the hardcore punk band Zero Defex, whose big hit was the eighteen-second masterpiece "Drop the A-Bomb on Me!" In the 1980s he released five albums of psychedelic rock under the band name Dimentia 13 (that's the way he spelled it), though Dimentia 13 was often a one-man band with Brad playing all the instruments. In 1993 he moved to Japan, where he landed a job with Tsuburaya Productions, the company founded by Eiji Tsuburaya, the man who created Godzilla. The following year Brad met Gudo Nishijima Roshi, who ordained him as a Zen monk and made him his dharma heir in 2000. Brad lived in Japan for eleven years. In 2003 he published his first book, *Hardcore Zen*, followed by *Sit Down and Shut Up!* in 2007 and *Zen Wrapped in Karma Dipped in Chocolate* in 2009. These days he travels around the world leading retreats, giving lectures, and looking for cool record stores. At last report he was living in Minneapolis with two rambunctious kitties.

He can be found on the web at **hardcorezen.blogspot.com**.